Studies in Major Literary Authors

Edited by
William E. Cain
Professor of English
Wellesley College

A Routledge Series

Studies in Major Literary Authors

William E. Cain, *General Editor*

"Somewhat on the Community-System"
Fourierism in the Works of Nathaniel Hawthorne
Andrew Loman

Colonialism and the Modernist Moment
in the Early Novels of Jean Rhys
Carol Dell'Amico

Melville's Monumental Imagination
Ian S. Maloney

Writing "Out of All the Camps"
J. M. Coetzee's Narratives of Displacement
Laura Wright

Here and Now
The Politics of Social Space in D. H. Lawrence and Virginia Woolf
Youngjoo Son

"Unnoticed in the Casual Light of Day"
Philip Larkin and the Plain Style
Tijana Stojković

Queer Times
Christopher Isherwood's Modernity
Jamie M. Carr

Edith Wharton's "Evolutionary Conception"
Darwinian Allegory in Her Major Novels
Paul J. Ohler

The End of Learning
Milton and Education
Thomas Festa

Reading and Mapping Hardy's Roads
Scott Rode

Creating Yoknapatawpha
Readers and Writers in Faulkner's Fiction
Owen Robinson

No Place for Home
Spatial Constraint and Character Flight in the Novels of Cormac McCarthy
Jay Ellis

The Machine that Sings
Modernism, Hart Crane, and the Culture of the Body
Gordon A. Tapper

Influential Ghosts
A Study of Auden's Sources
Rachel Wetzsteon

D. H. Lawrence's Border Crossing
Colonialism in His Travel Writings and "Leadership" Novels
Eunyoung Oh

Dorothy Wordsworth's Ecology
Kenneth R. Cervelli

Sports, Narrative, and Nation in the
Fiction of F. Scott Fitzgerald
Jarom Lyle McDonald

Shelley's Intellectual System and its
Epicurean Background
Michael A. Vicario

Modernist Aesthetics and Consumer
Culture in the Writings of Oscar Wilde
Paul L. Fortunato

Milton's Uncertain Eden
Understanding Place in Paradise Lost
Andrew Mattison

Henry Miller and Religion
Thomas Nesbit

Henry Miller and Religion

Thomas Nesbit

NEW YORK AND LONDON

Excerpts from Henry Miller's *Nexus* (Grove 1965), *Plexus* (Grove 1965), *Sexus* (Grove 1965), and *Tropic of Capricorn* (Grove 1961) used with permission of Grove/Atlantic, Inc.

Excerpts from a letter of Henry Miller to Herbert Muller, dated 2 July 1941, used courtesy of the Lilly Library, Indiana University, Bloomington, IN.

Excerpts from Henry Miller's *The World of Sex* (Ts. Henry Miller Papers, Columbia U.) used with permission of the Rare Book and Manuscript Library, Columbia University.

Excerpts from the Rosy Crucifixion Notes, Herbert Faulkner West Papers, Dartmouth College, used courtesy of Dartmouth College Library.

Excerpts from Henry Miller's *Notebooks* and "Scheme and Significance" (Henry Miller Papers, Collection 110) used with permission of the Department of Special Collections, Charles E. Young Research Library, UCLA.

Routledge	Routledge
Taylor & Francis Group	Taylor & Francis Group
711 Third Avenue,	2 Park Square
New York, NY 10017, USA	Milton Park, Abingdon
	Oxon OX14 4RN

First issued in paperback 2015

Routledge is an imprint of the Taylor & Francis Group, an informa business

© 2007 by Taylor & Francis Group, LLC

International Standard Book Number-13: 978-0-415-76249-6 (Paperback)
International Standard Book Number-13: 978-0-415-95603-1 (Hardback)

No part of this book may be reprinted, reproduced, transmitted, or utilized in any form by any electronic, mechanical, or other means, now known or hereafter invented, including photocopying, microfilming, and recording, or in any information storage or retrieval system, without written permission from the publishers.

Trademark Notice: Product or corporate names may be trademarks or registered trademarks, and are used only for identification and explanation without intent to infringe.

Library of Congress Cataloging-in-Publication Data

Nesbit, Thomas.
    Henry Miller and religion / by Thomas Nesbit.
        p. cm. -- (Studies in major literary authors)
    Includes bibliographical references and index.
    ISBN 0-415-95603-X
    1. Miller, Henry, 1891-1980--Religion. I. Title.

PS3525.I5454Z766 2007
818'.5209--dc22   2007008691

This book is dedicated to Julie Felty

Contents

List of Abbreviations   ix

Acknowledgments   xi

Chapter One
Introduction   1

Chapter Two
General Reception   13

Chapter Three
Avant-Garde Religion   27

Chapter Four
Tropic of Cancer   41

Chapter Five
Tropic of Capricorn   63

Chapter Six
The Rosy Crucifixion   93

Chapter Seven
Conclusion   127

Notes   129

viii	*Contents*
Bibliography	147
Index	155

List of Abbreviations

AMORC	The Ancient and Mystical Order Rosae Crucis
FBI	Federal Bureau of Investigations
KJV	King James Version
NIV	New International Version
OED	Oxford English Dictionary
OTO	Ordo Templi Orientis
UCLA	University of California at Los Angeles

Acknowledgments

Professor Susan Mizruchi dedicated countless hours to this project. From prolonged conversations to diligently edited drafts, she went far beyond what anyone would expect from an advisor. How wonderful it was to find someone who shares so many interests, who could see the logic uniting them. I will be forever grateful for her attention, curiosity, encouragement, enthusiasm, honesty, and trust.

As a careful reader and mentor, Professor Peter Hawkins refined my manuscript and my vision. He was always available, volunteering aid whenever he sensed it was needed. In addition to pointing out even more allusions to the Bible and Dante in Henry Miller's writings, Peter helped me articulate what is truly unique about Miller's religiosity. As Director of the Luce Program in Scripture and the Literary Arts at Boston University, he has developed an unparalleled program investigating the intersections of religion and literature. I am proud to be among its alumni.

Other colleagues have been helpful and generous. Professor Matthew Smith guided my project from conception to gestation, pressing me to pursue my intellectual investigations into excess. Beyond offering page-by-page comments on my manuscript, Professor Stephen Prothero had a major influence on my intellectual development, encouraging me to research sidestream religiosity. Professor Charles Lindholm also made valuable comments on my Miller work. Professor William E. Cain and Max Novick, Research Editor at Routledge, were both extraordinarily helpful in their efforts to ensure that this study was published.

Miller scholars past and present have also provided assistance. Mary V. Dearborn was always charitable with her notes, library, and time. Through chats and correspondence, Bertrand Mathieu and Karl Orend gave not only insight but courage. Discussions with the following also helped improve the study, pointing me in profitable directions: Sean Dempsey, Professor Abigail

xi

xii   *Acknowledgments*

Gillman, Christina Hoff-Kraemer, Professor Deeana Klepper, and Michal Luczewski. My students in "Henry Miller's Religious Journey," a graduate course in the Department of English and American Studies at Charles University in Prague, were kind enough to ask the right questions. In particular, I would like to thank Ondrej Skovajsa, a revered Miller translator and one of Charles University's finest.

This study was funded through the generosity of multiple entities. In May 2004, Boston University's Humanities Foundation honored my project with the Angela J. and James J. Rallis Memorial Award. Thanks to the James and Sylvia Thayer Fellowship from UCLA's Department of Special Collections, I was able to research their massive Henry Miller archive in the summer of 2004. Lucinda Newsome, Jeff Rankin, and all the staff at UCLA exuded kindness with their efficient aid. A Junior Visiting Fellowship allowed me to write my thesis at the Institut für die Wissenschaften vom Menschen (IWM) in Vienna. During my seven month stay in 2004–2005, the hard work of Managing Director Susanne Fröschl, Maria Nicklas, Ted Paul, and other staff made it possible to devote all my mental energy to Henry Miller and Viennese Actionism. I would personally like to thank IWM's Permanent Fellows, all of whom made valuable comments on my work: Cornelia Klinger, János Mátyás Kovács, Krzysztof Michalski, and Klaus Nellen.

The following made it possible to present archived material: Genie Guerard, Manuscript Manager, Department of Special Collections at UCLA; Sarah Hartwell of the Rauner Special Collections Library at Dartmouth College; Michael Ryan, Director of the Rare Book and Manuscript Library at Columbia University; and Saundra Taylor, Curator of Manuscripts, Lilly Library at Indiana University. I am especially grateful to George Boroczi, Henry Tony Miller, and Valentine Miller, who together gave me permission to publish excerpts from Miller's unpublished works. Thank you.

Many friends provided invaluable support to ensure this project was realized: Christoph Bärenreuter, Michael Ian Borer, Thomas D. Carroll, Sara Jaye Hart, Dan Smalheiser, Jennifer Smalheiser, and die Brüder Thaler. I am forever grateful.

Chapter One

Introduction

In a May 1959 issue of *Time,* an article titled "The Beat Friar" relates Bill Everson's conversion into Brother Antoninus, the Prior of a Dominican monastery. Speaking of *Lady Chatterley's Lover* and *Tropic of Cancer,* both then banned in the United States, Antoninus says, "They were the crystallizing books of my pre-Catholic formation. They have a kind of terrible vitality that enabled me to strip the merely conventional away and expose my soul so that when the moment of faith actually came, I was free within myself to make the act of faith" (61). While seemingly sensational, such testimony is common to devotees of American author Henry Miller. In fact, countless examples can be found in the sprawling correspondence housed in his personal archives. Erica Jong speaks for them all when she writes, "Again and again, people have said to me, in various ways: *I was dying in the prison of myself and Henry Miller freed me, gave me new life*" (*Devil* 7, emphasis Jong's). The conversion language used in these accounts demonstrates that reading Miller prompts more than a desire to toss inhibitions to the wind. The freedom inspired by his prose is, at least for some, a religious experience.

Only within this religious context can Miller's entire opus be understood and properly appreciated. Although many fans and scholars have noted the religious or "spiritual" dimensions of his writings, few have recognized how deeply religion is engrained in his life and work. Since the beginning of his career, he explicitly made his religiosity known to the public in lesser known works, such as *The World of Sex* (1941), in which he plainly states, "It goes without saying that I am essentially a religious person, and always have been."[1] This same study also argues that religion and sex are intertwined in his artistic creations, though he laments that readers tend to view him either as a liberator or a libertine. Critical history and popular renderings, however, have amplified the sexual facets to the point

1

of obscuring his religious motivation. The Miller most of us know comes not from his books; rather, he is a cardboard construction erected in the wake of the American sexual revolution.

If Miller's books, which sold in millions, were closely studied, it would have been difficult to support such one-dimensional renderings. He designates his religious sensibility in obvious ways, such as quoting Jesus and other religious figures, referring to saints and mystics, and calling his major work *The Rosy Crucifixion* (1949–60).[2] Despite these overtures, it is admittedly difficult to identify what he means by religion. One often finds perplexing statements such as, "I am a deeply religious man without a religion" (*Reflections* 123). A few pages after he calls himself a "religious person" in *The World of Sex*, he says that he hates all religions. While he is making an implicit distinction between esoteric and exoteric religious sensibilities, his lack of precision leaves the average reader puzzled. Opening both *Tropic of Cancer* (1934) and *Tropic of Capricorn* (1939) with insults against God exacerbates the problem for the casual reader. Most skip to the "dirty parts," leaving the bulk of the books unread.

Even those who catch Miller's more metaphysical intentions view them imprecisely through a loosely defined spiritual rubric. Because his most sensational publications were not sold in the United States until the early 1960s, the religious consciousness within them was identified with the spirit of a different time. To further confuse matters, Miller fans of the early 1960s read his works through the lens of the Beat books. This anachronistic presentation put his literature out of conversation with authors Miller himself was addressing, such as T. S. Eliot, James Joyce, and Marcel Proust. Further damage was done by associating Miller's religiousness with the "Beat Zen" expounded in such texts as Jack Kerouac's *Dharma Bums* (1958). We can understand the association: Miller wrote the preface to Kerouac's follow-up novel, *The Subterraneans* (1959). Although Miller's project is certainly in line with the Zen practice of "killing the Buddha," an idea he writes about himself in scattered texts, his religious consciousness can only be fully understood within the more complicated context that created it.

AVANT-GARDE RELIGIOUS MOVEMENTS

Miller's religiousness should be seen within the times that gave rise to it: Greenwich Village of the early twentieth century. In New York City, he was exposed to a variety of esoteric religions that integrated Christianity, assorted other religions, and even science. Finding commonalities between an assortment of religious beliefs and phenomena had been an ongoing

Introduction 3

quest in philosophy and the social sciences, a project that flourished in the late nineteenth and early twentieth centuries. Sometimes the distinction between science and belief was blurred, particularly with early psychoanalytic studies offered by C. G. Jung and Otto Rank. The religious beliefs of cosmopolitan folk in North America and Europe reflected this turn away from formal religion.

In the northeastern United States, new religious movements found some audience among the cultural elite. The tendency had some precedent in the mid-nineteenth century through Ralph Waldo Emerson and the New England Transcendentalists, who embraced Eastern teachings alongside their nature-oriented interpretation of Christianity. New Thought and Christian Science flourished in Boston shortly thereafter, reflecting more rigorous developments in the scientific studies of religion. Other practices on the periphery of philosophy, religion, and science also came to life during this time, including Mesmerism, Spiritualism, Phrenology, and Astrology.

Increasingly ecumenical religions were founded soon after. During the 1893 World Parliament of Religions in Chicago, Swami Vivekananda introduced Vedanta to a Western audience. Due to his popularity and the openness of Ramakrishna's beliefs, the Vedanta Society was successfully established in the United States by the end of the decade. Bahá'i was first brought to the United States in 1894, which led to the founding of the First Assembly in America the following year. Beginning in 1906, Elwood Worcester practiced psychotherapy and holistic medicine on his Boston congregants, leading to what became known as the Emmanuel Movement.[3]

With the establishment of the Theosophical Society in New York City in 1875, the most encompassing religion of them all—Theosophy—had landed on American shores. Attempting to circumscribe all esoteric knowledge, this religion was founded by Madame H. P. Blavatsky and spread throughout the United States by Henry Steel Olcott and other early followers.[4] Not until the leadership of Annie Besant in the 1920s, however, would it become a popular movement with over 9,000 adherents. Many artists, musicians, and writers in Western countries would find inspiration in Theosophy's teachings around this time, including T. S. Eliot, Wassily Kandinsky, Dane Rudhyar and Wallace Stevens.[5]

A heady mixture of Christian mysticism, Masonry, and science, Rosicrucianism also became popular with intellectuals of the age. The mid-nineteenth century had already witnessed the establishment of various Rosicrucian orders in the United States, but the most influential ones appeared after 1900. Some were splinter groups from the Theosophical Society, such as Max Heindel's Rosicrucian Fellowship, founded in 1907. The most famous organization—

The Ancient and Mystical Order Rosae Crucis (AMORC)—was founded in New York City in 1915 by H. Spencer Lewis. A writer and an artist, Lewis also helped establish the proto-Rosicrucian group called The New York Institute for Psychical Research in 1904, which also included writer Ella Wheeler Wilcox and dictionary publisher J. K. Funk among its officers. It was Lewis's AMORC, however, that would be the most successful, even resulting in a charter with Europe's Ordo Templi Orientis (OTO) in 1921.[6]

The Gurdjieff movement also became well known in the United States, as individuals sought to synthesize mystical teachings with self-development and body movement. Though Gurdjieff himself established the Institute for the Harmonious Development of Man outside of Paris in 1922, one of Gurdjieff's disciples—A. R. Orage—came to New York City in 1923 to recruit followers. The charismatic Orage was already popular in the United States as the editor of *The New Age,* an influential literary journal. Such notoriety made him quickly accepted among the Greenwich Village elite, including Margaret Anderson and Jane Heap, editors of *The Little Review,* a journal that first published essential modernist texts.[7] Throughout the remainder of the decade, Orage led many writers and literary figures to Gurdjieff's teachings, including *New Republic* editor Herbert Cowly, Hart Crane, Waldo Frank, Katherine Mansfield, critic Gorham Munson, and Jean Toomer.[8]

Living in New York City, Miller began his initial literary experiments during the heyday of Gurdjieff, Rosicrucianism, and Theosophy on the East Coast, movements he refers to throughout his work. While these religious phenomenon would directly give rise to West Coast esotericism, there are three major factors that distinguish Greenwich Village movements of the 1920s from Californian varieties of the 1950s and 1960s. First, the religious movements of the early twentieth century were linked with science and had some degree of genuine support from the intellectual community. Second, these religions attempted to encompass or expand Christianity, rather than exclude it by establishing themselves as alternatives. Third, artists and writers were intimately involved even on the organizational level with these groups. While West Coast spiritualities would certainly also give rise to artistic inspiration, these earlier manifestations were integrally tied with the arts. Journals placed esoteric ideas alongside paradigmatic Modernist poetry; religious meetings included discussions of avant-garde cinema and literature.

REVIVING RELIGIOUS GENRES

In the 1920s, an era in which religion and literature were intertwined, Miller wholeheartedly embraced both strands and created art that aimed to unite

Introduction 5

the two. These esoteric religious movements inspired him to create his own religious universe. For all the license he takes when approaching religions, liberties encouraged by the hodge-podge religious climate of the early twentieth century, he nevertheless engages the Christian tradition with the utmost sincerity. Erica Jong expresses how Miller's liberation theology connects with Christianity when she writes:

> What he was trying to do in *Sexus, Nexus, Plexus,* or *The Rosy Crucifixion,* was to offer up a man's life, his meanderings through the labyrinth, 'as a sacrifice.' [. . .] Here Henry becomes the man who died. Like Christ or Adonis, he dies for truth. But unlike Christ, he is both the sacrifice and its chronicler. He is reborn as a writer to write his own gospel. [. . .] He goes down into the underworld, is reborn, and his rebirth takes the form of writing. Writing becomes redemption. And redemption is the ultimate form of self-liberation. (*Devil* 239–40)

In this passage, Jong suggests that Miller's most sensational books can be read as religious works. Indeed, one of the obstacles to understanding him is a matter of categorization. When most critics try to access his work, they have attempted to force it into traditional genres like fiction, prose poem, or autobiography. These classifications distort his project; confession and testament suit him better.

By adopting a confessional mode of writing, Miller expresses his religiosity through a genre that unites American and European religious traditions. On the one hand, his autobiographical writings connect to the Puritan practice of personal journals, a tradition Emerson also adopted. Miller certainly puts himself in the Transcendentalist line by using an Emerson quote for the epigraph to his first published work, *Tropic of Cancer:* "These novels will give way, by and by, to diaries or autobiographies—captivating books, if only a man knew how to choose among what he calls his experiences that which is really his experience, and how to record truth truly" (3). On the other, Miller reaches back to the great European traditional of hagiographies and confessions, modes of expression that originate in the unabashed *Confessions* of Saint Augustine and continue through medieval mystical writings.

If we see Miller as a man on an esoteric religious quest for self-liberation, we can view his autobiographical books as confessions and testaments in an eccentric Christian mystical tradition. *Tropic of Cancer* and *The Colossus of Maroussi* (1941) chronicle his liberation and successive spiritual rebirths; they aim to inspire similar awakenings within their readers. *Tropic of Capricorn* and *The Rosy Crucifixion* trilogy are confessions of a misguided

6 Henry Miller and Religion

life, in which illusory sexual pursuits—personified in the female character "Mara"—sap one's sacred energy.[9] Once these books are rightfully seen as contemporary versions of ancient spiritual genres, scholarship can begin to advance and Miller may find his rightful place within the academy.

APPROACHING MILLER'S OPUS

Books like *Tropic of Cancer* challenge our perception of fiction and non-fiction. Less cautious readers have assumed that his experiences in France and the United States match what we find in his books. The author, however, advised his readers otherwise, as in an early piece titled "Autobiographical Note" (1939): "My aim, in writing, is to establish a greater REALITY. I am not a realist or naturalist; I am for life, which in literature, it seems to me, can only be attained by the use of dream and symbol. I am at bottom a metaphysical writer, and my use of drama and incident is only a device to posit something more profound" (371). Keeping this caveat in mind, I approach the classic distinctions of fiction and non-fiction with reservations. Nevertheless, they are helpful in classifying his sprawling literary output. When using the designation "fiction," I am referring to the works in which he took the most liberty with his autobiographical source material. Non-fiction means works that come closer to reflecting the factual events of his life.

Although drawing on life experiences, Miller's most celebrated and scandalous writings can be considered fiction: *Tropic of Cancer, Tropic of Capricorn, Black Spring* (1936), and *The Rosy Crucifixion*, itself comprised of three volumes: *Sexus* (1949), *Plexus* (1953), and *Nexus* (1960). Fiction also characterizes lesser known books, such as *Quiet Days in Clichy* (1956), *Aller Retour New York* (1935), the play *Just Wild About Harry* (1963), the novella *The Smile at the Foot of the Ladder* (1948), and two posthumously published novels composed at the beginning of his career: *Moloch: This Gentile World* (1992) and *Crazy Cock* (1991). Most of these works, both minor and major, read like completed works, although there are some exceptions. The most striking case is *Black Spring*, which appears to have been structured as a linear progression through various "colors," in which each step had a specific property closely tied to the development of the work.[10] The published version, however, is a loosely bound collection of short stories on his childhood and times in Paris. *Nexus* was to be supplemented with a second volume, a manuscript never completed.[11] Furthermore, he often stated that his opus would be capped by a thin work called *Draco and the Ecliptic*, a piece intended to highlight the religious and spiritual significance of his work. Unfortunately for this investigation, not to mention for

Introduction   7

our complete understanding of his life project, *Draco and the Ecliptic* never came to be.

The most famous works that tend closer to non-fiction are *The Colossus of Maroussi, The Air-Conditioned Nightmare* (1945), its follow-up *Remember to Remember* (1952), and *Big Sur and the Oranges of Hieronymous Bosch* (1957). Although Miller certainly reconfigures events to meet his literary aims, these works come closer to matching what actually took place in his life. Each book was conceived with sophisticated aims and designs, but the finished products turned out to be essay collections, with the exception of *The Colossus of Maroussi*. The following straightforward collections can also be classified as non-fiction: *The Cosmological Eye* (1939), *Stand Still Like the Hummingbird* (1962), *The Wisdom of the Heart* (1940), *Sunday After the War* (1944), *Sextet* (1977), and the *Book of Friends* trilogy (1976–79). There are also a few literary studies, such as *The Time of the Assassins: A Study of Rimbaud* (1956), the posthumously published *The World of Lawrence* (1980), a philosophical investigation into the themes of his work entitled *The World of Sex,* and a study of some of his most beloved books: *The Books in My Life* (1952). Many volumes of correspondence were published both during his lifetime and after his death, including letters between him and Anaïs Nin, Michael Fraenkel, Lawrence Durrell, Alfred Perles, and others. Lastly, this non-fiction category includes many chapbooks and rare editions too numerous and obscure to list.

In this study, I focus on works from the first category: *Tropic of Cancer, Tropic of Capricorn,* and *The Rosy Crucifixion* trilogy. My investigation is limited to these for two primary reasons. First, these books offer Miller's boldest experiments in constructing his own religious universe. Unlike what we find in his more accessible essays, religion in these works is developed in a sophisticated and somewhat elusive manner, thereby increasing the need for scholarly examination. Second, even though these works are the most misunderstood, they are nevertheless the most popular. In order to bring about a sea-change in the way he is perceived, I focus our attention on his most important and well-known writings, even though more obscure texts and even unpublished materials also attest to his complicated affair with religion. When appropriate, I have referenced these less familiar pieces to enhance my argument.

METHODS

To accomplish the aims of this study, I developed a four-step method of interpreting Miller. First, I situate the author and his works in their proper historical contexts. Second, I examine the materials that helped him construct his religious universe. Third, I use theory developed from sources that inspired him to understand the architecture of Miller's own vision. Fourth, I undertake close readings of individual texts. In the final section of this chapter, I elaborate on these methods and acknowledge precedents that gave rise to this approach.

New Historicism has been helpful in establishing the appropriate contexts in which to view Miller's work.[12] Guided by Michel Foucault's work on the construction of knowledge and its relationship to power, New Historicists acknowledge that history is forged with a political agenda. Accessing the past through marginalized or overlooked sources could provide more illuminating contexts for certain works of literature. Unfortunately, some New Historicist work has simply replaced more old-fashioned histories with alternative but equally problematic ones. In my study, I have attempted to construct historical contexts that are suggested by the literature under consideration.

Stephen Greenblatt and Louis Montrose have been most responsible for the success of New Historicism through their influential studies of Shakespeare and Elizabethan England. In approaching Miller, however, I have gained inspiration from scholars who have applied New Historicist strategies to the life and work of William Blake, who shares many of Miller's sensibilities and traits. Considering print technologies and their role in the transmission of religious literature in Blake's England, Joseph Viscomi convincingly analyzes *The Marriage of Heaven and Hell* as a polemic against Swedenborg and shifts in the New Jerusalem Church around 1790.[13] E. P. Thompson reads Blake's early illuminated works as a response to rising antinomian sentiments in late-eighteenth century England.[14] Jerome McGann sees Blake's *Marriage of Heaven and Hell* as a reaction to new biblical criticism, especially Alexander Geddes's *Prospectus of a New Translation of the Holy Bible* (1786).[15] These recent approaches to Blake have demonstrated how complex religious climates can be reconstructed in order to better understand the equally complex religiosity expressed in his own writings. They offer a more informed discussion of religion than the generic references to Christianity and religion that we find in previous landmark studies of the English poet.

In this study, I use similar strategies to reconstruct Miller's religious universe. I begin with traditional published sources, including biographies and studies of religious and cultural history in the United States and Europe. This is supplemented by extensive archival research into unpublished materials, including the private and professional papers of Miller and members of his circle, such as Anaïs Nin. The extant notebooks and his annotated library were particularly helpful in revealing his approach to difficult religious and

Introduction 9

philosophical materials. Despite the ambition of his reading, Miller surveyed these materials in the spirit of an amateur, lacking the precision of a scholar. He nevertheless often grasped the essential teachings of the texts, which would then inform his writings in creative ways. As a record of how he encountered these texts, the archival materials have precluded unwarranted connections between Miller and religion. One might easily be misled by unrestrained immersion in the esoterica of his age.[16]

Writings that inspired Miller also inspired numerous theorists; their works, in turn, helped guide my interpretations. Among these are the philosophical pieces of Georges Bataille, along with studies by Gilles Deleuze and Felix Guattari. Bataille's work has allowed me to envision a religion of immanence guided by flows within a "general economy."[17] His related notion of "nonproductive expenditure," particularly its relationship to sacrifice, has demonstrated how moments of excess have a sacred quality within Bataille's admittedly unsystematic system. This has been especially helpful in seeing how Miller uses symbols of flow and crystallization to express a religious worldview positioned between immanence and transcendence. Studying Bataille's work also encouraged me to return to philosophical sources that directly inspired both Miller and Bataille, especially Henri Bergson and Friedrich Nietzsche. Living as contemporaries in the same city, Bataille and Miller encountered similar ideas and knew one another's writings.[18]

Deleuze and Guattari have had an even greater impact on the way I envision Miller's religiosity.[19] Scholars are wary of acknowledging religiousness in Deleuze's writings, preferring to view him as a staunch materialist.[20] While this interpretation is certainly sound, Deleuze's materialism comes out of a zeal to take Protestantism to its ultimate conclusion: the complete absence of God. This becomes all the more pertinent when one considers that Deleuze was practicing philosophy in French-Catholic environs. Building upon Nietzsche's *Anti-Christ,* Deleuze and Guattari's *Anti-Oedipus* (1972) continues Nietzsche's protest against any appeal to authority. Furthermore, their work builds upon the Judeo-Christian writings of Bergson and Spinoza, both of whom attempt to systematically render the divine in immanent terms, almost to the point of absence. When we view Deleuze and Guattari through their "nomadic" lineage, these traces of religion surface, though perhaps against their will.

From this perspective, we can read Deleuze and Guattari's attack against traditional religions in "587 B.C.-A.D. 70: On Several Regimes of Signs" from *A Thousand Plateaus* (1980) as a radical extension of Protestant Christianity. Even iconoclastic remarks, such as the "God is a lobster" pronouncement, make sense in this light. While seemingly trivial, the phrase challenges not only the strict measures found in the Torah (lobsters are not kosher) but also notions of height and transcendence in Christianity, as lobsters are bottom feeders. Less jocular moments in their work are in dialogue with Bergson and Spinoza. In the opening section of *Anti-Oedipus*, we are first introduced to the concept of "Body without Organs," an undifferentiated mass of energy that may extend "lines of flight" extending to other zones of concentrated energies. Deleuze and Guattari write, "The body without organs is not God, quite the contrary. But the energy that sweeps through it is divine, when it attracts to itself the entire process of production and serves as its miraculate, enchanted surface, inscribing it in each and every one of its disjunctions" (13). In this passage, Deleuze and Guattari have simply translated the charisma of a religious leader into their specialized materialist terms, which nevertheless retain traces of the religious terminology we find in their predecessors.

As with Bataille's concept of "nonproductive expenditure," Deleuze and Guattari's ideas have been helpful in understanding the architecture of Miller's elusive religiosity. Instead of the all-inclusive mystical oneness we find in Miller and Bataille, Deleuze and Guattari render energy in ways that preserve multiplicity, in which the sundry zones are connected in a web configuration via "lines of flight."

Because Deleuze and Guattari's philosophy evolved in conversation with Miller's writings, we can identify similarities between them. While caution should be exercised, Miller's travel narratives clearly provide source material for Deleuze's rendering of the nomad. Miller's "*Tropic of Cancer*" and "*Tropic of Capricorn*" can be seen as Deleuze's "lines of flight"; Miller's "Happy Rock" becomes Deleuze's "Body Without Organs." In Deleuze's works, we find him repeatedly quoting or alluding to Miller, particularly a scene from *The Rosy Crucifixion* in which Miller becomes "intoxicated" with water. Intriguingly, Deleuze and Guattari claim elsewhere that Miller enters "feminine" zones. After reminding us of Virginia Woolf's responses to the gender question, they write, "The rise of women in English novel writing has spared no man: even those who pass for the most virile, the most phallocratic, such as Lawrence and Miller, in their turn continually tap into and emit particles that enter the proximity or zone of indiscernibility of women. In writing, they become-woman" (*Plateaus* 276). Such comments not only complicate feminist critiques of Miller, but recast his project in a hermaphroditic light with the male author entering both "masculine" and "feminine" areas. From this position, we can begin to see how his literary project seeks to move from a sexual union of male and female to a metaphysical androgyny, a purpose that extends throughout his writing.

Introduction 11

Deleuze and Guattari's concept of "minor literature" has also been pivotal in understanding Miller's marginalized writings, which fit the philosopher's three criteria for designating the genre.[21] His work fulfills the first qualification as a literature formed by a minority out of a major language. Raised in a working-class German-American household, he dared to write in English and break into the bourgeois world of letters. Second, his work is intimately political, if politics are conceived on the personal level as individual freedom from any form of authoritarianism. Lastly, his project is fueled by a desire to liberate others from all forms of constraint. These qualifications, and the genres that Deleuze and Guattari associate with minor literature, help to reveal Miller's works as confession and testament. Although Deleuze and Guattari would be uncomfortable with categorizing traditional religious genres as minor literature, they nevertheless fulfill their requirements, even if religious texts appeal to higher authorities.

Miller's persistent use of traditional religious symbols and ideas, along with the complicated tension he preserves between transcendence and immanence, ultimately distance his work from the amorphous philosophy of Deleuze and Guattari. Yet their theories provide valuable tools for understanding Miller's world.

The next two chapters will examine Miller's reception and recompose his religious milieu. The following three chapters will address his work, beginning with *Tropic of Cancer,* continuing with studies of *Tropic of Capricorn,* and ending with the three volume *Rosy Crucifixion.* In the concluding chapter, I offer my final reflections on his affair with religion.

Chapter Two
General Reception

Henry Miller studies often begin with some lamentation over his status as an undervalued author. The truth of the matter, however, is that no scholar has made a convincing case for his importance.

To be fair, there are obstacles that inhibit profitable debate. In this chapter, I narrate the history of Miller's reception, beginning with the initial praises of the 1930s and continuing through the present. I aim to demonstrate that his reputation in the United States has hinged upon factors that have little to do with his creative output. Rather, distorted perceptions in mass culture, coupled with bad choices he made in response to these depictions, have made it difficult to access his work accurately. If his reputation had been based on serious critical analysis, the religious elements in all his writing would not have gone unexamined.

Although Miller's literary importance has been under-acknowledged in the United States, he has always received praise from the French literati. Blaise Cendrars, one of the most important modernist poets in French literature, wrote the first review of *Tropic of Cancer* (1934), triumphantly titled, "Un écrivain américain nous est né" (1935). Miller also knew Raymond Queneau and other leading figures in the Surrealist movement in Paris. For these reasons, Miller found support in 1946 when his books were brought up against the charge of pornography. Georges Bataille, Albert Camus, Jean-Paul Sartre, and other leading French intellectuals, with whom Miller did not even have direct contact, testified in his favor.

By associating with prominent French minds in the 1930s, he was able to insure a lasting reputation in France and the Continent at large, quite a contrast to his reception in America. While reduced to living in a shanty on the California coast, France invited him to judge the Cannes Film Festival in 1960! Antonio Bibalo produced an opera on Miller's short piece, *The Smile at the Foot of the Ladder* (1948), which debuted in Hamburg on 6 April 1965

13

as *Das Lächeln am Fuße der Leiter.* More recently, Miller's unfinished *Nexus 2* (2004) was posthumously published in French translation, whereas the text has never been released in English.

Even before the publication of *Tropic of Cancer,* Miller was poised to join the expatriate pantheon of authors in Paris. Although unknown at the time, he was included in a volume promoted to an audience that wanted to learn about the Parisian literary moment. In *Americans Abroad* (1932), he found himself among Ernest Hemingway, F. Scott Fitzgerald, and other literary greats he diligently followed. A series of ill-conceived strategic moves in the years that followed thwarted this trajectory to long-term literary success, jeopardizing his rightful position among the Modernist elite.

At first, Miller's published work received favorable reviews. In his 1935 appraisal of *Tropic of Cancer,* George Orwell advances the opinion that Miller's work is not pornographic. Speaking about Miller's sex scenes, he writes, "These are interesting not because of any pornographic appeal (quite the contrary), but because they make a definite attempt to get at real facts" (155). When reviewing *Black Spring* (1936), Orwell admits that he admires above all the vivacity of Miller's language, praising the author's ability to "cast a kind of bridge across the frightful gulf which exists, in fiction, between the intellectual and the man-in-the-street" (230).

The most riveting review of Miller's work during this era, however, remained unpublished until decades later. In contrast to the sensational French takes, Ezra Pound's 1935 review of *Tropic of Cancer* offers some of the first judiciously restrained praises of Miller.[1] A large portion of the review consists of a diatribe against the poor standards of contemporary fiction, citing James Joyce and Wyndham Lewis as among the few writers of high caliber, D. H. Lawrence occupying a middle tier, and H. G. Wells, George Bernard Shaw, and Arnold Bennett as all "third rate." Pound raises this scaffolding to evaluate Miller's book, which he sees of the same vintage as Joyce and Lewis. But perhaps the most remarkable aspect of this brief essay is Pound's insistence that Miller is a *moral* writer who "has very strongly a hierarchy of values" (88). This is a judgment that rings true in Miller's essays and work produced after the Paris years but is difficult to perceive in *Tropic of Cancer*'s haze of outlaw language.

T. S. Eliot privately sent Miller great praise upon reading *Tropic of Cancer.* Eliot writes, "*Tropic of Cancer* seems to me a very remarkable book . . . a rather magnificent piece of work. There is writing in it as good as any I have seen for a long time. Several friends to whom I have shown it, including Mr. Herbert Read, share my admiration . . . Without drawing any general comparisons, your own book is a great deal better both in depth of insight and

General Reception 15

of course in the actual writing than *Lady Chatterley's Lover*" (qtd. in Martin 317). Eliot later trimmed his comments for the jacket of *Tropic of Cancer's* second edition, but he continued to hold Miller in high regard. In 1936, Eliot attempted to publish *Black Spring* on the Faber & Faber imprint, but could only release an essay by Miller in his journal *Criterion* (Martin 319).

As the 1930s came to an end, two crucial events prompted Miller's critical downfall in the opinion of British and American readers. First, Miller attacked the wife of prominent critic Malcolm Cowley in published correspondence.[2] Although this collection was not widely read, the scandalous remark was likely spread to Cowley and other intellectual patriarchs in the English speaking world. A second blow was dealt through the publication of "Inside the Whale" (1940) by George Orwell. Although Orwell had praised Miller before, this essay damned his work for its seemingly immature hedonism. Upon return from the Spanish Civil War, Orwell believed that authors should take moral stands against political regimes, particularly during the opening gambits of World War II. These new views resulted in a polemical attack against Miller's work. Orwell's heavily anthologized piece effectively blacklisted Miller from serious intellectual consideration, dismissing his work as childish.

Although World War II helped bring about the demise of Miller's critical reputation, soldiers helped his work reach a massive reading audience. Americans on the Western front found solace in the eyebrow-raising parts of *Tropic of Cancer* and *Tropic of Capricorn* (1939). They began to smuggle copies into the United States, where Miller's most controversial work remained banned. A survey of his archives at UCLA reveals letters from GIs who were struck by the powers of his work both abroad and at home. While this helped boost sales and make Henry Miller a household name, this newfound fame forever linked him with pornography. Even though less sensational works, such as *The Cosmological Eye* (1939) and *The Colossus of Maroussi* (1941) had long been available, he became known as a producer of "smut."

A pathetic attempt to rectify Miller's stature in the United States came from Bern Porter, a nuclear physicist who worked at Oak Ridge National Laboratory, Princeton University, and the University of California Radiation Laboratory at Berkeley. Porter punctuated his resignation from the Manhattan Project by publishing Miller's anti-war piece, "Murder the Murderer" (1944). Although passionately inspired, Porter's effort to find peace by supporting California-based artists did little to help Miller's standing. Porter's first major venture as an amateur publisher, *The Happy Rock* (1945) was an ill-conceived mishmash of critical pieces about Miller and fawning remarks from major literary figures. Although some pieces shed new light onto his work, most contain overstated praise, such as Lawrence Durrell's following exaggeration: "Certainly there is no doubt that this towering, shapeless, sometimes comic, figure completely overtops the glazed reflections cast by those waxworks of contemporary American fiction—Hemingway, Dos Passos, Faulkner" (1). Although only 750 copies of the collection were printed, the most noteworthy critics and writers in the United States and the United Kingdom knew of its embarrassing existence, as Porter shamelessly asked them to contribute to his volume. While the project was aimed to be a surprise gift for Miller, he heard of the undertaking and did nothing to halt the misfired endeavor.

When his anti-American diatribe, *The Air-Conditioned Nightmare* (1945), appeared at the end of World War II, Miller succeeded in losing the audience he found among soldiers. Considering the patriotism sweeping in the United States, such a bilious indictment of America could not have been more ill-timed for mass market circulation. Miller's brand of anti-Americanism did not even find favor from the perspective of members of the American Communist Party. In their newspaper *The Daily Worker*, a 1945 article published by Albert E. Kahn accuses Miller of being "a fascist, anti-Semitic propagandist and a former labor spy." The piece was penned in opposition to a laudatory article published in the anticommunist socialist paper, *The New Leader*. Kahn's commentary portrays Miller as a Nazi sympathizer, noting his German heritage and linking him with other literary supporters of Fascism, including André Gide, Knut Hamsun, and Ezra Pound. The most damning part of the feature, however, relates Miller's visit to Dartmouth at the request of Professor Herbert Faulkner West, whom we are told "is a devoted member of the Miller cult." Kahn says that Miller lectured to military men studying under the Navy V-12 Program, uttering such statements as: "The Nazis are no different than you are. They're fighting for the same things that you're fighting for. [. . .] You're in uniform not because you want to be but because there's an authority that forces you to be. The only authority I believe in recognizing is the authority of one's own will." Although these statements are not inconsistent with *The Air-Conditioned Nightmare,* the language was likely manipulated to fabricate a more menacing Miller. Exaggerated or not, his utterances at Dartmouth, along with his portrayal in Kahn's article, sparked the FBI's interest and further tarnished his reputation.[3]

In the years following World War II, Miller devoted time to projects unable to be published in the United States, such as *The Rosy Crucifixion* trilogy (1949–60), and minor works of questionable literary merit, released on the New Directions imprint. Remotely stationed at Big Sur, surrounded by artistic charlatans and dropouts, he further diminished his stature by drifting

General Reception *17*

into the periphery. Journalists helped to seal his doom through slander. Building upon Kahn's "Miller cult" accusations, Mildred Edie Brady published a piece in *Harper's* entitled, "The New Cult of Sex and Anarchy," a sensational expose portraying Miller as a Big Sur guru. This supercilious work steered intellectuals away from his writings and prompted disenchanted youths to seek his remote station, only to be turned away by Miller himself.[4]

Brady's piece was followed by a series of even more damning articles published a month later in the *San Francisco Examiner.* Clint Mosher begins his first of four columns with the front-page headline: "Group Establishes Cult of Hatred in Carmel Mountains." Incorporating Brady's work as fact, Mosher features Miller as the cult's leader:

> And with Miller perched high atop a mountain at Anderson Creek and his disciples sprawled along the coast highway, the cult is producing an anarchistic credo [. . .] At night, they sit about their clapboard shanties, sparring for the right to utter the well turned phrase and, on occasion, playing such Mid-Victorian parlor games as charades. (1)

Although it is difficult to see charade-playing artists as a major threat, Mosher continues to argue that Miller corrupts the youth with his "doctrine of doom." The feature is accompanied with a picture showing a grimaced Miller seated beside an attractive young woman, well-groomed and dressed in white. With sharp shirt-collars pointing at the downcast girl, he seems poised like a hawk, ready to descend upon the unwitting innocent.

Other columns in Mosher's series associate Miller with Communism and anarchism, titling the second of four: "Emma Goldman Inspired Carmel Hate Cult Chief: Anarchist Eulogized by Henry Miller; Escapest [sic] Doctrines Spread Here." Such accusations did not fare well with an increasingly paranoid America, as the second "Red Scare" was in the gestation process. Although he amazingly emerged unscathed from the Communist whichhunt of the 1950s, his reputation remained severely damaged. Various sensational articles that popped-up periodically only helped seal his fate.[5]

As the McCarthy era waned, it seemed that Miller could establish a respectable reputation, even though his most important books remained unavailable in English speaking countries. In 1957, the National Institute of Arts and Sciences elected him, a gesture indicating the United States was primed to be receptive. In the summer of 1958, Stanley Kubrick and James B. Harris contacted Miller, expressing interesting in making films of *Tropic of Cancer* and *Tropic of Capricorn.* He refused, however, claiming he would "hold out to the day when we have freedom of expression" (qtd. in Martin

450). With Kubrick as director and Harris as producer, the duo would instead make *Lolita* (1962), perhaps the most successful screen adaptation of a controversial literary work. One can only speculate how Miller would be received today, if he had greenlighted the project.

At the dawn of the 1960s, some believed Miller's sensational works could at last be published in the United States. A pivotal court case in late 1960 regarding D. H. Lawrence's *Lady Chatterley's Lover* gave Grove Press enough courage to release *Tropic of Cancer* in 1961, prefaced by Karl Shapiro's adulatory essay, "The Greatest Living Author." The ensuing trials are a storied affair, a pivotal moment in American arts and letters well chronicled in a handful of publications.[6] McCarthyite entities, such as the Citizens for Decent Literature, popped up across the nation. In 1964, the Supreme Court eventually overruled all state rulings on Miller's controversial writings, thereby allowing his entire oeuvre to be readily available.

Miller appears to have been drained by the censorship trials and his newfound fame, leading to circumstances that further damned his reputation. His literary powers had all but disappeared, making him unable to complete *Nexus 2*. In comparison to earlier compositions, all new pieces were poorly executed. Although he had found fame, he became known as the grandfather of the sexual revolution, rather than the literary pioneer he was. By the mid-1960s, his books were considered smut, despite court rulings that stated otherwise. Intellectual attempts to counterbalance negative portrayals fell flat. One such entity was the Minnesota-based Henry Miller Literary Society, which printed newsletters preaching the American author's importance. In Chicago, an art gallery called "M, the Studio for Henry Miller" sold his watercolors, writings, and the work of his associates.[7]

The scant scholarly treatments of Miller in the 1960s failed to examine his early work within its original contexts. Some attempts to examine him seriously were horribly botched, such as *His World of Urania* (1960) by Sidney Omarr, a Hollywood astrologer who continues to publish annual star guides. Miller's own introduction to the book reveals that he reluctantly gave his blessings to Omarr's project.

Kate Millett's *Sexual Politics* (1970), a bestselling feminist study of American literature, greatly damaged Miller's reputation. In *The Prisoner of Sex* (1971), Norman Mailer demonstrates how Millett often quoted Miller out of context, even fabricating a citation.[8] Mailer's brash voice, however, added more heat to the argument, making his rejoinder to Millett less than convincing. Any potential advances Mailer accomplished were short-circuited by Miller's own bad judgment, such as accepting to write an article on female sexuality for *Mademoiselle*.[9] In this piece, he defends his books

General Reception 19

by portraying women as the more oversexed sex: "they dream about it in the waking state as well as asleep. Unless they are extremely inhibited they seem ready to make love any time." Such outbursts were obviously not well received in the era of the Equal Rights Amendment.

Abominable cinematic adaptations also disparaged Miller's credibility. Among these was *Tropic of Cancer* (1970), a soft-porn film starring Rip Torn. *Stille dage i Clichy* (1970), a Danish adaptation of Miller's *Quiet Days in Clichy* (1956), flopped as a pathetic experiment in art-porn, even though *The Evergreen Review* released and promoted the film.[10]

In the 1970s, Miller continued to humor the public in a series of ill-inspired endeavors. Some of these involved *Playboy*, whose subscription base increased sevenfold during the decade. One project was a coffee table book released by Playboy Press entitled *My Life and Times* (1971), which was tangentially linked to Robert Snyder's film, *The Henry Miller Odyssey* (1969).[11] The *Playboy* book featured Miller retelling pivotal moments of his life, snippets already fictionalized or retold in other forums. The most eyebrow raising photos include a clothed Miller posed with a nude centerfold. In one, she poses as a subservient secretary; in another, she plays ping-pong with the 80+ year old author.

While Miller's reputation was in turmoil, his intellectual compatriot Anaïs Nin became a lodestar of the second-wave feminist movement. The Nin renascence began in 1969 with the publication of her diaries, culminating in seven volumes released through 1980. To protect everyone involved, the more licentious passages describing her extramarital sexual affairs with Miller in 1930s Paris were removed for this edition. Nevertheless, the first volumes attest to the strong artistic companionship between Miller and the famous diarist. With this in mind, one cannot underestimate how Millett's book functioned as a hermeneutical tool. In order for Miller to remain so scandalous, one has to overlook the mutually respective relationship he shared with Nin. Considering that sex was excised from the diaries, his sensitivity and creativity should have been clearly perceptible. In an odd coincidence, Nin's rise in popularity correlates with Miller's downfall. While Nin was asked to visit college campuses throughout the United States, Miller sunk into further obscurity and ridicule.

Although he made an appearance on the respectable television show *60 Minutes* in the summer of 1975 and publicly defended Erica Jong's *Fear of Flying* (1973), most of the 1970s remained a low point. *Henry Miller: Asleep and Awake* (1975), however, marks rock bottom. Most of the footage is shot in Miller's bathroom, where the American author and his visitors tacked flotsam on the walls, seemingly at his invitation. Embarrassing

20 Henry Miller and Religion

moments abound for both actor and director Tom Schiller. Zooming in on a portrait of Blaise Cendrars, Schiller asks if it is Bing Crosby, a question that infuriates Miller. The author humors the camera by toweling off his young Asian bride, who tries to escape without being captured on film. He also tries to retell a "Zen parable," most likely of California origin, about a monk called "Master of Fuck." Despite a somewhat intriguing discussion on Gurdjieff, such moments only show traces of a man once deeply engaged in religion and literature. The movie sadly ends with the author cursing New York City as he walks through a Hollywood set, meant to represent his old Brooklyn neighborhood.

Shortly before the end of the decade, Miller did receive some sincere acknowledgement in the critical arena. In *A Literature Without Qualities: American Writing Since 1945* (1979), Warner Berthoff devoted two chapters to Miller's work. The first one, entitled "Old Masters: Henry Miller and Wallace Stevens," treated both authors on equal ground. The final chapter in the book, "Coda: A Note on the Influence of *Tropic of Cancer*," strikingly suggests the direct impact of this novel on contemporary literature, as Berthoff compares passages from Miller's most famous work with lines from T. S. Eliot, Allen Ginsberg, Jack Kerouac, Robert Lowell, Walker Percy, Sylvia Plath, Thomas Pynchon, and even Adrienne Rich. Showing his influence in unlikely places, this stunning chapter demonstrates that Miller made an impression on many beyond the familiar company of Durrell, Mailer, and Nin.

The last honor came when Issac Bashevis Singer nominated Miller for the 1979 Nobel Prize in Literature, only to win it himself. Besides the latecoming praise of Berthoff and Singer in 1979, Miller died the following summer with a marred reputation, relegated to literary backwater. In death notices, he is remembered as a sexual emancipator instead of a pioneering man of letters.

By the 1980s, Miller was all but forgotten. As the footage was filmed before his death, he had a respectable posthumous appearance as a witness in Warren Beatty's acclaimed film *Reds* (1981). The remainder of the decade was not so kind. In a 1984 issue of *Granta*, Salman Rushdie published an article entitled "Outside the Whale," revisiting Orwell's own "Inside the Whale." Rushdie scathingly writes, "In the forty-four years since the essay was first published, Miller's reputation has more or less completely evaporated, and he now looks to be very little more than the happy pornographer beneath whose scatological surface Orwell saw such improbable depths" (95–96). The release of Miller's pornographic writings—under the title *Opus Pistorum* (1983)—likely prompted Rushdie's scathing comments. Two year later, Miller reappeared in *Playboy*, thanks to a feature on Brenda Venus, billed as

General Reception   *21*

"Henry Miller's last great love." A collection of love letters was also timely released under the title, *Dear, Dear Brenda* (1986).[12]

The 1990s found Miller poised for another renaissance. Upon the death of her first husband, Hugo Guiler, Nin's unexpurgated diaries were prepared for publication. The first volume, *Henry and June* (1990), coincided with a cinematic adaptation of the same name. Like the diaries, the film *Henry and June* (1990) focuses on the love triangle among Nin, Miller, and his wife June Smerth. Philip Kaufman directed the film after finding success with his adaptation of Milan Kundara's *Unbearable Lightness of Being*. *Henry and June* also profited from a stellar cast comprised of Fred Ward as Miller, Maria de Medeiros as Nin, and, most notably, Uma Thurman as Smerth. A major advance from prior renderings, the movie is a fairly accurate portrayal of the author and his circle, depicting Miller not as a simple, licentious character, but a dedicated writer who spends more time before the typewriter than in Parisian cafes. Nevertheless, the film is ultimately a clichéd Hollywood love story, a verdict captured in the tagline: "A true adventure more erotic than any fantasy." Receiving the first ever "NC-17" rating by the Motion Picture Association of America demonstrates that any endeavor associated with the controversial writer still remains taboo. Once again, he was distinctly associated with sex and artistic censorship.

Building upon the success of *Henry and June,* the early 1990s also saw the publication of scholarly materials on the American author. Rediscovered in 1988, two of Miller's first projects—*Crazy Cock* (1991) and *Moloch, or This Gentile World* (1992)—were published complete with informative introductory materials. The poor quality of these books, along with their rampant anti-Semitism and homophobia, ultimately did little to help his reputation. In 1992, Ronald Gottesman's edited volume *Critical Essays on Henry Miller* was published as part of the "Critical Essays on American Literature" series. Containing newly commissioned pieces, the attractive hardback called for more academic treatments to follow in its wake. Gottesman writes, "It is still the case that with all of the recent movement of the margins to the center, Henry Miller appears only in one major anthology of American literature" (24). Unfortunately, Gottesman's pleas for critical examination ultimately fell on deaf ears.

Marking the centennial of Miller's birth, two new biographies were released, including Robert Ferguson's *Henry Miller: A Life* (1991). In April, Mary V. Dearborn published *The Happiest Man Alive: A Biography of Henry Miller* (1991), the first of a still unfinished trilogy on Miller, Normal Mailer, and Ernest Hemingway.[13] Despite some passing attacks at Miller's "theology of the cunt" by Sandra M. Gilbert and Susan Gubar, it seemed that feminists of the 1990s, beginning with Dearborn, were ready to treat the American author in a more balanced manner.[14] However, Dearborn's preface to *The Happiest Man Alive* refers to Millett through paraphrasing her famous thesis.

Such prefatory remarks could lead one to believe that Dearborn's biography is as bilious as Millett's study. What follows Dearborn's preface, however, is the most empathetic treatment offered by any biographer to date. She portrays Miller as an oversensitive child who is deeply disturbed by his mother's abusive treatment of his mentally handicapped sister Loretta. She writes, "Often Miller changed places with his sister imaginatively, and suffered her tortures in his own hypersensitive soul. In fact, he developed an ability to hypnotize himself when [. . .] his mother beat Lauretta. Instead of experiencing the horrible spectacle, he would escape into a dream world" (28–29). Dearborn's language, especially "hypersensitive soul," depicts him as sympathetic to women's suffering, even to the point of identification with it.

Dearborn continues to portray Miller more sympathetically. Consulting his *Book of Friends* trilogy, she unearths passages on his childhood and the occurrence of homosexual relationships. Quoting him, she says that the author and his friend Joey "had acquired the habit of buggering one another" (qtd. in Dearborn 31). She also points out sexual abuse he received from a scoutmaster of the Boys Brigade, a group that met in the Miller family's Presbyterian church. She includes this information to suggest psychoanalytical takes on his writings, emphasizing their anti-authoritarian leanings and defiantly heterosexual tone. Although her comments could lead one to reductive interpretations, she consciously elected to render him a "hypersensitive," bi-curious, and victimized child. Curiously, male biographers who had access to this same information chose not to report it.

Dearborn's book also rightly highlights the anti-Semitic and misogynist strains within Miller's work and life. She even maintains he was simply unable to see women—even Anaïs Nin—as equals. These claims would later be addressed by Erica Jong in her Miller book, *The Devil at Large* (1993). A mix of biography, panegyric, critical study, cultural history, and memoir, it contains many critical insights. Jong contends that Miller's major work was not only officially banned in the United States for decades, but remains unofficially boycotted due to Millett's impact. Although Jong detests the aftershock of Millett's work, she does agree with both Millett and Dearborn that "Miller's entire apprehension of sex was misogynistic" (13). But like Dearborn, Jong continued the trend of making Miller more personable. Jong goes further than Dearborn, however, by suggesting that Miller was not anti-Semitic, referring to her personal experiences with him as evidence. A Jewish author herself, Jong shields him by showing how he often defended Jews,

General Reception 23

even occasionally claiming to be Jewish. After suggesting that he often criticized Jewish culture with the lightheartedness of an insider, she accounts for Miller's more severe jabs by claiming they issue from jealousy, as he was born into a gentile environment suspicious of education. In addition to addressing this difficult subject, she additionally civilizes him by poignantly recounting their friendship, calling the controversial author her "spiritual grandfather."

Another high-profile defense is Louise DeSalvo's introduction for the Signet Classic edition of *Tropic of Cancer* (1995). Instead of focusing on his childhood, DeSalvo casts light on obstacles Miller overcame as an adult, especially due to his working-class background. Examining him from this perspective, she suggests that his language is not only a reflection of voices that surrounded him, but a howling rage against oppressive forces in general.

DeSalvo goes on to consider the sacrifices and humiliation Miller experienced when becoming a writer, as he often looked to friends, family, and even his wife for financial assistance. She writes, "In a patriarchal culture, this dependency 'unmans' the male working-class writer. It forces him to use charm, guile, and seduction to keep himself fed, clothed, and housed—attributes ordinarily ascribed to dependent women" (x). According to her, he had to assume a manly voice not only to compensate for his feminine artistic sensibilities, but also to counterbalance economic dependency. Considering his Protestant upbringing and inherited work-ethic, he must have felt like a failure, as he was neither able to care for his family in New York nor support himself in Paris. Living abroad, he mostly survived through Nin's generosity, but he also depended upon wires from his wife, June Smerth.

DeSalvo treats Miller's traumatic affair with Smerth, recalling how she encouraged him to quit his job as employment manager. Although Smerth supported him, she was soon discouraged by his uneven efforts at writing. According to DeSalvo's account, Smerth continued to belittle him by taking a lesbian lover—Jean Kronski—who moved into their tiny apartment and would eventually leave with Smerth. DeSalvo includes this negative portrait of the women to show Miller as a victim to infidelity and cruelty. In DeSalvo's eyes, *Tropic of Cancer* is to be read as a reaction to these horrific moments. Like Dearborn and Jong, DeSalvo compensates for his faults by presenting a vulnerable Miller. She, however, uniquely traces his misogyny not to childhood, but to adult traumatic experiences stemming from his working-class past and tumultuous affair with Smerth.

DeSalvo also surpasses prior sympathetic renderings by showing incongruities between Miller's fabricated *übermensch* and the author portrayed in Nin's diaries. On the final page of her introduction, DeSalvo writes: "Yet Anaïs Nin had recorded in her diary that Miller punished women in his work because he let himself be violated by them in his life. She saw *him* as the victim of a woman's mistreatment" (xvii). By using Nin's voice as an authoritative witness to the Miller who wrote *Tropic of Cancer,* DeSalvo depicts him as a man-child who uses big talk to compensate for a throbbing internal wound. Her introduction is effective, as she incorporates the same materials handled by second-wave feminists.

Despite the wide exposure of these materials, negative portrayals in pop culture continued to make a deeper impact. The 1991 remake of *Cape Fear,* directed by Martin Scorsese, recasts the tale of Max Cady (Robert de Niro), a released rapist who seeks revenge on his prosecutor, Sam J. Bowden (Nick Nolte). One of the most intense moments comes when Cady attempts to seduce Bowden's fifteen-year-old daughter, Danielle (Juliette Lewis). With Bible verses tattooed all over his body, Cady seductively reads passages from Miller's *Sexus.* As the first volume of *The Rosy Crucifixion, Sexus* is presented as a perversion of Christianity, just as Cady's body-text conflicts with his actions. On a level accessible to general audiences, Miller's writings are again as a literature of defilement, able to contaminate and corrupt the innocent. Scorcese's film suggests that criminals, including those who rape young girls, read Henry Miller.

In a lighter manner, an episode of *Seinfeld* premiering the same year imparted a similar lesson. "The Library" is framed around an overdue fine Jerry Seinfeld receives for *Tropic of Cancer,* a book he checked out decades before but never returned. In high school, Jerry allowed George Costanza to borrow the book, which he then lost in a scuffle with his gym teacher. Years after the teacher lost his job over this incident, Costanza rediscovers him homeless outside of the New York Public Library. The show ends with a close-up of *Tropic of Cancer,* suggesting the book hastened the instructor's downward spiral. A "dirty book" received when losing his job, *Tropic of Cancer* turns him into a "dirty man."

Although his Seinfeld appearance and cameo in *Cape Fear* may seem insignificant, these were the most popular depictions of Miller in the early 1990s. Though tempered by *Henry and June* the year before, these 1991 representations once again framed his work as pornography, books that will somehow contaminate the beholder. Sadly, since the solid scholarly considerations did not receive major exposure for the remainder of the decade, his reputation remains tied to these pop culture depictions.[15] To be fair, *Tropic of Cancer* was listed at #50 on the Modern Library's list entitled "One Hundred Best Novels of the Twentieth Century," published in the *New York Times* in July 1998. Miller's inclusion, however, is merely a symbolic gesture rather than a convincing argument. The following year, *Tropic of Cancer* was

General Reception 25

portrayed not as a literary landmark, but as a sex aid in the box-office sensation *American Pie* (1999). A recent article on American censorship in *Newsweek* entitled "From Henry Miller to Howard Stern" (2004) demonstrates that Miller remains etched a pornographer in the popular imagination.[16]

In this chapter, I sketched a story of an important writer's reputation that has been steered not by rigorous analysis, but by representations in pop culture. If people actually read his books, rather than thumbing the "dirty parts," perhaps this crucial author would have been rightfully seen as a pivotal writer.

Chapter Three
Avant-Garde Religion

As a denizen of New York City during the first decades of the twentieth century, Henry Miller participated in numerous avant-garde groups devoted to art *and* religion. Public lectures and publications gave the Brooklynite a window into a realm dominated by the cultural elite of Greenwich Village. Arriving in Paris around the age of 40, he gained entrance into the post-Lost Generation intellectual world, finding himself surrounded by writers, painters, and other artists who shared his spiritual interests.

In this chapter, I begin by taking us to 1910s and 1920s Greenwich Village, a place where avant-garde religious movements—including Gurdjieff, Rosicrucianism, and Theosophy—were popular among the literati. I discuss Miller's involvement as an outsider, and suggest how the movements' intermingling of art and religion helped him establish a relationship between these two fields. Next, I analyze books he encountered during his formative years that helped him develop this connection. Unpublished notebooks are examined throughout to help us understand how he read these texts. Although the books that excited him came from different fields—including philosophy, art criticism, literary criticism, and psychoanalysis—they all assisted in developing a vision, in which art, religion, and sex are seen as three manifestations of one sacred creative energy.

AVANT-GARDE RELIGION

United by a vague conception of liberation, the avant-garde cultural centers of the early twentieth century often commingled art and religious thought. In New York's Greenwich Village, any source potentially capable of liberating the individual—from politics to psychoanalysis—was in high demand. Historian Robert Humphrey, in his *Children of Fantasy: The First Rebels of Greenwich Village,* vividly describes this scene: "Although Greenwich Villagers held diverse views on art and politics, they agreed that the individual should be liberated. To this end, they encouraged artistic freedom, violated conventional mores, and supported a radical reorganization of society" (251). Religion was not exempt from this mad pursuit of liberation. As Leslie Fishbein argues, some included religion in their lives because "they desired a life of intensity and commitment" (221). During this critical period in American cultural history, many disciplined artists used both art and religion as ways to emancipate the self.

Miller, however, was situated between avant-garde pioneers and bohemian charlatans. Most of his association with the pretenders came through his marriage to June Smerth, who had adopted the name of June Mansfield to suggest some relation to Katherine Mansfield, a writer adored by Greenwich Village eccentrics. Miller biographer Jay Martin relates that some even called Smerth "Queen of the Village," an appellation that perhaps came through her profession as a "taxi dancer," a type of prostitution in which lonely men would pay a small fee to dance with sultry women in dark clubs (119). Under these conditions, Smerth supposedly met Miller in the Roseland Ballroom during the summer of 1923.[1]

Once married, Miller became part of the more capricious facets of Greenwich Village life. Smerth encouraged him to abandon his job as employment manager of the Western Union Telegraph Company, thereby giving him more time to write. To support themselves, they devised a number of unconventional schemes, including selling candy on the streets and opening a speakeasy called "The Pepper Pot," in which Smerth would allegedly entertain clients in the back office. Other plots involved selling Miller's prose poems, collectively titled *Mezzotints,* under her name. One of her devotees even commissioned her to write a novel, which Miller ghostwrote.[2] When he failed to produce dazzling works of art, however, their relationship suffered. Smerth became close with a lesbian friend, a marionette maker who eventually moved into their apartment. Eventually, the two ladies departed for Europe, leaving Miller alone in New York City.

Despite Miller's bohemianism by association, he became tangentially involved with the serious intellectual circles of Greenwich Village. Working-class and without substantial publications, he was barred from elite societies, such as A. R. Orage's Gurdjieff group. He was able to follow their movements, however, through New York journals, in which art and literature were printed alongside articles that engaged metaphysical concerns. In *The Dial,* we find Kenneth Burke's translation of Oswald Spengler's *Decline of the West* garnished by works from distinguished poets.[3] The first issue of *The Little Review* includes pioneering fiction alongside an article on Henri Bergson's

Avant-Garde Religion 29

principle of *élan vital*.[4] Because Margaret Anderson and Jane Heap, the editors of *The Little Review*, were intimately involved with the Gurdjieff movement, Miller may have first heard of the group from them. Arriving in Paris in 1930, he became increasingly acquainted with the movement during his decade-long stay. His familiarity with the esoteric school is confirmed in his preface to Fritz Peters's *Boyhood with Gurdjieff*, an account of life at the Prieuré—the center for Gurdjieff work—from the vantage point of the eleven-year-old Peters.

During the 1910s and 1920s, Miller attended many public lectures in New York City that advocated a radical form of religiosity. Biographical remembrances confirm the effects of lectures by W. E. B. DuBois, Emma Goldman, and lesser-known intellectuals, such as John Cowper Powys and evangelical minister Benjamin Fay Mills. Little is known about Mills, his congregation at Oakland's First Unitarian Church, and his legacy after abandoning institutionalized religion. Swami Vivekananda's eight lectures at his Oakland church in 1899, however, attest to Mills's acceptance of Eastern ideas.[5] Biographer Jay Martin tells us more: "Particularly stressing New Thought, Mills assembled a *mélange* of spiritist ideas—telepathy, hypnotism, mental suggestion, the 'divinity within,' and the 'transmigration of mental powers'—tied loosely to Christian Science and expressed in a tone of moral earnestness" (35). The notion of "divinity within" resonated with Miller, who was twenty-one years old when first introduced to Mills. According to a story he often recounted, Miller was so moved during the first Mills lecture he attended, he offered his services in exchange for private lessons.[6] Mills, in turn, allowed the spirited Miller to attend exclusive sessions on the condition that he help collect donations. This story underscores not only his youthful enthusiasm for esoteric religious teachings, but the obstacles he had to overcome to gain entrance into the inner sanctum of these movements.

Miller was also involved with the Theosophical Society in both New York City and Paris. Most likely, he was introduced to Theosophy through his childhood friend Robert Hamilton Challacombe, who was a member of the Theosophical Society and also a follower of Mills, New Thought, the Ethical Culture movement, and Bahá'í.[7] Although it is difficult to determine the intensity of Miller's involvement with the Theosophical Society in New York City, an incident related in *Sexus* has him delivering a powerful speech after being inspired by a lecture at the Society. So moving was this outburst that an official supposedly invited him to give another oration at a later date. Later in Paris, he continued to follow the Theosophical Society; one of his first letters home describes watching a Surrealist film by Luis Buñuel at their meeting house.[8]

Because they are mentioned throughout his published works and some copies are preserved in his archives, we know Theosophical books, such as Madame Blavatsky's *Secret Doctrine* (1888), had a tremendous impact on Miller's religious awareness.[9] David Edger, one of Miller's friends in Paris, presented him with two Theosophical texts that shaped the themes, symbols, and even character names in his later work: A. P. Sinnett's *Esoteric Buddhism* (1883) and Blavatsky's *The Voice of the Silence: Chosen Fragments from the "Book of the Golden Precepts" for the Daily Use of Lanoos (Disciples)* (1889).[10] These texts introduced him to the Theosophical project of unifying all religious and philosophical understanding into one essential doctrine. The variety of ideas and the totalizing way in which they were presented made a monumental impression on him, giving the American author license to make cross-cultural comparisons between such seemingly divergent religious figures as Jesus Christ and the Buddha. These books introduced Miller to Eastern religious figures, such as Lao-Tzu and Ramakrishna, whose works he went on to examine for himself. While other Modernists, such as T. S. Eliot, James Joyce, and Ezra Pound, would absorb the encyclopedic spirit of Theosophy by including many languages in their work, Miller seriously engaged the movement's philosophy in order to develop his own religious thinking. His writings demonstrate that he draws upon these resources to develop his own religious consciousness and intricate symbolism.

Early in his intellectual life, Miller also learned the principles of Rosicrucianism, mystical teachings that he incorporated into his own literary achievements. In the basic Gnostic renderings of Rosicrucianism, one acknowledges that the world is corrupt but nevertheless journeys towards salvation through the body rather than the spirit. Initiate P. R. Koenig writes of this sensual path: "The sensual gnostic embraces sin in order to experience the decaying of the world, and to rise as the Phoenix from the ashes. Sexual orgies are sweating out the divine Pneuma/Logos which rises to the Pleroma."[11] This reveals Miller's confessional project as a sensual way to salvation through embracing sex and the negative dimensions of existence. Although he probably knew of Rosicrucianism in New York City, he began intensively to research this tradition during his stay in Paris. On the opening page of his copy of the key Rosicrucian text, Max Heindel's *The Rosicrucian Cosmo-Conception,* he wrote an inscription that conveys his enthusiasm for this mystical religion: "Sacred Property of Henry Miller, 18 Villa Seurat, Paris (XIV) who has just discovered that he has been a Rosicrucian all his life. [...] Dedicated to conquest of Desire Body. [...] Paris 3/5/39."[12] Rosicrucianism had a major effect on his artistic and religious sensibilities, inspiring him to title his magnum opus *The Rosy Crucifixion.*

Avant-Garde Religion 31

In Paris, Miller encountered many alchemical and mystical texts pivotal to Rosicrucian consciousness, all collected by his astrologer friend Conrad Moricand in a handwritten manuscript entitled *Pages curieuses des grandes occultists* (circa 1938). This document contains texts in French translated from multiple ancient philosophers and mystics throughout the ages, including Hermes Trimestigus, Plato, Paracelsus, Jacob Boehme, Swedenborg, and a host of lesser known occultists.[13] Some of the ideas included within the folio, especially those of Boehme, were to play an integral role in the metaphysics of Miller's writings.

Also through Moricand, Miller had some connection to the Ordo Templi Orientis (OTO), a Rosicrucian faction led by Aleister Crowley. Crowley aficionado J. Edward Cornelius believes Moricand introduced Miller to the spiritual leader's work in 1933. Cornelius bolsters his claim by citing a section from Anaïs Nin's diary dated 2 November 1934, in which she writes of the pair: "Henry has fallen under the spell of a remarkable old man [Crowley] who is fantastic and psychic, a painter gone mad in Zurich." This scholar also mentions that Miller refers to Crowley in a letter to his friend Emil Schnellock in October 1935. Biographer Robert Ferguson also confirms that Crowley and Miller met through Moricand, and that the American author even tried to borrow money from the cult figure![14] Cornelius, however, is more cautious in asserting that the two actually met, as he notes that Crowley was banished from France in 1929. Nevertheless, Miller's work shows that he was acquainted with Crowley's writings and thus the practices of the OTO described.

MILLER AND SECULAR SOURCES

A concern for self-liberation united Miller's varied reading, both religious and secular. Not coincidentally, liberation was a key theme in foundational texts in art and religion published in 1930s Paris. Mircea Eliade's *Yoga: Essai sur l'origine de la mystique indienne* (1933), for example, claimed that yoga is used to liberate people from limitations physical and spiritual. An acquantance of Miller and close companion of Nin, Antonin Artaud began to conceive of a "Theatre of Cruelty" that would liberate people from inhibitions and self-imposed constraints through artistic shock. Many other publications persuaded Miller that self-liberation is a preoccupation of both art and religion, leading him to believe that art and religion derived from the same source.

Evidence for this transcendental claim was to be found in scientific literature of the time, particularly psychoanalysis. In *Two Essays on Analytical Psychology* (1928), a text that Miller cites in published correspondence and unpublished notes, C. G. Jung develops the concept of the collective unconscious, a repository of archetypes that reappear in both art and religious myth.[15] *Art and Artist* (1932) by Otto Rank, a close acquaintance of Miller and paramour of Nin, makes an even stronger case for the esoteric interrelationship between these two worlds.[16] In the preface to his text, Rank identifies an inborn urge to create that "does not find expression in works of art alone: it also produces religion and mythology and the social institutions corresponding to these" (xiii). In his book, he goes on to argue that art is the fulfillment of religion, and that it is the artist's task to unite these divergent streams. Since such works were heralded as science, they invested Miller's literary endeavor with the authority to assume Rank's challenge of synthesizing these disparate realms.

Miller found further inspiration in the work of Henri Bergson, a philosopher whose work he had known since his early adulthood.[17] Bergson's concept of *élan vital*—"life spirit"—provided him with a metaphorical conception of the impulse behind creative acts, whether natural, religious, or artistic. In *Two Sources of Morality and Religion* (1932), a treatise published while Miller began to write *Tropic of Cancer,* Bergson used his idea of *élan vital* to identify two types of religion: dynamic and static. He associates static religion with institutional forms of worship, claiming that such organizations restrict the flow of *élan vital.* Dynamic religion, on the other hand, promotes the vital surge.

Bergson suggests that dynamic religious experience, in which one becomes liberated, involves a sort of rupture, as in Jesus's parable of the wine skins. In fact, he often presents *élan vital* in liquid metaphors, conjuring fluid images such as currents, rivers, and streams. In one passage, for example, his description of dynamic religious experience is enhanced by such visuals: "And all great mystics declare that they have the impression of a current passing from their soul to God, and flowing back again from God to mankind" (53). Applied to both art and religion, the image of creative force would reappear in the fiction Miller wrote after Bergson published this treatise.

Similar liquid conceptions of energy are to be found in esteemed art criticism of the age. In a letter to Jean Paulhan dated 25 January 1936, Artaud discusses "the pool of energies which constitute Myths." While only a private account, it suggests a broader use of liquid metaphors to render religious motifs in 1930s Paris. A much larger reservoir is Elie Faure's five-volume study *History of Art* (1909–27), a massive work that had a tremendous impact on Miller.[18] This study attempts to trace "l'esprit des formes" from prehistoric art to contemporary art, disregarding distinctions between different genres. As with the psychoanalytic writings, Faure's study posits a tight interrelationship

Avant-Garde Religion

between art and religion, going so far as to claim, "Religion does not create art; on the contrary, it is developed by art" (1: 22). In his attempt to trace the evolution of art, he often referred to this energy binding art and religion as the "great rhythm," but he also uses other metaphors.[19] The following passage, which begins with a discussion of the "creative spirit," shows his tendency to use energy metaphors of light, sound, and liquid interchangeably:

> Whatever god he adores, or even if he rejects all the gods, the man who desires to create cannot express himself if he does not feel in his veins the *flow* of all the *rivers*—even those which carry along sand and putrefaction, he is not realizing his entire being if he does not see the *light* of all the constellations, even those which no longer *shine,* if the primeval *fire,* even when locked in beneath the crust of the earth, does not *consume* his nerves, if the hearts of all men, even the dead, even those still to be born, do not *beat* in his heart, if abstraction does not mount from his senses to his soul to raise it to the plane of the laws which cause men to act, *the rivers to flow, the fire to burn, and the constellations to revolve.* (2: xix-xx, emphasis added)

In this passage, itself an example of literary flow barely channeled by punctuation, we find Faure shifting from metaphors of flowing, illumination, burning, and pulsating all in one sentence! Miller's fiction, particularly *Tropic of Cancer* (1934), will incorporate each of these images as metaphors for the creative impulse, although flow will be the predominate one. In addition, his use of obscene language preserves the impurities—the "sand and putrefaction"—that Faure maintains *must* be expressed in this creative surge.

To art and religion, Miller added a third tributary flowing from the sacred source of creativity: sexual desire. To make this connection, he was again guided by the writings of C. G. Jung, who envisioned the libido through the same liquid metaphors employed by Bergson and Faure. A quotation attributed to Oswald Spengler, which we find in one of Miller's unpublished notebooks, demonstrates how he was able to make a connection between Jung's libido and Bergson's *élan vital:* "Jung saw in the term (libido) a concept of unknown nature, comparable to Bergson's *élan vital,* a hypothetical energy of life, occupying itself with all human activities and interests."[20] In another notebook, he devotes many pages to Jung's thoughts not only on the flow of libido but on its blockages through fixation.[21] He admits his own fixation on his wife June Smerth, a realization that, in turn, shapes the form and content of his work. In *Tropic of Cancer,* which chronicles his break from Smerth, we find him merging with the river at the end of the novel, signifying spiritual purification and a healthy flow of sexual desire once he is able to release himself from captivity. In *Sexus* (1949), whose narrative occurs years before the Parisian events, seemingly unfocused passages are saturated with sexual thoughts of a fictionalized Smerth, representing his inability to direct his creative stream into the creation of art at the outset of his literary career.

The fiction and writings of D. H. Lawrence also shaped Miller's view of the relationship between art, religion, and sex. In fact, as he extensively revised *Tropic of Cancer* for publication in the early 1930s, he explored the connection between these three fields in a study on Lawrence. Miller's publisher, Jack Kahane of Obelisk Press, encouraged him, believing it would establish him as a serious man of letters before the appearance of *Tropic of Cancer.*[22] Unfortunately, he could not complete his meditation.[23] His personal archives reveal that the work consumed him, resulting in fragmentary manuscripts and notebooks that together amount to nearly a thousand pages. *The World of Lawrence,* however incomplete, had a fruitful effect on his work. In trying to grasp Lawrence, he formed a clearer understanding of his own views and literary mission and was able to synthesize various influences into a coherent vision. These revelations allowed him to conceptualize *Tropic of Cancer* as a religious testament, rather than simply an account of his Paris days.

By culling what remains of the Lawrence manuscript, we gain a better sense of what Miller aimed to accomplish in his own fiction. In excerpts published during his lifetime, he develops an amorphous conceptualization of the artist, a figure loosely designated as "artist," "poet," "Dionysian type of artist," or, as we find in *Tropic of Cancer,* "inhuman."[24] This vague notion of artist includes novelists, poets, philosophers, architects, painters, dancers, musicians, and composers. He frequently includes major religious figures as well, as illustrated by the following passage on Lawrence's predecessors: "Jesus certainly, and Nietzsche, and Whitman and Dostoievski. All the poets of life, the mystics" ("Creative" 2). Similar lists of "the poets of life" appear throughout Miller's writings of the early 1930s.

What ultimately binds these extraordinarily diverse figures is their willingness to break artistic and moral boundaries. In Miller's work, these figures are often presented as messiahs, individuals who have sacrificed themselves to art or ideas in order to save the living. As he writes in *The World of Lawrence,* "The savior and the artist type are fundamentally one and the same" (126). In his essay "Creative Death," he maintains that in contemporary times, we are not in as much need for "Apollonian" artists, those concerned with form and representation, as we are "Dionysian" ones, who can bring

Avant-Garde Religion

about the destruction of civilization and its ills through their sagacity. Out of their "creative deaths," in which they bury themselves with the tombs of their texts, can emerge a new, flourishing culture. Employing images at once biblical and anthropological, he writes:

> Once again man must re-enact the mystery of the god, the god whose fertilizing death is to redeem and to purify man from guilt and sin, to free him from the wheel of birth and becoming. Sin, guilt, neurosis— they are one and the same, the fruit of the tree of knowledge. The tree of life now becomes the tree of death. But it is always the same tree. And it is from this tree of death that life must spring forth again, that life must be reborn. (11–12)

Dionysian artists are avant-garde in the truest sense: shock troops whose deaths pave the way for descendents.[25] Through art, the individual sacrifices himself to save the next generation.

Miller's apocalyptic outlook was inspired by the millennial philosophy of Oswald Spengler.[26] In "Creative Death," he uses Spengler's distinction between the epochs of "Culture" and "Civilization," which spin into one another on the grand wheel of time. In unpublished notes related to his study of D. H. Lawrence, Miller quotes Spengler on how "Culture" is identified with religion and "Civilization" with the irreligious consciousness. Although "Civilization" may take place in an era of irreligiousness, the artists within it generate the seeds that lead towards a full flowering of religious awakening in the next period of "Culture," a new beginning or "Second Religiousness." Spengler identifies these two periods with the figures of Apollo and Faust, which Miller in turn associations with Apollo and Dionysus, as the American author muses on the different types of artists he associates with each epoch.[27]

Miller derived this distinction most directly from Friedrich Nietzsche's writings. *The Birth of Tragedy,* in which he first makes the distinction between the Apollonian and the Dionysian, immensely influenced Miller, beginning in his youth.[28] In fact, one of his extant notebooks contains twenty pages of notes on the text, mostly consisting of lengthy quotations. Nietzsche's aesthetic treatise convinced him that tension between divergent poles gives rise to tragedy, leading him to establish related dichotomies in his own work, such as oppositions between horizontality/verticality and transcendence/immanence. In writings such as *Tropic of Cancer,* he translates these metaphysical tensions into concrete symbols, manufacturing polarities out of man/woman and rock/river. By exploring the friction between these extremities, he was able to express his personal tragedy—his "rosy crucifixion"—in which the mundane drama becomes mythic.

The stress placed on music and dance as Dionysian forms of art shaped Miller's perception of how a text can break the constraints of two-dimensionality. This is particularly the case in *Tropic of Cancer,* a book that shouts in the opening pages, "I will sing while you croak, I will dance over your dirty corpse. . . ." (24). Furthermore, he explicitly conceived of this book to be a "song that contaminates," meaning that it would break down our resistances, injecting us not with disease but life-affirming freedom (233). Nietzsche often presents music as a liberating force, as in the following passage from *The Birth of Tragedy* that Miller underlines and quotes in one of his notebooks: "What was the power which freed Prometheus from his vultures and transformed the myth into a vehicle of Dionysian wisdom? It is the Heracleian [sic] power of music."[29] Naturally, this passage must have made an impression, as it mixes music with the image of the river, through alluding to Heraclitus, and posits that this force can liberate the bounded Prometheus, himself chained to a rock.[30]

In addition to Prometheus, *The Birth of Tragedy* introduced Miller to the mystical figures of Dionysus and Orpheus.[31] Reviewing Nietzsche's text around 1932 prompted his search for additional sources on Dionysus, Orphic myths, and most particularly the practice of omophagia. Again in his notebooks, we find pages of notes on these subjects. When recopying the Orpheus myth from the *Encyclopedia Britannica,* he includes his own parenthetical explication in which he connects the consumption of Orpheus with Christian rites: "omophagia is ritual of consuming the totems, the gods—*the communion*" (emphasis added).[32] His ability to link the pagan rite with the Christian Mass demonstrates his tendency to translate myths into a Christian schematic. Although Miller scholar Bertrand Mathieu has noted the influence of Orphic materials on the form and content of his fiction, he overlooks this fundamental act of translation, in which he first processes the myths in Christian terms before applying them to fictionalizing his own life as a "rosy crucifixion."[33]

Out of the concept of omophagia and its relationship to Nietzsche's idea of "Dionysian art," Miller developed the figure of the "Dionysian artist," whose "creative death" helps feed the next generation by replenishing the modern wasteland. He was consciously employing a conceptualization of self-sacrifice enacted through one's art, in which the writer buries himself in his creation not only to become immortal through its literary afterlife, but also to become resurrected as a liberated individual in the immediate present. He found additional inspiration for these ideas again in the writings of Jung.

Avant-Garde Religion

Consider the following passage, which refers to his particular notion of the artist, from one of Miller's notebooks:

> The demands to free himself from [the] bond of childish dependency [are] so strong that [he] frequently produces the severest conflicts, the period being characterized symbolically as a *self-sacrifice* by Jung. This struggle and conflict gives rise to the unconscious phantasy of self-sacrifice which really means the sacrificing of the childish tendencies and love type in order to free libido. (emphasis Miller's)[34]

Miller's "phantasy of self-sacrifice," however, was to become a program of chronicling his struggle to harness libido into religious art, a process that would liberate him from the ghosts of his past.

The philosophy of Emerson would inspire Miller to use writing to liberate not only his own "divinity within," but the divine in those who read his work. He may have gained access to Emerson's thought, if only indirectly, through the poetry and prose of Walt Whitman; most likely it came through Ludwig Lewisohn's *Expression in America* (1932). Published the same year that Miller began writing *Tropic of Cancer*, this history of American literature is cited in the Lawrence manuscript as well as in correspondence from the early 1930s, suggesting that he frequently referred to this work in Paris.[35] Furthermore, he took over twenty pages of notes on the contents, attesting to the mighty influence of Lewisohn's study.[36] The book begins with Emersonian musings on the poet, which Lewisohn renders as someone preoccupied with catharsis and liberation:

> He starts from an inner fact of his individual consciousness. Out of that consciousness, which is both perceiver and thing perceived, both container and content, there arises the impassioned need for the release and communication of experience, for the *liberation* from that experience and its projection for the contemplation and *salvation* of his fellows. (qtd. in Miller, emphasis added)[37]

Such words must have resounded in Miller's mind, as he wanted a book like *Tropic of Cancer* to be a "container" whose "content" would not only hold the story of his own liberation, but would also bring about a similar transformation within his readers. There are, however, even more striking correspondences between Lewisohn and the American author. As quoted by Miller, Lewisohn writes of the poet: "For the modern poet has not chosen a subject, grateful or ungrateful, which he can determine to treat in this or that fashion. He and his subject are one. He has descended to the depth of his soul and so to the core of the world whence, if the world is organic or even continuous, all roads must be roads to God" (qtd. in Miller).[38] Not only is this idea in accord with Miller's conviction that he and his work were one, but that access to the divine comes through self-exploration.

Lewisohn also discusses how writers create a literary "double" who is able to carry out actions that the author is otherwise unable to perform himself. Referring to Edgar Allen Poe, in particular his story "William Wilson," he writes: "This double personifies the 'I's' terror of itself and contempt for itself, comes between the 'I' and the object of its passions and thus *liberates* that 'I' from the consciousness of both impotence and guilt" (qtd. in Miller, emphasis added).[39] Miller's attraction to this passage reveals how he was consciously creating a literary double in his own fiction. Take it this way: by painting a portrait of himself as a virile man in books like *Tropic of Cancer*, Miller was simultaneously confessing his guilt for abandoning June Smerth and, at the same time, compensating for his inability to win her devotion. By considering this concept of the double, we can more precisely understand the important distinction between Miller the man and Miller the character.

The most intriguing passage he quotes from this study, however, pertains to the artist's use of traditional symbols. Lewisohn describes how an artist must not be preoccupied with creating new symbols, but instead must update old ones for modern times. Nuanced by his understanding of Bergson and Jung, Miller accepted Lewisohn's indictment and presented a contemporary vision of Christianity. Unlike many of his contemporaries, who saw ancient symbols as broken and mute, Miller believed they were salvageable. Indeed, he updates the story of Christ's crucifixion and resurrection by applying this framework to his own biography. His understanding of Christ is admittedly tinted by other myths, such as those from the Orphic tradition, and by alternative religious concepts, including the Buddhist figure of the bodhisattva—a saint who postpones his own spiritual release to help others experience nirvana. Building upon Jesus's idea that "the Kingdom of God is within," Miller believed that self-emancipation allows this sacred energy to issue forth in the forms of art, religion, and sexual desire.[40]

Avant-garde religious movements introduced Miller to many of these concepts and afforded him the freedom to envision the Christ myth in unorthodox ways. Furthermore, these groups promoted a sincere religious cosmopolitanism that encouraged him to freely select concepts that he would synthesize into a choate entity. As we have seen, his religiosity was additionally colored by what he uncovered in secular texts, ranging from psychoanalytical works to literary criticism. Such sources helped him to conceive the

Avant-Garde Religion 39

sacred as an effortlessly flowing energy, albeit channeled into specific endeavors, such as the creation of art. Blockages damming this flow, whether sexual obsessions or rigorous moral systems, must be eliminated, because they are antithetical to the evolutionary force promoting diversity and multiplicity. As a writer, then, he purports to unleash this holy energy within him through art, hoping that his literary afterbirth will also promote spiritual rebirths within those who encounter his texts.

Chapter Four
Tropic of Cancer

Tropic of Cancer (1934) chronicles Henry Miller's self-liberation, narrating his emotional departure from the people, places, and situations constraining his development.[1] According to the story, he escapes the confinement of his New York past, particularly his overbearing mother, alcoholic father, and tumultuous affair with his wife June Smerth, who appears in the book as "Mona." He smashes all manacles to become a writer, leaving behind a series of respectable jobs ranging from proofreader to English instructor. Although he had already written three unpublished novels and a handful of published pieces, he realized in Paris that these works were imitative, impeded by traditional design. He consciously set out to develop a style that would reflect the disorder around him, a form that would grow organically out of the formlessness. His new format, however, would employ techniques used in the centuries-old genres of confession and hagiography. In the tradition of religious autobiographies, he would include himself as the protagonist and narrator of the account.

Scanning the subjects of *Tropic of Cancer*—abandoning one's wife, globetrotting, changing careers—one could dismiss the work as a simple personal account of a midlife crisis. There is, however, much more amiss. Like Dante, whose *Divine Comedy* begins "in the middle of the journey of our life," Miller attempts to elevate his autobiography to a testament of spiritual transformation.[2]

In this chapter, I offer an interpretation of *Tropic of Cancer* as a narrative of Miller's rebirth as a liberated individual. The novel charts his journey, in which he transfigures himself into a divine artist. The guiding principle in his quest is creative energy, a sacred power symbolized in the image of the river. He guides us through his voyage, taking us from the confinements of his apartment at the Villa Borghese to the open air banks of the Seine, where he becomes one with the river—his prime symbol—at the end of the narrative. Before this moment of mystical union, he relates how this pent-up energy had been misspent. While he taps into a primal energy that he sees as the root of art, religion, and healthy sexual desire, he confesses periods of blockage—particularly his fixation on Mona—and scathingly critiques civilization for investing itself in military exercises, the accumulation of capital, and perverse sexual endeavors. By examining critical passages from his most famous book, I aim to chart this pilgrim's progress. The chapter ends by address how he sought to promote spiritual awakenings within those who read *Tropic of Cancer.*

THE MISSION OF *TROPIC OF CANCER*

Since freeing oneself and becoming an artist are equivalent in Miller's mind, the narrative of *Tropic of Cancer* tells two stories in one, namely, the tale of the author's liberation and the genesis of the book itself. In other words, it simultaneously details the trauma of his rebirth and the birth of the text, as did Dante in *The Divine Comedy* and Marcel Proust in *Remembrance of Things Past.* Towards the beginning of the second chapter, Miller explicitly uses birthing terms to describe the writing process: "Perhaps it is because the book has begun to grow inside me. I am carrying it around with me everywhere. I walk through the streets big with child and the cops escort me across the street. Women get up to offer me their seats" (43). Contrasting his current work with previous attempts at writing a novel, this passage allows us to see this text as an organic product rather than a forced literary endeavor. But to see *Tropic of Cancer* as the story of his own spiritual rebirth, we have to examine the opening pages in detail.

The first two pages serve as a roadmap to the work, showing the transition from spiritual death to renewed life, the story to be chronicled at length in *Tropic of Cancer.*[3] Although unadvertised, Miller begins his book with the convention of the opening argument, a thematic summery that helps us navigate a taxing work of literature. Another writer who rendered energy sacred, William Blake also employed this device, and it is likely that Miller was consciously emulating *The Marriage of Heaven and Hell.*[4] In a letter to a Norwegian lawyer who tried to defend his books in court, Miller calls his autobiographical novels "a sort of modern 'Marriage of Heaven and Hell'" (White 13). Although this statement comes two decades after the initial publication of *Tropic of Cancer,* he most likely read *The Marriage of Heaven and Hell* while composing his manuscript, as biographer Jay Martin tells us that he found Anaïs Nin's bookcases filled with "everything written on William Blake" (240). Regardless of whether he knew this specific work at the time,

Tropic of Cancer 43

he could have known the convention of the argument from other sources, including the second edition of Milton's *Paradise Lost*.

Miller begins his argument with the themes of death and stagnation, conveying a sensation of living death. He writes, "I am living at the Villa Borghese. There is not a crumb of dirt anywhere, nor a chair misplaced. We are all alone here and we are dead" (23). After these sterile images, the theme of disease—one interpretation of "cancer"—opens the second paragraph: "Last night Boris discovered that he was lousy. I had to shave his armpits and even then the itching did not stop" (23). Then he gives us a clearer picture of what is amiss:

> Boris has just given me a summary of his views. He is a weather prophet.
> The weather will continue bad, he says. There will be more calamities,
> more death, more despair. Not the slightest indication of a change any-
> where. The cancer of time is eating us away. Our heroes have killed
> themselves, or are killing themselves. The hero, then, is not Time, but
> Timelessness. We must get in step, a lock step, toward the prison of
> death. There is no escape. The weather will not change. (23)

As a "weather prophet," his roommate Boris becomes a John the Baptist figure who accurately senses the spiritual conditions. The message is that one must accept the world as it is, that nothing can be used to change the climate. We may, however, change ourselves, even if the conforming drum of the world commands us to march like sleepwalkers into death. A strange version of "repentance" is at hand.

Because Boris is a prophet, his pronouncements straighten the path for the appearance of a messianic figure. After a clear line break from the opening paragraphs, we are presented with the following: "It is now the fall of my second year in Paris. I was sent here for a reason I have not yet been able to fathom" (23). This announcement gives the impression that his sojourn is in fact a divine quest. Not only is there the implication that this mission may have cosmic origin, but Miller situates these events in the autumn, the season frequently used by English Romantics and American Transcendentalists to symbolize the crumbling of empires. The message is that the pessimism outlined in the opening will "fall." Death will give rise to life.

Then appears Miller's testament, his great declaration: "I have no money, no resources, no hopes. I am the happiest man alive. A year ago, six months ago, I thought that I was an artist. I no longer think about it, I *am*. Everything that was literature has fallen from me. There are no more books to be written, thank God" (23). On the surface this seems to be a simple declaration of his authenticity in contrast with the thousands of charlatans who moved to Paris in the 1920s and 1930s. The author has in mind, however, a specific notion of the artist as a holy figure, whose book is more than "literature." Instead, it is an organic product of himself, the afterbirth of his own spiritual genesis. The "I am" pronouncement signifies his connection to God through allusion to the Book of Exodus, in which God reveals himself as "I AM," as well as Christ's self-identification in The Gospel of John: "Before Abraham was, I am."[5]

After these prefatory remarks, and without announcement, the narrative flashes back to a time before Miller became a liberated artist, though most of the opening chapter's action continues to take place in this same Villa Borghese. The time-shift is signaled when he writes, "It is the twenty-somethingth of October. *I no longer keep track of the date*" (24, emphasis added). We find confirmation that we have reverted back to a prior time in his artistic development when he admits, a few pages after the opening, "I have been looking over my manuscripts, pages scrawled with revision. Pages of *literature*" (29). In this moment, he realizes that he has been a derivative practitioner of literature, rather than one who channels his own authentic voice into his writing. The chapter's remaining pages attest to his increasing awareness, prompting him to make more declarations, such as "I have made a silent compact with myself not to change a line of what I write. [. . .] There is only one thing which interests me vitally now, and that is the recording of all that which is omitted in books" (31). These are stepping stones toward the realization that he relates in the opening pages of the second chapter, in which he has decided to begin composing, with his friend Boris, what he calls "The Last Book." This text is *Tropic of Cancer* itself, organically growing inside the pregnant Miller. In contrast with empty literature, he maintains that this book will be holy: "A cathedral, a veritable cathedral, in the building of which everybody will assist who has lost his identity" (44). Like James Joyce's *Finnegan's Wake* (1939), published serially while *Tropic of Cancer* was being written, the progressive narrative of Miller's sacred text circles back on itself. Ending with the image of the author as a resurrected artist, *Tropic of Cancer* becomes a venerated chronicle of its own creation, renewing itself with each subsequent reading.

BETWEEN NARRATIVE AND MONOLOGUE: MILLER'S OSCILLATORY TEXT

In between the opening and closing moments, the text oscillates between narrative and monologue. The actions described within the flowing story

Tropic of Cancer 45

give rise to the monolithic diatribes in which Miller reflects on the events. In chapter seven, for example, he first relates an incident in which a "young Hindu," whom he accompanied around Paris, commits a *faux pas* at a brothel by defecating in the bidet. This action gives rise to a grand rumination lasting for a few pages, in which Miller gains religious consciousness, prompting him to make statements he will begin to actuate, such as "One must burrow into life again in order to put on flesh. The word must become flesh; the soul thirsts" (104).[6] His personal religion is contrasted with what he considers to be the empty rituals and practices of Hinduism, referring to chants as "mumbojumbo" (91). Since we are told that the Hindu "was one of Gandhi's men," Miller also spotlights his hypocrisy since, despite his affiliation with the Indian spiritual leader, he desires to be with prostitutes and soak up the Parisian nightlife (97). This juxtaposition between Miller's own religious articulations—presented in the monologues—and his encounters with hypocrites occurs in several other passages. In the chapter that immediately follows the longest monologue in the book, he relates an incident in Florida where he and a friend, both of whom were flat broke, were turned away by both a Christian church and Jewish temple.[7] Each moment underscores the vitality of Miller's personal religion in contrast with institutionalized ones that have become ineffectual.

In this same section, we flash forward to find Miller as a member of an institution, namely, an English instructor at a Lyceé. The scene reads as a trial to determine if he will forfeit his esteemed position, effectively practicing what he preaches. Set in winter, the season suggests a momentary stasis of the life flow, as he tells us that even the school's pipes have frozen (256). Describing the environs, he writes, "The Lyceé itself seemed to rise up out of a lake of thin snow, an inverted mountain that pointed down toward the center of the earth where God or the Devil works always in a strait-jacket grinding grist for that paradise which is always a wet dream" (253). In this description, the institution is identified with Dante's *Inferno,* as Miller's description recalls the inverted spiral of Hell. Also suggestive is the "strait-jacket," a symbol of restraint and insanity. But this hell is a temporary stop on the way to his ascension, the merging of his vertical frame with the undulating waters of the Seine.

Miller's propensity for oscillating between narrative and monologue is linked to the persistent tension between time and timelessness in the novel. He first presents this opposition in the opening argument, in which he writes, "The hero, then, is not Time, but Timelessness" (23). Recalling that this sentence is situated within the section identified with entrapment within the "prison of death," it follows that timelessness from this perspective would be

46   *Henry Miller and Religion*

"the hero," since death marks a definitive succession of time. Because they suspend the action of the narrative, his monologues are linked to timelessness, as they arise vertically like monoliths, attempting to articulate the author's own timeless thoughts, the fancies taking place within his upper registers. Conversely, narrative action is linked with time; it chronicles life as it unfolds on a horizontal plane. It comes as no surprise that in the life-affirming section of the opening argument, he becomes concerned with concrete time again, as he tells us, "It is now the fall of my *second year* in Paris" and later, "*A year* ago, *six months* ago, I thought that I was an artist" (23, emphasis added). As the book continues toward the end, there will be a constant struggle between time and timelessness, just as the form switches from narrative to monologue.

FROM CONFINEMENT TO EXPANSE:
THE RIVER OF LIBERATION

The book's narrative generally moves from images of confinement to images of liberation. At the opening of the book, Miller is cloistered and stagnant in his apartment; at the end, he becomes one with the Seine, declaring that he can feel the river flowing through him. In between these depictions of confinement and liberation, we find dramas developing these themes. For example, at the first of the novel, he misses his wife Mona who has remained in America. When he decides to remain in France at the end, even when he has the financial resources to return to the United States, we receive confirmation that his wife is no longer of great concern. As he writes, "I wondered in a *vague* way what had ever happened to my wife" (285, emphasis added). By selecting the word "vague," he highlights how his memory of her has begun to fade. He opens the next paragraph by stating, "After everything had quietly sifted through my head a great peace came over me" (285). Following this moment of contemplating New York, a traumatic terrain that remained an open wound in his mind, he was able simply to accept America and move on.

During his journey, which begins in an apart-ment and ends in union, we find Miller roaming the streets of Paris, the vast network of avenues connecting to the open road such as Whitman sang about when thinking of New York City. Even at the beginning of Miller's third chapter—the first moment in which he breaks out of his apartment's confinements—we find him delivering a Whitmanesque pronouncement: "Salute! Salute, O Cosmos!" (54). In what follows throughout the novel, he becomes a great *flaneur* who endlessly wanders around Paris. As readers we walk with him, reading chronicles of lost evenings, encounters with prostitutes, conversations with

Tropic of Cancer 47

friends, and dialogues with art and literature. Each event mark periods in which he becomes increasingly free; they function as various stops on the pilgrim's progress, each imparting a lesson.

The most crucial symbol in the transition from restriction to expanse is the river.[8] On the first of his many walks, Miller finds the Seine to be a "tarnished mirror" (27). Distorted as it may be, he finds a slight reflection of himself in its waters, suggesting a hazy identification. This should be seen in contrast with what he related a page before: "I have moved the typewriter into the next room where I can see myself in the mirror as I write" (26). These two passages show a movement from placid narcissism to identification with the flowing river, a transition from confinement to liberation, from chamber to open expanse.

The river theme continues to be developed as the novel progresses. Towards the end of the fifth chapter, Miller writes, "The river is still swollen, muddy, streaked with lights. I don't know what it is rushes up in me at the sight of this dark, swift-moving current, but a great exultation lifts me up, affirms the deep wish that is in my [sic] never to leave this land" (78). Although the river here remains muddy, there is a suggestion of additional identification with its movement, as the sight inspires his emotions.

The river image appears again in the longest monologue in the novel, which functions as a paean to flow. At first, Miller expresses his disdain of static morality and transcendental thinking through the image of the mountain. He writes, "I want to make a detour of those lofty arid mountain ranges where one dies of thirst and cold, that 'extra-temporal' history, that absolute of time and space where there exists neither man, beast, nor vegetation, where one goes crazy with loneliness, with language that is mere words, where everything is unhooked, ungeared, out of joint with the times" (235). In place of mountains, he tells us that he wants us to be aligned with rivers:

> I want a world of men and women, of trees that do not talk (because there is too much talk in the world as it is!) of rivers that carry you to places, not rivers that are legends, but rivers that put you in touch with other men and women, with architecture, religion, plants, animals—rivers that have boats on them and in which men drown, drown not in myth and legend and books and dust of the past, but in time and space and history. I want rivers that make oceans such as Shakespeare and Dante, rivers which do not dry up in the void of the past. Oceans, yes! Let us have more oceans, new oceans that blot out the past, oceans that create new geological formations, new topographical vistas and strange, terrifying

continents, oceans that destroy and preserve at the same time, oceans that we can sail on, take off to new discoveries, new horizons. (235)

As specified towards the end of this passage, rivers and oceans are meant to be used as ways of transporting the self to new zones. Furthermore, by eroding geological formations and seeping through cracks, water diligently searches for ways to break out of confinement.

By the end of the novel, Miller's identification with the river becomes complete. At first, he finds the Seine "like a great artery running through the human body" (285). In the final paragraph, however, the simile has become a personal reality: "I feel this river flowing through me—its past, its ancient soil, the changing climate. The hills gently girdle it about; its course is fixed" (286). In these last two sentences of the novel, he has experienced a complete identification with the current. Initially trapped in an apartment, then freed into the network of Paris's streets, he renders himself as one with nature, thereby signaling his liberation in this grand moment of acceptance. From this moment onward, he is able to channel his creative energy into a sacred enterprise, the very book we hold in our hands.

The persistence of the river image is an integral part of *Tropic of Cancer*, as flow itself remains a holy attribute for Miller. Opposed to conformity, his version of "going with the flow" entails becoming connected to the natural movement of the universe. This means being aware of one's natural desires, those not suppressed through acculturation. In his romanticism, anything related to the conforming powers of civilization is considered profane; anything in line with the effusion of the universe is deemed sacred. Sometimes, flow is aligned in the text to the great rhythm of the universe, to its grand circuit. Although each metaphor has its peculiar properties, what unites them all in his consciousness is their tendency towards change.

Miller's identification with water seems counterintuitive since water is traditionally considered a feminine metaphor.[9] Two compendiums that influenced him—Blavatsky's *Secret Doctrine* (1888) and Jung's writings on archetypes—indeed argue that water is a female symbol. As a water sign, "Cancer" is meant to be a more feminine or "moody" counterpart to the bedrock earth sign of "Capricorn," identified with grounded relationships. *Tropic of Cancer* might be seen as Miller's journey from the masculine parade that will be *Tropic of Capricorn* (1939), its narrative set in his early New York days, towards becoming feminine. In the final crucifixion, in which his "course is *fixed*," he is penetrated by a phallus of water, which then merges within him. Like the body of Christ, which has a vulva-like piercing in its side, the messianic Miller presents himself as a fusion of woman and man.[10]

Tropic of Cancer 49

In the midst of his watery symbols of change and immanence, Miller often includes traces of stability and transcendence. We see this in passages such as the following: "The river is still swollen, *muddy*, streaked with *lights*. I don't know what it is rushes up in me at the sight of this dark, swift-moving current, but a great exultation *lifts me up*, affirms the *deep* wish that is in my *never to leave this land*" (78, emphasis added). Traces of solid earth in the form of mud are found in the water, which is itself "streaked with lights," sparkling symbols of enlightenment (78). Viewing the horizontal flow of the current, he experiences intimations of elevation while, at the same time, expressing his yearning to remain stationary on the earth's horizontal plane.

This tension between transcendence and immanence foreshadows the great merger at the novel's end.[11] In this section, Miller first looks at the Seine and reports, "In the wonderful peace that fell over me it seemed as if I had climbed to the top of a high mountain; for a little while I would be able to look around me, to take in the meaning of the landscape" (285–86). From these sentiments and images of transcendence and elevation, albeit qualified in the subjunctive mood, he follows with a mixture of immanent and transcendent symbols. He writes, "The sun is setting. I feel this river flowing through me—its past, its ancient soil, the changing climate. The hills gently girdle it about; its course is fixed" (286). Although the sun, signifying enlightenment, is present, it is fading over the horizon. The river again contains traces of earth, "its ancient soil." Most strikingly, he ends the novel by telling us that it is on a fixed course. This final message shows that he is self-critical; by chronicling his story of self-liberation, he has also trapped himself in a black and white world of words. Although his identity is in flux throughout the novel, as he undergoes his own creative evolution, the tale itself has become solidified or "fixed"—a static representation of his own dynamic religion.

DIRECTING CREATIVE ENERGY

Although some Miller enthusiasts may be tempted to render him a champion of pure immanence, a close reading of his work shows this is not the case. In the paragraph immediately following the one in which he first reveals how the river uplifts him, he decries his native New York City for being a sprawling mass of undirected movement. He writes, "There is a sort of atomic frenzy to the activity going on; the more furious the pace, the more diminished the spirit. . . . Nobody directs the energy. Stupendous. Bizarre. Baffling. A tremendous reactive urge, but absolutely uncoordinated" (78). Miller's work and life move from this inherited chaos into an authorial order.

He views all new creations—both of natural and human design—as attempts to harness chaotic energy.

Miller believes sprawling and undirected energy to be the result of blockages; his controversial rendering of sex should be seen in this light. Ultimately, he wants us to see sex as a holy act, as it stems from the same energy source that gives birth not only to children, but to other creative endeavors, including art and religion. When one reads *Tropic of Cancer* carefully, one clearly sees that he is against instrumental sex, because he feels that sex without passion does not involve a clean transferal of energy.

In chapter eight, Miller presents us with Van Norden, a perverted friend who is angry because women want to feel emotions when having sex. Van Norden must be seen in contrast with Miller, who refuses to have sex with a prostitute that Van Norden procured. Miller lingers on the impersonal transaction, especially the price haggling. Another layer of detachment forms as he watches Van Norden have sex with the prostitute:

> As I watch Van Norden tackle her, it seems to me that I'm looking at a machine whose cogs have slipped. [. . .] The sight of them coupled like a pair of goats without the least spark of passion, grinding and grinding away for no reason except the fifteen francs, washes away every bit of feeling I have, except the inhuman one of satisfying my curiosity. (141–42)

Although Miller does claim that the two are "coupled like a pair of goats," implying some degree of bestial naturalness to the act, the overwhelming impression is one of dispassionate machines.[12] The natural arousal one could potentially feel in this situation has been obscured by capitalistic thoughts; sacred sex has been reduced to a pagan economy. The author, of course, implicates himself in the act. He is able to preserve himself enough, however, to observe that there is something fundamentally flawed in this transaction, thereby learning yet another lesson on his journey. He comes to celebrate sex only where there is a free exchange of healthy sexual desire.

Passages relating Miller's feelings about his wife Mona attest to another variety of energy blockage. In the novel, he gives us the impression that he has fetishized his wife, turning her into an object of devotion. In one passage, he writes, "Were there a Christian so faithful to his God as I was to her[,] we would all be Jesus Christs to-day" (170). Fully cognizant of Jung's psychoanalytical writings, Miller realizes that in order for him to become liberated, he must let his libido flow naturally rather than clinging to an empty memory. Thinking about Mona is often a source of pain, opening ancient wounds: "When I realize that she is gone, perhaps gone forever, a great void

Tropic of Cancer 51

opens up and I feel that I am falling, falling, falling into deep, black space. And this is worse than tears, deeper than regret or pain or sorrow; it is the abyss into which Satan was plunged. There is no climbing back, no ray of light, no sound of human voice or human touch of hand" (170). We are not meant to see this vagina-like abyss as a tomb in which Miller has buried himself. By clinging to the ghost of his wife, he has become paralyzed. Worshipping her as an object, rather than following his natural desires, he has contravened dynamic religion, a sin akin to worshipping Christ instead of becoming Christ-like by releasing one's creative energy.

Miller marks Judaism as another type of energy blockage. In order to have a more accurate understanding of his problematic anti-Semitism, his prejudice should be examined within this rubric of liberation. Although he had many lifelong Jewish friends, as many of his defenders are quick to mention, his work features a persistent undercurrent of anti-Semitism. While some resentment may stem from the personal trauma of his marriage to the Jewish June Smerth—the inspiration for *Tropic of Cancer*'s Mona—these feelings may also derive from his gentile German working-class upbringing in Brooklyn. His anti-Semitism was elaborated by an ideological distinction he made between Judaism and Christianity, in which Christianity is trumpeted as liberation theology.

Influenced by various evolutionary thinkers—including Henri Bergson, Havelock Ellis, Elie Faure, D. H. Lawrence, Herbert Spencer, and Oswald Spengler—and the common understanding of Friedrich Nietzsche's philosophy at this time, Miller constructed a firm distinction between Judaism and Christianity, basing this dualism on a concrete adherence to Torah in opposition to the promptings of a more amorphous Holy Spirit.[13] In short, he saw Judaism as a rigid religion unable to promote the natural flow of energy integral to all religious experience. One passage in *Tropic of Cancer* conveys this notion through the metaphor of entrapment. He writes, "For the Jew the world is a cage filled with wild beasts. The door is locked and he is there without whip or revolver. His courage is so great that he does not even smell the dung in the corner. The spectators applaud but he does not hear. The drama, he thinks, is going on inside the cage. The cage, he thinks, is the world" (30). As the passage continues, he juxtaposes these images of confinement with lions that tear the Jews apart. The author tells us, "The lions, too, are disappointed. They expected blood, bones, gristle, sinews. They chew and chew, but the words are chicle and chicle is indigestible" (30). In contrast to the gristle of the Jew, Miller proposes "the Word made flesh," to recall the prologue to John's Gospel. He comes closer and closer to his spiritual ideal as the narrative unfolds, himself becoming a wild beast, declaring, "The dawn

52 Henry Miller and Religion

is breaking on a new world, a jungle world in which the lean spirits roam with sharp claws. If I am a hyena I am a lean and hungry one: I go forth to fatten myself" (105). To paraphrase Blake, he disturbingly sees the fleshy "tygers of wrath" as wiser than the Jewish "horses of instruction."[14] By accessing his primal desires, he believes himself to be more connected with sacred energy, as well as to supersessionist prejudice against the Hebrew Law.

METAPHYSICAL HYPERTROPHY: HARNESSING ENERGY

In contrast to complete blockages, Miller documents objects of resistance that allow him to channel and harness creative energy. Considering his metaphysics, one should not be surprised to see that sex and art provide sufficient means. As he presents himself as coming closer to self-liberation, he uses artworks and women as places of confinement out of which he emerges a stronger individual. They should be envisioned as caves that he enters, only to emerge with increased might. Within this section, I discuss the problematic way in which women and literature become aids of his quest for self-liberation.

In the first sustained meditation on a prostitute named Germaine, whom he has just visited, we find sex presented as a vehicle for channeling energy. In this small section from the third chapter, Miller quotes a passage from an earlier piece called "Mademoiselle Claude," telling us that it was really Germaine whom he was describing: "All the men she's been with and now you, just you, and barges going by, masts and hulls, the whole damned *current of life* flowing through you, through her, through all the guys behind you and after you, the flowers and the birds and the sun streaming in and the fragrance of it choking you, annihilating you" (59, emphasis added). In this description, we find Germaine to be a nodal point to a vast network connected by flows of *élan vital*. The vagina is rendered a holy place when he calls it "a God-given thing" and, more suggestively, a "flaming bush," harkening back to the burning bush Moses encounters in Exodus (58, 60).[15]

Later in the passage, Miller dangerously suggests that the only way Germaine can experience life herself is through this connection. In words oozing with sexism, he writes, "A man! That was what she craved. A man with something between his legs that could tickle her, that could make her writhe in ecstasy, make her grab that bushy twat of hers with both hands and rub it joyfully, boastfully, proudly, with a sense of connection, a sense of life. That was the only place where she experienced any life—down there where she clutched herself with both hands" (60). What makes this excerpt so sinister is not simply his objectification of women, but that the

Tropic of Cancer 53

prostitute can experience *élan vital* only by plugging into the phalluses of paying customers. Although one should not necessarily assume that he envisions all women this way, his language invites such conclusions. Consider the following excerpt, when he writes of the prostitute's drinking habit, "the fire of it penetrated her, it glowed down there between her legs *where women ought to glow,* and there was established that circuit which makes one feel the earth under his legs again" (61, emphasis added). It is implied that women are the earth, insatiable and stationary ports on journeys available only to nomadic men.

Miller punctuates this point when he explicitly connects women with geography. The title "*Tropic of Cancer*" itself refers to the geographic line surrounding the northern hemisphere, suggesting some arc of travel between his native New York and Paris. One biographer tells of how he, perhaps jokingly, once mentioned that the title refers to the name of one of his wife's breasts, the other naturally being "Tropic of Capricorn."[16] Whether or not Miller was serious, this anecdote demonstrates a strong and perhaps subconscious association in his mind. In the fifth chapter, he explicitly develops the relationship, beginning with a prophetic vision that recalls Emerson's transparent eyeball: "Standing in the courtyard with a glass eye" (74).[17] In this sequence, he finds himself in a strange room lined with ancient maps and charts, including depictions of "Knossus and Carthage, of Carthage before and after the salting" (74). These locations are suggestive not simply because they signal the death of civilizations, but because of the powerful women associated with each local. Sources available during his time, such as *The Story of the World's Greatest Nations and the World's Famous Events,* would have informed him that the early civilizations at Knossus, under the rule of King Minos, "worshipped a female deity, the 'Great Mother,' the productive force of Nature" (Ellis and Horne).[18] Carthage was allegedly founded by Dido, a woman famous for her passion and destructive thirst for revenge. Such powerful female images underscore their connection to nature and locale.

A woman also appears in the room filled with maps. Among other surrealist gestures, she swallows a goldfish, whereupon we are told, "Slowly the room begins to revolve and one by one the continents slide into the sea; only the woman is left, but her body is a mass of geography" (74). Again we find women as concentrated masses in an ever changing sea of energy. In addition to connoting bulk, "mass" may also suggest that her body has a holy quality, a space in which sacred rites can occur.

In the long monologue located in chapter twelve, we find Miller again associating women with geography. The passage begins not unlike the one described before, as it includes a mystical experience brought upon by looking into a woman's vagina, the mysterious depths out of which life flows. This is meant to be seen in contrast to the earlier episode with Van Norden, in which he inspects a prostitute's vagina with a flashlight exclaiming, "You'd imagine I'd never seen one before. And the more I looked at it the less interesting it became. It only goes to show that there's nothing to it after all, especially when it's shaved. It's the hair that makes it mysterious" (138). Opposed to Van Norden's comments, Miller's language in this later episode is dramatically impassioned. Looking into a prostitute's vagina, he finds that this "whore of Babylon," what he calls "great whore and mother of man," has given rise to his own revelation, a private apocalypse (227).[19] He announces this mystical experience in plain terms: "the world ceases to revolve, time stops, the very nexus of my dreams is broken and dissolved and my guts spill out in a grand schizophrenic rush, an evacuation that leaves me face to face with the Absolute" (227). Before and afterwards, however, the language is not as straightforward. With an overflow of imagery inspired by John the Divine's Revelation, he tries to recreate the madness of the encounter, complete with its chaos. Within these surrealistic moments, there are nevertheless recurrent themes.

In fact, the combination of women and geography unites many of the fleeting images. As women are undressing, Miller looks up at a picture of his wife Mona, where "she is facing northeast on a line with Cracow written in green ink. To the left of her is the Dordogne, encircled with a red pencil" (227). Because photos freeze life rather than letting it flow, he is suggesting that his wife symbolizes some sort of permanence, an anchor to use the familiar metaphor.[20] The particular stations have import, as Cracow represents the Eastern Europe from which she came. When we consider that the Lascaux caves of Dordogne were considered by the author to be the birthplace of art, we can then see Mona identified with the origin of his creativity. Certainly, his most important literary output was devoted toward imagining his affair with the real-life Mona, June Smerth, and the relationship's aftershocks. These observations aside, his imprint of place and direction suggests that he views Mona as terrain.

In addition to this passage, a few pages later we find a tighter connection between geography and the feminine. Miller writes, "The earth is not an arid plateau of health and comfort, but a great sprawling female with velvet torso that swells and heaves with ocean billows; she squirms beneath a diadem of sweat and anguish" (230). Traversing the paths within and without women as an explorer would conquer terrain, he finds passages that transport him to the uncharted waters of freedom and ecstasy. Keeping in mind

Tropic of Cancer 55

the astrological resonance of "Cancer," we can see him freeing himself to travel in all directions like a crab.[21]

On the following page, Miller again brings together Mona and geography when he writes, "I moved along under the Equator, heard the hideous laughter of the green-jawed hyena, saw the jackal with silken tail and the dick-dick and the spotted leopard, all left behind in the Garden of Eden" (231). In this passage, he conveys that he travels between the Tropic of Cancer and the Tropic of Capricorn—Mona's "hemispheres"—through the passage under her "Equator"—her vagina—to encounter the primeval paradise. Although he is traveling in a rather tight area, one imagines that Mona and other women deliver a reborn Miller through the birth canal. Once the umbilical cord is cut, he may then move on to other women, to further terrain. Besides promoting the construction that women are more in touch with the earth, his portrayal raises additional gender trouble. Sometimes it is difficult to distinguish whether he is traveling through women towards greater experience or simply trampling on them. Either way, his women are discarded like cocoons once Miller emerges with the awareness their terrain provided.[22]

With Mona in mind, we see in this monologue Miller's ability to transform women alchemically from tombs of trauma into wombs of rebirth. Rekindling the image of Satan in the darkness, found earlier in the novel, he writes, "Out of that dark, unstitched wound, that sink of abominations, that cradle of black-thronged cities where the music of ideas is drowned in cold fat, out of strangled Utopias is born a clown, a being divided between beauty and ugliness, between light and chaos, a clown who when he looks down and sidelong is Satan himself and when he looks upward sees a buttered angel, a snail with wings" (228). Able to look upwards out of the abyss, Miller has the potential to fly, as he sees that even lowly creatures like snails have wings. He continues, "Out of nothingness arises the sign of infinity; beneath the ever-rising spirals slowly sinks the gaping hole. The land and the water make numbers joined, a poem written with flesh and stronger than steel or granite. Through endless night the earth whirls towards a creation unknown . . ." (231). Infinite potential issues from trauma's nothingness; he inverts his pain. Through revisiting Mona in memory, through traveling "to the open wound, to the festering obscene horror," the tomb of memory becomes a womb of rebirth (229). Channeled through geography, he fabricates a network of energy, an assemblage "stronger than steel or granite" (231).

Art performs a similar directive function. Framed by his own book, Miller becomes confined within a concert hall and a library. The first moment comes when he attends a performance at the Salle Gaveau. Finding himself in a den of somnambulists, he describes their complacency in contrast to his own attentiveness. As the music plays, his body opens and his organs, symbols of mechanistic processes, are replaced by pure light. He writes, "It's as though I had no clothes on and every pore of my body was a window and all the windows open and the light flooding my gizzards. I can feel the light curving under the vault of my ribs and my ribs hang there over a hollow nave trembling with reverberations" (84). By transforming his solar plexus into a "nave," music morphs his body into a temple. He then becomes an embodiment of the music hall, describing the sensation in almost mystical terms, writing "I have lost all sense of time and place" (84). First presenting himself as transformed into a lake, his body becomes a baptismal font, a self-purifying apparatus. Out of this vessel come "huge birds of passage," indicating that he has taken flight out of the confines not only of the auditorium but his internal temple. When the music comes to a halt, his body returns to earth, organs reappear, and flight is halted by shut windows (84). Nevertheless, for a brief moment, confining himself to the auditorium allows him to escape inwardly towards infinity.

Books also serve as modes of transportation. Miller often discusses them using metaphors of descent, reminiscent of his metaphoric encounters with women. Describing his escape inside the labyrinthine universe of Marcel Proust, Miller writes, "Lost as when once I sank into the quick of a budding grove and seated in the dining room of that enormous world of Balbec" (156). With more potency, he elaborates on this feeling of immersion when describing his experiences reading Strindberg's *Inferno*, another perplexing autobiographical work about finding one's personal religion in Paris.[23] He writes, "We came together in a dance of death and so quickly was I sucked down into the vortex that when I came to the surface again I could not recognize the world. When I found myself loose the music had ceased; the carnival was over and I had been picked clean . . ." (172). Again we find a cycle of decent and assent similar to his journey to and through the womb. The last part of this passage suggests that reading Strindberg was not only a performance—a dance—but also a Dionysian omophagy in which Miller was devoured by the book.

In the passage that follows, he then reaffirms the baptismal theme by flying in his imagination to the Ganges, reminding us of purification rites. From the sacred river, he journeys to the astrological zodiac, again through text. The passage also attests to his increasing awareness of the poet's mission, particularly the "bloody struggle to liberate himself" (173). In the sentence that follows, he announces, "It was no mystery to me any longer

Tropic of Cancer 57

why he and others (Dante, Rabelais, Van Gogh, etc., etc.) had made their pilgrimage to Paris" (173). By naming this precession of artists on a holy quest to the French capital, the stage is set for the author to identify himself with this tradition.

Visual art also functions as portals for voyage. Describing his experience upon walking into an art gallery on the Rue de Sèze, Miller writes, "I have the sensation of being immersed in the very plexus of life, focal from whatever place, position or attitude I take my stance" (157). In this sentence, he places himself in a field of immanence, a network that allows him to freely move. Speaking more about Matisse, he notes the sensation of travel in the artist's work, just as Miller's book will adopt the same theme. His art fields a panoptic eye, new vistas of vision. Miller goes on to write specifically about Matisse's liberating powers: "He is a bright sage, a dancing seer who, with a sweep of the brush, removes the ugly scaffold to which the body of a man is *chained* by the incontrovertible facts of life" (158, emphasis added). Calling him a sage and a seer, Miller lends messianic attributes to the painter, claiming him as a liberator, as the French Revolution incarnate, who is capable of smashing our manacles.[24]

In Miller's mind, both women and artworks help to save us through their liberating powers. As vessels to be entered, however, they are ultimately to be discarded once the individual is renewed. His treatment of art is similar to Milton's practice in the elegy, whereby he established himself as a poet by writing about the death of his beloved Lycidas. Miller often directly quotes prior writers and artists, including two passages by Emerson and an unattributed citation from J. P. Eckermann's *Conversations with Goethe.* Without scare quotes, he even integrated a selection from what became Joyce's *Finnegan's Wake!* More often, however, Miller simply alludes to past writers, such as Proust and Rabelais. These tactics not only acknowledge his influences, but they also place his writings in conversation with them. Their work is the scaffolding that lifted him to his highest vision, but the structure ultimately must be dismantled to give rise to his own work.

Throwing a book against the wall will not harm anyone. Using women as dispensable vessels for self-expansion, however, is more noxious. Although women, like artists, give birth, Miller cannot see them as equals. Through June Smerth fronted the fare to Paris and helped fund his stay, as did Anaïs Nin, the fictionalized Mona is rendered an anchor pulling him back to America. While the violence of this act is less bilious when we consider the amount of trauma she put him through, it is frighteningly consistent with his prohibition of women from journeys of freedom; they must remain forever bound to the earth.

TROPIC OF CANCER AS SELF-SACRIFICE

Like the tools of liberation cast away once the artist is liberated, Miller's book is shed at completion. Becoming one with the river, he is baptized and cleansed from the afterbirth. The construction of the novel was, in part, simply the means by which he could become freed. While the novel holds tension between time and timelessness, the last words—"its course is fixed"—shift from the endless present—"is"—to the past "fixed," preserving a friction reminiscent to the Easter catchphrase, "Jesus Christ is risen" (286). Referring to the water running through him, the passage also suggests a movement from Heraclitean flux towards permanence, a shift punctuated with a period. Being "fixed," the final words also hark back to cruci*fixion*, Christ's moment of mortal conclusion, suggesting that Miller can now remain in the world in pure spirit.

This concept of self-sacrifice through writing becomes amplified when we consider an earlier moment in which Miller encounters a book called *A Man Cut in Slices*. In a chapter that begins with the single sentence word "Sunday!," he comes across this very title in a store window (53). He writes, "*A man cut in slices* . . . You can't imagine how furious I am not to have thought of a title like that! [. . .] I wish to Christ I had had brains enough to think of a title like that" (55). This appellation, which he presumably wants for *Tropic of Cancer*, is certainly suggestive of sacrifice. Coupled with "Christ," the sentence conveys some identification between the author's work and the self-sacrifice achieved on Golgotha. The connection becomes accentuated when he reprises the opening of his book, as if his book has been renamed to *A Man Cut in Slices:* "I'm living at the Villa Borghese. We're all dead, or dying, or about to die" (55). In addition to identification with Christ, this passage marks a new beginning, a moment in which Miller can reflect on his literary mission. He continues, "I'm going to remember this title and I'm going to put down everything that goes on in my noodle [. . .] And I'll tell no one why, after I had put everything down, I suddenly went home and chopped the baby to pieces" (55). Recalling the section in which he claims to be "pregnant with book," he suggests that he is willing to sacrifice his own child, his Word made flesh. While this ritualistic slicing helps explain why *Tropic of Cancer* is not a linear account of his time in Paris, it also points to the book's deeper significance as a chronicle of the author's liberation and the testament of his messianic mission.

Cutting himself into slices and burying them in a textual tomb, Miller is also symbolically attempting to replenish the soil of his contemporary wasteland. His paean to flow counters the cries of Eliot's "Waste Land," in

Tropic of Cancer   59

which we are told "But there is no water" (line 359) and later, "the dry stone [gives] no sound of water" (line 24). Through the sacrificial theme and Miller's use of metaphor, we can see *Tropic of Cancer* as a direct response to Eliot's poem.[25] In fact, Miller associates stone with Eliot; writing about dead trees in the Square de Furstemberg, he describes them as "nourished by the paving stones. Like T. S. Eliot's verse" (54). Although his apocalypticism is as bleak as Eliot's, Miller believes there will be a rebirth of culture and, in turn, the individuals who live within it. By replenishing the soil, he hopes his book will promote a collective rebirth.

To put this cycle into motion, Miller's text is meant to shock his readers out of stasis. This is accomplished by creating a literature that breaks traditional confines. To pull this off, we frequently find him convoluting visual art with music, poetry, and even dance. Beyond attempting to manufacture confusion, a synaesthesia that short-circuits our reasoning, he maintains the romantic faith that Art is one, that each tributary flows into the great stream of inspiration.

To exacerbate the confusion, Miller specifically tells us that *Tropic of Cancer,* is not literature, a position he explains in the final paragraphs of the opening argument. First, he tells us, "This is not a book. This is libel, slander, defamation of character. This is not a book, in the ordinary sense of the word" (23). Already he is admitting that his novel distorts his own character, thereby suggesting the narrative is not a faithful account. After attempting to convince us that we are not reading, he tells us we are witnessing an unroutine song and dance: "I am going to sing for you, a little off key perhaps but I will sing. I will sing while you croak, I will dance over your dirty corpse. . . ." (23–24). Here he is claiming that his book is a performance, a notion that underscores that it is a living work of art. As a dance among corpses, he suggests his book comes to a plagued age, recalling the dance of death that victims would spasm before giving up the ghost. His words also suggest his song to be an incantation, making him a modern Orpheus who will lead us to new awakenings. With its ability to permeate walls and barriers, song is the perfect metaphor for the type of outreaching literature he proposes. A book extending beyond the boundaries of textuality, his *bildungsroman* seeks to serve as a model while, at the same time, breaking our internal restraints.

Miller believes that song can destroy barriers. In his longest monologue, he calls those who do not adhere to a slave morality "inhuman," a species of true artists. He writes, "Side by side with the human race there runs another race of beings, the inhuman ones, the race of artists who, goaded by unknown impulses, take the lifeless mass of humanity and by the fever

Henry Miller and Religion

and ferment with which they imbue it turn this soggy dough into bread and the bread into wine and the wine into song. Out of the dead compost and the inert slag they breed a song that contaminates" (233). The passage fuses Christian and Dionysian symbolism, a perverted transubstantiation in which the artist is credited with creating a "song that contaminates." Now we can fully see the significance of his alleged obscenity; by writing a "dirty book," he was manufacturing an art that would contaminate his readers, as his words extended beyond the written page. Throwing this "filth" onto the readers, his text becomes the dung that we, like Ezekiel, must consume in order to have vision:

> I love everything that flows, everything that has time in it and becoming, that brings us back to the beginning where there is never end: the violence of the prophets, the obscenity that is ecstasy, the wisdom of the fanatic, the priest with his rubber litany, the foul words of the whore, the spittle that floats away in the gutter, the milk of the breast and the bitter honey that pours from the womb, all that is fluid, melting, dissolute and dissolvent, all the pus and dirt that in flowing is purified, that loses its sense of origin, that makes the great circuit toward death and dissolution. (236)

Filth can become purified through movement. His "dirty" books are meant to purify us. In trying to create a "primitive" literature inspired by post-Impressionist and Modernist painters, he uses obscenity and a willed disorder to promote the flow of *élan vital* in the hopes of creating a sacred literature for modern times.[26]

Miller's Bible presents the author as messiah, a Christ whose mission is "to erect a world on the basis of the *omphalos*, not on an abstract idea nailed to a cross" (224). The conversion testifies to the author's own transformation. Quoting from Boris's epistle, he relates: "What happened between us—at any rate, as far as I go—is that you touched me, touched my life, that is, at the one point where I am still alive: my death. By the emotional flow I went through another immersion. I lived again, alive. No longer by reminiscence, as I do with others, but alive" (161). Although Miller is as yet unable to grasp his salvific power, he does baptize the Baptist, who goes "through another immersion." While this is a reversal of the biblical account, in which John the Baptist baptizes Christ, Miller is confirmed messiah, an individual able to rekindle the lives of all. In *Tropic of Cancer,* the seemingly profane author has been deified, from his filth has come purity.

Close analysis of *Tropic of Cancer* in the context of biography and history reveals the text as Miller's chronicle of his spiritual rebirth. Beginning with *Tropic of Capricorn,* his works become even more self-consciously religious, as they are increasingly in conversation with traditional religious symbols.

Chapter Five

Tropic of Capricorn

As his work on *Tropic of Cancer* (1934) came to a close, Miller continued to delve further into religion. Having moved away from the influence of friends Michael Fraenkel and Walter Lowenfels, whose "death philosophy" helped shape his concept of "creative death," he became more intimate with the astrologist Conrad Moricand.[1] Moricand provided astrological readings for many in the Villa Seurat circle, including Anaïs Nin, and even composed birth and death charts for famous figures who captured Miller's imagination. Miller was drawn to the complex symbolism and metaphysics underpinning astrology.

In fact, he attempted to incorporate these astrological materials into his own creative work. Already we have seen how he uses basic astrology to lend pathos to *Tropic of Cancer*. When we look at the early plans for *Black Spring* (1936), we find him attempting to use astrological symbols in an even more elaborate manner.[2] On the back of a chart made for *The World of Lawrence*, we find that he, probably around 1934, also used astrology to offer a preliminary plan of *Tropic of Capricorn* (1939), the companion volume of *Tropic of Cancer*.[3] If he planned to arrange the book on this astrological schematic, he appears to have abandoned it along the way, even though many of the characters and themes appear in the final version of *Tropic of Capricorn*. As with the *Black Spring* layout, these sketches show how he persistently tried to map his autobiography onto a spiritual plane. Even if he did not stick with this specific scheme, astrological symbols nonetheless do appear in the published book.

As we will see, Theosophical and Rosicrucian texts inspired Miller's religious philosophy and provided additional afflatus for character development. Furthermore, his turn to Rosicrucianism allowed him to frame his life in Christian terms. Although he had positioned himself as a messianic figure in *Tropic of Cancer*, in which we find multiple allusions to Christ, *Tropic of Capricorn* concretely fuses the author with Christ, forging a project essentially Christian in nature. Uniting these sources and shaping them with Eastern

64 *Henry Miller and Religion*

religious thought, he advanced his religiosity in *Tropic of Capricorn*. In this chapter, I offer an interpretation of this work informed by the author's use of these antecedents.

CREATING A CHRISTIAN UNIVERSE

Tropic of Capricorn presents a more refined variety of the religious system first proposed in *Tropic of Cancer*. When reflecting on *Tropic of Capricorn* years later, Miller sincerely wrote about it as a work dictated by "the Voice," adding "it was all given, straight from the celestial recording room" (*Big Sur* 127–8). Perhaps to help us better understand this Voice and the peculiar type of religiosity presented in *Tropic of Capricorn*, he identifies the philosophy of Henri Bergson as an immediate inspiration. Reflecting on his youth, he discusses his devotion to Bergson's *Creative Evolution* (1907) and even describes it in religious terms. Calling it a "new Bible," he recalls reading passages to the Jews working in his father's Tailor Shop: "Reading to them from this new Bible in the way Paul must have talked to the disciples" (221). The passage becomes an interesting play on the biblical story of the young Jesus discussing scriptures in the Temple or in what he calls his "Father's house."[4] He also tells us how fervently he read the book, literarily devouring it like Ezekiel swallowing God's scrolls: "My understanding of the meaning of a book is that the book itself disappears from sight, that it is chewed alive, digested and incorporated into the system as flesh and blood which in turn creates new spirit and reshapes the world" (221). He even frames the experience in communion terms when he writes, "It was a great communion feast which we shared in the reading of this book" (221).

In both of these passages, we discover that Bergson's word has become flesh in the form of Henry Miller. Later in *Tropic of Capricorn*, he again refers to Bergson's text as a Bible, saying that it "is to instruct me, initiate me into a new way of life" (225). Although he does not directly address how scriptures shaped him, he underscores how the Bible distinguished him from others, as the American author increasingly found himself alone in his love of these ideas. Nevertheless, as we have seen in *Tropic of Cancer*, he takes Bergson's concept of *élan vital* to envision a triune interrelationship of creative energy broken into the streams of sex, religion, and art.

Beginning with *Tropic of Capricorn*, however, we find Miller situating his brand of liberation theology in the traditional language of Western religions. We can see this clearly in a passage in which he reflects upon his rebirth in Paris. He says that he becomes "born anew, born and baptized by my right name: Gottlieb Leberecht Müller!," a name which, when translated, means

Tropic of Capricorn 65

"Loved-by-God, Right-living Miller" (228). Biographer Jay Martin notes that Miller was most likely inspired by a 1932 German film called *Mensch ohne Namen,* in which the main character, who has lost his identity, selects Gottlieb Leberecht Müller as his name (227). But Martin does not acknowledge that Miller, who was raised in a German-speaking household, uses the literal meaning of this name to claim that he has changed his misguided ways.

Miller's self-proclaimed righteousness is confirmed in many passages within *Tropic of Capricorn,* in which his manufactured holiness is situated in specific Christian contexts. He clearly wants us to connect his life to that of Jesus Christ, such as when he writes the following regarding his birthday: "Slated for Christmas I was born a half hour too late. It always seemed to me that I was meant to be the sort of individual that one is destined to be by virtue of being born on the 25th day of December. Admiral Dewey was born on that day and so was Jesus Christ . . . perhaps Krishnamurti too, for all I know" (61). When we check the dates, we find that Admiral George Dewey, an American war hero popular during Miller's childhood, actually shares his birthday of December 26th, not the 25th. Such an error could only be deliberate. By stating that Dewey and Christ have the same birthday, there is a suggestion that Miller and Christ were also born on the same day. As an explorer traversing the Tropics, Dewey is a proper candidate for the pantheon, which includes Christ, the fisher of men, along with Miller himself.

This connection between Miller and Christ via their common birthdates is echoed in the remarks of his Jewish friend Kronski. As he and Miller go for a walk, his friend confesses, "Sometimes I think you were born in the wrong time. [. . .] if you had just a little more confidence in yourself you could be the biggest man in the world today. You wouldn't even have to be a writer. You might become another Jesus Christ for all I know" (88). By saying he was "born in the wrong time," Kronski suggests Miller was born in the wrong epoch. There is also a hint that he was born *at* the wrong time, meaning he was destined to arrive on the holiest day of the Christian calendar (88). Like a prophet preparing for the coming Messiah, Kronski is also able to perceive the alleged inner divinity within the author.

In addition to such faint echoes, Miller explicitly connects his life to Christ's mythology. One passage in the book has the author rendering himself in the substance of God: "What is your name? shouts someone. *My name? Why just call me God—God the embryo*" (204). In this statement, there is an implied connection between a fully realized God and its embryonic form, which one could say is another way of conceiving of the Christ child. This phrasing implies that the two entities are the same substance, just as God and Christ are identified in the Christian conception of the Trinity.

66 *Henry Miller and Religion*

Even stronger allusions to the life of Christ are rendered into Miller's autobiography. Just as Christ had twelve disciples, Miller surrounded himself with twelve men while first attempting to write a novel: "Clipped Wings," a collection inspired by men he hired during his tenure as employment manager of the "Cosmodemonic Telegraph Company." These twelve messengers are presented as fallen angels who are never able to relate Miller's message. We also find an allusion to the Last Supper in *Tropic of Capricorn*. Recounting the bread he would share with his Polish friend Stanley, he transubstantiates this seemingly secular moment into a holy event. He writes, "The wonderful sour rye went into the making of our individual selves; it was like the communion loaf in which all participate but from which each one receives only according to his peculiar state of grace" (130). Like Proust's famous taste of the tea-soaked madeline, such tender events led Miller on a voyage of individuation, helping him to become his own Christ-like self. A few pages later, he talks about the need to break out of the confinement of his job in New York City to return to this voyage. The language is peculiarly reminiscent of Jesus's words spoken at the Last Supper: "I must do this in remembrance of a life beyond all comparison with the life which was promised me, in remembrance of the life of a child who was strangled and stifled by the mutual consent of those who had surrendered" (145).[5] In this passage, Miller resurrects the message of the bread shared with Stanley. His life will now commence with the enthusiasm of his childhood, though at the cost of crucifixion.

In fact, this communion serves as a prelude to Miller's own crucifixion, an event anticipated throughout the novel. Many passages in the novel explicitly connect his experiences with Christ's sacrifice, such as the following citation, in which Miller accounts for his apathy: "I felt exactly like Jesus Christ would have felt if he had been taken down from the cross and not permitted to die in the flesh. I am sure that the shock of crucifixion would have been so great that he would have suffered a complete amnesia as regards humanity" (67). On the following page, we find another moment connecting him with the ancient martyrdom: "At night the streets of New York reflect the crucifixion and death of Christ" (68). One can imagine dirty pools of water reflecting his suffered, world-weary visage, as he walks the streets of Manhattan. In this sentence, Manhattan becomes the stage for the crucifixion drama.

Miller also talks about his rebirth, the transformation that he chronicles in *Tropic of Cancer*, in terms related to Christ's crucifixion and resurrection. Early in the novel he confesses in light of his birthday, "One thing seems clear, however—and this is a hangover from the 25th—that I was born with a crucifixion complex" (62). Discussing his born-again experience in a passage in which he also mentions the "Miracle of Golgotha," he writes: "What

Tropic of Capricorn 67

fascinates me is that anything so dead and buried as I was could be resuscitated, and not just once, but innumerable times. And not only that, but each time I faded out I plunged deeper than ever into the void, so that with each resuscitation the miracle becomes greater. And never any stigmata!" (230). Although he does not have the sacred wounds, he bleeds his confession into his texts, themselves testaments of resurrection. Towards the conclusion of the novel, he again refers to these experiences of liberation within a Christian rubric, writing: "All my Calvaries were rosy crucifixions, pseudo-tragedies to keep the fires of hell burning brightly for the real sinners who are in danger of being forgotten" (325). As we will see, what makes his crucifixion "rosy" or a "pseudo-tragedy" is that he voluntarily led himself into suffering through his relationship with Mara. During the time chronicled in *Tropic of Capricorn*, Miller had the chance to become liberated by relinquishing everything, but decided instead to worship Mara, the embodiment of illusion ("Mara" in Sanskrit means "illusion"). His relationship with her becomes the subject of *The Rosy Crucifixion* trilogy, which documents his voluntary sacrifice thorough his passionate affair.

MILLER'S APPROPRIATION OF DANTE

Many passages in *Tropic of Capricorn* connect Miller's own experiences to that of another pilgrim moved by love: Dante. Like him, Miller attempts to construct his own religious universe deeply informed by the Christian tradition. In fact, there are two moments in which he recounts reading Dante's *Inferno,* the first being a boyhood reminiscence: "I had been poring all week over Dante's *Inferno* in English" (249). Another recalls adult years: "I tried reading the *Inferno* at night, but it was in English and English is no language for a Catholic work" (297). Beyond attesting to his familiarity with the poem, these moments demonstrate that he was interested in translation, particularly in the way he calls attention to English renderings of the *Commedia.* This suggests that he knew of Dante's bold decision to pen his testament in the vernacular, knowledge that inspired the American writer to use his Brooklynite English when writing his contemporary *Inferno.*

Indeed, one can read *Tropic of Capricorn* as Miller's chronicle through hell.[6] He splits his "inferno" into the two zones of Brooklyn and Manhattan, locations respectively associated with home and work. Twice he specifically connects Myrtle Avenue, a street he knew well in Brooklyn, to Dante's *Inferno:* "For the genuine Inferno [. . .] I give you Myrtle Avenue, one of the innumerable bridlepaths ridden by iron monsters which lead to the heart of America's emptiness" (298). Later on the page, he directly addresses the reader, a trope that parodies Dante, when mentioning the Italian poet directly: "Dear reader, you must see Myrtle Avenue before you die, if only to realize how far into the future Dante saw" (298). Towards the end of the novel, he speaks about all Brooklyn streets when writing, "The hydra-headed dog barks with all his mouths and though there are no swamps I hear the frogs croaking everywhere" (337–38). This "hydra-headed dog" alludes to Cerberus, the beast guarding the entrance to the third circle of Dante's Hell, a mythological figure that is the underworld's guardian in classical mythology.[7] Through this reference, his native Brooklyn, where Miller continued to live with wife and child, is implicated as the entrance into his own private hell.

The center of Miller's adult employment, Manhattan forms the second locus of his Inferno. Many pages of *Tropic of Capricorn* are devoted to chronicling his life as employment manager at "the Cosmodemonic Telegraph Company of North America" (16). He often suggests through colloquial slang that "the Cosmodemonic" is swarmed with demons. In one passage, he sympathetically refers to the telegraph messengers he would hire as "poor devils" (27). Later, he refers to those in charge of the company as "demons on high" (33). Recalling his first days in the managerial position, he also implicates himself by stating that he was a "lucky devil" complete with "a tail and a pair of horns," earlier claiming that he was "hiring and firing like a demon" (324, 19). Speaking of the place in general, he states, "From the moment I arrived at the office it was one long uninterrupted pandemonium" (21). "Pandemonium" captures the howling chaos that is the Cosmodemonic Telegraph Company, but it also conjures images of the Hell presented in *Paradise Lost,* namely, Milton's own "Pandemonium," a place removed from enlightenment and God. As Miller become increasingly aware of the evils lurking within the Company, he tries to deliver an optimistic message. With the idea of comforting prospective messengers, he tells us that he had put a sign above his desk stating, "Do not abandon all hope ye who enter here!" (321). Naturally, it is an allusion to the placard above the gates of Hell in Dante's *Inferno.*[8] Although his sign negates the message found in the *Inferno,* Miller throughout the text, as we have seen, acknowledges that the office was unmistakably a modern Hell.

Miller saw the Brooklyn Bridge as a pathway attaching the two Hells of Manhattan and Brooklyn. For him, the commuter train he rode everyday along the structure offered little more than a station to station journey between painful places. As he writes, "Instead of joining me to life, to me, to the activity of men, the bridge seemed to break all connections: either way was hell" (60). In more surrealistic moments, he refers to this passage as "on the ovarian trolley," which itself recalls conversations he would have on the

Tropic of Capricorn 69

train with his friend Hymie, who would often discuss his wife's diseased ovaries (53).[9] In Miller's mind, Brooklyn and Manhattan were sick zones incapable of producing a liberated individual. The back and forth travel between home and work gives the illusion of progress, that one is going somewhere with one's life, but people remain trapped within a much greater entity, unable to see that to exit, one must jump off the train. Miraculously, one can become born again in this Hell in which the reproductive organs (i.e., ovaries)—sources of creation—are diseased. In this mythology, the East River below the Brooklyn Bridge becomes a canal linked to the vagina, a passage that can lead one to rebirth if one takes a leap of faith. Considering that he reads his "new Bible"—Bergson's *Creative Evolution*—as he journeys across this stream of *élan vital* underscores such associations.[10]

From the vantage-point of the ovarian trolley, however, such a leap appears to be suicide. On a page in which Dante is mentioned, he records an inner dialogue typical of this moment in his life, writing "don't die yet, wait another day, a stroke of luck, river, end it, down, down, like a corkscrew, head and shoulders in the mud, legs free" (50). The first part of the passage alludes to Hart Crane's poem, "Proem: To Brooklyn Bridge," in which a man jumps to his death.[11] But the overall message of Crane's poem is that the Bridge and its river are pathways to God, themes that Miller-the-character will identify once conscious of the creative stream's powers. From his perspective at this point in the novel, however, such a leap seems to be a suicidal plunge. By conjuring the image of one's torso stuck into the ground with legs and feet above, one is reminded of various moments in Dante's *Inferno*. He could be referring to the Simonists of Canto 19, who are trapped in what he would see as false vessels—baptismal fonts—since they contain water used in empty rituals rather than the holy water one finds in the dynamic flow. The task is to break these fonts in order to restore one to life, just as Dante recounts how he broke one to save a drowning child.[12] A couple of pages later, when Miller takes a mental leap into these waters, he conjures up images of those who are frozen in similar positions at the end of the *Inferno*, referring to it as "the skating rink of hell."[13] He writes, "each buttoned ovary produced a subterranean chill, the skating rink of hell where men stood upside down in the ice, the legs free and waiting for a bite. Here Dante walked unaccompanied, weighed down by his vision, and through endless circles gradually moving heavenward to be enthroned in his work" (52). Although he was certainly aware that the narrative presents Dante accompanied by Virgil, just as Miller is accompanied by his friend Hymie, he is suggesting that such inner explorations led Dante to God. By noting the inverted legs, he recalls Dante and Virgil's exit from Hell, in which they see Satan with his legs in the air.

Because Miller's leap into the river took place only in his imagination and the full plunge will not occur until he arrives in Paris, he writes that his journey, at least at this stage, remains distinct from (not to mention of less significance than) Dante's own. Rather than connecting to *élan vital* by fully immersing himself into the East River, he remains trapped on "the current of life" as he navigates the passage between work and home (54). Although he maintains that his journey and Dante's are not at this moment identical, this passage and Miller's own mental plunge intimates some identification with the Italian poet, as they are both eternally lodged in the self-constructed Christian worlds of their autobiographical texts. As we find later in *Tropic of Capricorn*, he equates his painful experiences of becoming a liberated individual with Dante's vexations. He writes, "It was some such gigantic collapse which Dante must have experienced when he situated himself in Hell; it was not a bottom which he touched, but a core, a dead center from which time itself is reckoned. Here the comedy begins, from here it is seen to be divine" (207–08). In this passage, he implies that we should read his work as a Christian text and in the light of Dante's magnum opus.

Keeping with his appropriation of Dante's schematic, Miller includes an inverted Beatrice figure who nevertheless serves a similar role to the Italian poet's beloved.[14] As Mara, the personification of illusion, she is far from the virtuous female found in *The Divine Comedy*. Nevertheless, her influence encourages Miller to leave his dual-hell of the Cosmodemonic Telegraph Company and Brooklyn to become a writer in Paris, a city that can be interpreted as his Paradiso. She guides him to the abyss in which he can apprehend God directly, just as Beatrice leads Dante to the light, only to behold the Trinity alone. Miller's relationship with Mara, chronicled in *The Rosy Crucifixion*, can be seen as his Purgatorio, a claim he makes in *Tropic of Capricorn*. Referring to this period as "the Land of Fuck," in which he evolves into a person who understands that he must plunge alone into the waters of creative energy, he writes, "The interlude which I think of as the Land of Fuck, a realm of time more than of space, is for me the equivalent of that Purgatory which Dante has described in nice detail" (208). There are also suggestions that we are supposed to associate Mara with Beatrice. Her work as a taxi dancer in "Roseland Ballroom" evokes the image of the mystic rose in *Paradiso*, which itself becomes an auditorium (105).[15] Also, since this venue is where he first encountered her, the hall functions as the opening of his "rosy crucifixion." But perhaps the most palpable association between Mara and Beatrice relates to their author's thirst to immortalize these women. This project, just like Dante's *Divine Comedy*, would drive most of his creative output throughout his life.

Tropic of Capricorn 71

Additional associations to Dante come through Miller's citations of Peter Abelard. Dante alludes to the love affair of Abelard and Heloise through the scene in which the Pilgrim encounters Francesca da Rimini and Paolo Malatesta, lovers moved to amours by reading.[16] By reminding us of these love affairs, Miller suggests that *Tropic of Capricorn* should not be used to move one to sexual stimulation. Instead, one should remember the lessons of these famous lovers and let their example remind us that these accounts should lead one towards God. He makes this known by selecting a passage from the opening of Abelard's *Historia Calamitatum,* his confession of his relationship with Heloise, as a prelude to his own text. It is unfortunate that this epigraph was removed from American editions of the book, as it provides essential clues into Miller's intent.[17] The passage clearly suggests that sex in *Tropic of Capricorn* is not to titillate but to show how his mishaps, including robbing his child's bank and hitting his wife, eventually led him closer to God.

Abelard's quote also gives us a clue into the nature of Miller's text. Here is but a selection: "This I [write] so that in comparing your sorrows with mine, you may discover that yours in truth naught, or at the most but of small account, and so shall you come to bear them more easily." By putting these words at the front of his own book, Miller tries to frame his work as a confession written with hopes of helping others become liberated.[18] Lastly, Abelard's phrasing distinguishes actions and words, implying that his *Historia Calamitatum* is more than words but rather a representation of himself. As we have seen in *Tropic of Cancer,* the conundrum of creating a "living book" is at the heart of Miller's work. Naturally, he would identify with Abelard's confessional work, which aims to fuse word with flesh, than do more contemporary genres, such as the novel or prose poem.

THE FORM AND STRUCTURE OF *TROPIC OF CAPRICORN*

Because it chronicles events that happened when Miller went astray, *Tropic of Capricorn* is best classified as a confession. Unlike *Tropic of Cancer,* which reads as if the reader accompanies the author on a journey, most of *Tropic of Capricorn* is situated in the distant past. There are, however, two major exceptions. Occasionally he reflects on experiences from his contemporary standpoint. At other times, he charts the evolution of his perspective as if such growth were taking place in the present—the technique employed throughout *Tropic of Cancer.* Naturally, it takes a careful eye to identify the moments in which he shifts time.

One can place sharp divisions in the text to better demarcate these points of view. In fact, it seems that Miller originally divided the manuscript into three parts. When we reinstate these partitions, we find that Part One discusses pivotal moments from his childhood and his life as employment manager at the "Cosmodemonic Telegraph Company."[19] This section is the most linear: it begins with youth, then quickly moves to his adult working life, before ending with earlier childhood moments that brought about illumination. The second part, which begins with the heading of "An Interlude" in the published version, contains his inner thoughts as he edges closer to uniting himself with creative energy.[20] Charting his internal evolution, this entire passage is written in the present tense. Part Three reverts to discussions of his childhood and life in New York City, but he switches between these two periods with greater frequency.[21] He begins by discussing moments that give his life direction and the "new Bible"—Bergson's *Creative Evolution*—that leads him to his alleged transfiguration into Gottlieb Leberecht Muller. The last moments of this section detail his experiences with women as a young adult and grown man, eventually ending with a Coda devoted first to a childhood love, then to his wife in New York, and finally with Mara. In both the first and third part, he oscillates between chronicling and commenting on the past. His "present" voice is often easy to locate, as these two sections—the first and third—are not as stylistically complex as the second.

By breaking the book into three components, *Tropic of Capricorn* further resonates with Christian mythology. It recalls the trinity theme, which we will see replicated in *The Rosy Crucifixion,* as the magnum opus is divided into three volumes. Such partitions also underscore Miller's preoccupation with Dante, who employed three-line *terza rima* and broke his grand poem into three canticles, two of which contain 33 cantos. In fact, the second division of *Tropic of Capricorn* describes the author's own visions in the "Land of Fuck," a realm he associates with Purgatory.[22]

Splitting his narrative in such a manner, Miller was also trying to structure his narrative in accordance with Rosicrucian doctrines. Around this time, he was familiar with French sources outlining three general movements that a Rosicrucian has on his spiritual journey: *vie purgative, vie illuminative,* and *vie unitive.* When we compare this schematic with the twin novels *Tropic of Cancer* and *Tropic of Capricorn,* we can see Parts One and Three of *Tropic of Capricorn* representing the "*vie purgative,*" as they are confessional expurgations, detailing the author's misspent life in Hell. The second part of *Tropic of Capricorn,* the so-called "Purgatorio" or the "Land of Fuck," refers to the "*vie illuminative,*" as it details his inner awakening. *Tropic of Cancer* becomes his "*vie unitive,*" established by the author's hermaphroditic union with the Seine at the end of the novel. When we examine the novel's content carefully, this unification quest dictates the metaphysics of *Tropic of Capricorn.* In the

Tropic of Capricorn 73

next part of this chapter, I show how he appropriates mystical concepts to inform his vision of liberation.

TOWARDS METAPHYSICAL UNION: LOGOS AND THE LAND OF FUCK

Throughout *Tropic of Capricorn,* we find Miller preoccupied with the Christian concept of "Logos," the divine Word that gave birth to creation. As his text concerns his childhood and the moments that prompted him to become creative, it follows that he would appropriate such creation myths. On the first page, we discover him addressing his own creation *ex nihilo,* the birth of form through chaos. The opening words state, "Once you have given up the ghost, everything follows with dead certainty, even in the midst of chaos. From the beginning it was never anything but chaos: it was a fluid which enveloped me, which I breathed in through the gills" (9). In these initial sentences, he appropriates not only the content but also the language of biblical creation myths when discussing his own birth. Although occasionally used in common parlance, the phrase "given up the ghost" is most closely associated with the King James Bible and, in particular, Christ's terminal moment on the cross. "From the beginning" recalls "in the beginning," the opening words of Genesis and of John's Gospel, the latter being where the concept of Logos is introduced.

Miller's interest in Logos was likely prompted through his association with Aleister Crowley's Ordo Templi Orientis (OTO), especially their peculiar rendering of the concept of "Spermatikos Logos." According to OTO ideas, sperm is the literal vessel of Logos and it is man's duty to reform the Androgyne through a union of "Logos Spermatikos" and the "Pleroma."[23] Crowley even suggested using sperm to create a literal "Elixir of Life" to be imbibed ritualistically through Gnostic Mass, a variation on the Eucharist.[24] While Miller is certainly inspired by these ideas, he shies away from taking them literally, using them in the metaphorical sense to build his religious world. His use of "Logos" was certainly nuanced by these occult renderings.

In *Tropic of Capricorn,* Miller frequently mentions Logos or its common variations, "Word" and "Verb." There are two passages, however, in which he directly quotes John 1.1. One instance is when he describes his childhood acquaintance Grover Watrous, who left a lasting impression on the author. He laments that Watrous had to use "Christ for a crutch" to find salvation, though Miller concedes that the ends are more important than the means, perhaps recalling how he himself used others—particularly Mara—to achieve liberation. He describes Watrous as someone completely overtaken with love for God, preaching to anyone he encountered:

74   *Henry Miller and Religion*

God only asked of Grover Watrous that he reveal himself alive in the flesh. He only asked of him to be more and more alive. And when fully alive Grover was a voice and this voice was a flood which made all dead things into chaos and this chaos in turn became the mouth of the world and the very center of which was the verb *to be*. *In the beginning there was the Word, and the Word was with God, and the word was God.* (173)

In this sequence, we move from an undirected flow of energy—the flood—through a channeling of this chaotic flux into the mouth, an organ that shapes the energy into form. His name itself—Watrous—whispers "water us," as if the preacher is a fountain spewing Logos. In opposition to Miller's father, whom we learn turned to religion to achieve sobriety, Watrous is not interested in keeping us dry. Miller continues pontificating on the Word: "Starting from this Verb what difference did it make which road he traveled? To leave the Verb was to travel away from the center, to erect a Babel" (174). In these two sentences, he establishes two groups: one composed of people who travel with the Word, another of those who stray. Those who break away fabricate false concretizations of the spoken word by attempting to transcend the world, an act he likely identified with the construction of Manhattan skyscrapers. Rather than harnessing the Word's power into brick and concrete, he insists following its flow onto the open road.

The second passage in which we find John 1.1 also connects Logos to a channeling of flow. This moment comes when Miller is "on the ovarian trolley" above the East River:

In the beginning was the Word. . . . Whatever this was, *the Word,* disease or creation, it was still running rampant; it would run on and on, outstrip time and space, outlast the angels, unseat God, unhook the universe. [. . .] In every word the current ran back to the beginning which was lost and which would never be found again since there was neither beginning nor end but only that which expressed itself in beginning and end. (53–4)

He critically connects Logos with current, identifying this Christian concept with *élan vital,* the creative energy developed in *Tropic of Cancer.* When we consider that this passage appears when he is on the Brooklyn Bridge, we can see the East River itself as a manifestation of Logos.[25] Situated towards the "east," this river symbolically transports him to Paris, where he becomes one with the Seine.[26]

Tropic of Capricorn 75

By identifying Logos with the river, the vast ocean becomes associated with the chaos found before creation. Through this concordance, we are better able to grasp the opening of *Tropic of Capricorn,* in which he writes that chaos is "a fluid which enveloped me, which I breathed in through the gills" (9). Yearning to become a modern Christ, a savior himself symbolized by a fish, the aquatic author foreshadows his own creative powers as an artist who channels the chaos surrounding him. Before he can undertake such a task, however, he must undergo the inner awakening we find detailed in Part Two of the book.

This second part is the most challenging section of *Tropic of Capricorn.* To signal the challenges ahead, Miller opens with a warning that states, "Confusion is a word we have invented for an order which is not understood" (176). Here he suggests that one should not dismiss the passage as confusing nonsense, but should try to understand the order within. Because he uses the present tense, as if the transformation chronicled takes place contemporaneously, the section is additionally difficult. To trace this inner change, he begins this interlude with ideas inconsistent with other parts of the novel and, in fact, the end of Part Two itself. Caught within chaotic oceans, the ideas and images presented at the first of the passage are distorted, as if he peers at the sun from the bottom of the sea. He acknowledges his position in this metaphysical space by writing, "I lay like a dolphin on the oyster banks" (183). One of the pearls of wisdom he misapprehends concerns Logos. He writes, "There was Logos, which somehow I had always identified with breath: I found that on the contrary it was a sort of obsessional stasis, a machine which went on grinding corn long after the granaries had been filled and the Jews driven out of Egypt" (184). Contradicting what he had written just pages before, he erroneously identifies Logos with stability rather than flow, a machine instead of water. He commits a similar error on the following two pages when he discusses Noah's Ark as a place of comfort and slothfulness, which will differ sharply from his vision at the end of the passage (185–86). Although it is difficult to perceive this false standpoint from which he is writing these distorted thoughts, he provides a clue when writing, "It was going on this way all the time, even though every word I say is a lie" (190). The "was" indicates that the thoughts presented before this sentence belonged to the past, though the act of writing "I say" indicates again the present moment. In short, this particular sentence serves as a point of demarcation; after it things begin to become clearer, albeit not yet completely precise.

The confusion of this passage continues as Miller expresses his desire to become fixed in the quicksand that is the Land of Fuck. In a whirl of words, he recalls symbols and figures from what Bergson would refer to as static religions, including the Anglican Church, the Egyptian bull god Apis, Absalom, the Seventh Day Adventists, the Roman fertility god Priapus, and the controversial Christian group called the Holy Rollers of Oregon (192–95). Christ is also mentioned multiple times, albeit not as living divinity but rather as a stagnant entity. Miller writes that Priapus, a figure most often depicted with an erect phallus, sees "a huge slate on which was written the body of Christ" (193). Even though he tells us that Christ arose and "danced like a mountain goat," one does not associate goats with great vitality (194). Rather, it is through the astrological sign Capricorn that goats are associated with stability. Later on the page, Christ's lifelessness is again underscored when Miller writes, "Up with the thorns and the manacles! Christ is dead and mangled with quoits" (194). These passages show Christ not as a living savior imbued with *élan vital,* but wed to rock and bound by manacles.

Out of this mythical tour, we arrive at places significant to Miller's upbringing in Brooklyn. He writes, "It is Sunday morning around the corner from Evergreen Cemetery. It is Sunday morning and I am lying blissfully dead to the world on my bed of ferroconcrete" (196). Through these lines, he substitutes himself with the dead Christ image, though Miller also remains languid, as if positioned on the Brooklyn Bridge above holy waters. He tells us that here "everything is in rock crystal," emphasizing the rigidity of this position (197). A few pages later, he continues his vision: "Everything was absolutely clear to me because done in rock crystal; at every egress there was written in big letters ANNIHILATION. The fright of extinction solidified me; the body became itself a piece of ferroconcrete. It was ornamented by a permanent erection in the best of taste" (202). Everything belonging to him had become completely solidified; even the prospect of making a change paralyzed him with fear, especially if it meant jumping into the waters of *élan vital* at the risk of dissolving one's ego. From this perspective, taking a leap of faith seemed suicidal.

In the next paragraph, however, we find that Miller has assumed a new name. As he writes, "It was about this time, adopting the pseudonym Samson Lackawanna, that I began my depredations" (202). Through incorporating the name of Samson, he positions himself as a character from the Old Testament, signifying a prelude to becoming Christ. The particular choice of Samson, however, is critical for many reasons.[27] First, Samson submitted to Delilah rather than following the ways of God. But even more critical to these images, Samson was a rock-solid man who broke his shackles in order to bring down the temple of the Philistines. Through his alleged transformation into Samson Lackawanna, one no longer driven by sexual desire (i.e., lack-

Tropic of Capricorn 77

a-want), he is able to commence smashing the stony entity his body and life have become. Confirmation is found on the following page, when he relates an experience of illumination:

> It was like a blaze of pure consciousness, thought became God. And God, for the first time in my knowledge, was clean-shaven. I was also clean-shaven, flawless, deadly accurate. I saw my image in the marble black lakes and it was diapered with stars. Stars, stars . . . like a clout between the eyes and all remembrance fast run out. I was Samson and I was Lackawanna and I was dying as one being in the ecstasy of full consciousness. (203)

Rather than thought being crystallized, knowledge is now fiery, a "blaze of pure consciousness." Miller also becomes increasingly identified with God via the "clean-shaven" Samson whose deadly accuracy brought down the temple. His "black marble lakes," symbols for Samson's gouged out eyes, are pierced with light, another metaphor for Logos. "Marble lakes" also insinuates rock that may potentially flow.

In fact, at the beginning of the paragraph immediately following this passage, we find Miller flowing down a river. He writes, "And now here I am, sailing down the river in my little canoe" (203). In this moment during the Land of Fuck interlude, he has positioned himself as a spermatozoa, the seed for his rebirth. He underscores the potential within this form:

> At the very bottom of the ladder, *chez* the spermatozoa, there is the same condition of bliss as at the top, *chez* God. God is the summation of all the spermatozoa come to full consciousness. Between the bottom and the top there is no stop, no halfway station. The river starts somewhere in the mountains and flows on into the sea. On this river that leads to God the canoe is as serviceable as the dreadnought. From the very start the journey is homeward. (204)

Soon afterwards, we find additional correlations between this potential divine entity and Christ in a passage quoted before: "Sailing down the river. . . . Slow as the hookworm, but tiny enough to make every bend. And slippery as an eel withal. What is your name? shouts someone. *My name? Why just call me God—God the embryo.* I go sailing on" (204). This marks a moment of complete identification of Miller with the son of God.

Soon after this instant, Miller introduces images and symbols related to the climax of *Tropic of Cancer.* Out of the flowing river, the liberated self

78   *Henry Miller and Religion*

begins to crystallize into an entity with a hard shell but who nevertheless contains the flow of *élan vital* within. He may have envisioned such a creature in *Tropic of Cancer* via the crab symbol, as crabs have a rigid exterior filled with fluid, tender muscles.[28] But to return to *Tropic of Capricorn,* he develops this crystallization process by comparing sperm to mustard seeds, alluding to passages in the New Testament, in which Christ claims that faith even as small as mustard seed can move mountains.[29] Through this reference, Miller suggests a correlation between mustard seeds and rock. Also, this simile insinuates that each person contains the "kingdom of God," as the image alludes to additional passages in which Christ made analogies between heaven and mustard seed.[30]

These allusions anticipate concrete associations between becoming rock and the liberated self. Describing this free individual, Miller writes, "In this strange Capricornian condition of embryosis God the he-goat ruminates in stolid bliss among the mountain peaks. The high altitudes nourish the germ of separation which will one day estrange him completely from the soul of man, which will make him a desolate, rocklike father dwelling forever apart in a void which is unthinkable" (204–05). In addition to being situated within mountain peaks, the entity is identified with the "he-goat," a play on the astrological "sea-goat" symbol linked with "Capricorn." Having risen out of the waters, this regenerated self has again become hard, albeit containing fluid life within.

In Miller's complex symbolism, this rock-like being is associated with Noah's Ark. He mentions the Ark narrative numerous times in the text, including the "Land of Fuck" interlude. At the end of the novel, however, he recalls the image to describe the self emerging from streams of creative energy:[31]

> This monster which rose now and then to fix its target with deadly aim, which dove again and roved and plundered ceaselessly [sic] would, when the time came, rise for the last time to reveal itself as an ark, would gather unto itself a pair of each kind and at last, when the floods abated, would settle down on the summit of a lofty mountain peak thence to open wide its doors and return to the world what had been preserved from the catastrophe. (321)

Similar to Noah's Ark, which unified opposites within its planks while charting the chaotic seas, the liberated self he proposes fuses contraries: it is crystallized yet holding *élan vital.* Like the biblical vessel, the liberated individual must also give birth to the next generation.[32] In Miller's case,

Tropic of Capricorn 79

the well-fashioned book becomes the vessel, a form that can be transferred generation to generation.

To return to the "Land of Fuck" interlude, Miller contrasts his own textual Ark with the work of James Joyce. Miller continued his obsession with what would become *Finnegan's Wake* (1939), a text steeped in the Genesis narratives. In the following passage, Miller seems simply to be decrying rampant capitalism and New York bourgeois tastes when ranting about Bloomingdale's department store. A close reading, however, suggests that he is critiquing Joyce, the architect of Leopold and Molly *Bloom,* characters in his celebrated *Ulysses.*

> There is the smell, not of decomposition, but of misalliance. Man, the miserable alchemist, has welded together, in a million forms and shapes, substances and essences which have nothing in common. Because in his mind there is a tumor which is eating him away insatiably; he has left the little canoe which was taking him blissfully down the river in order to construct a bigger, safer boat in which there may be room for everyone. His labors take him so far afield that he has lost all remembrance of why he left the little canoe. The ark is so full of bric-à-brac that it has become a stationary building above a subway in which the smell of linoleum prevails and predominates. Gather together all the significance hidden away in the interstitial miscellany of Bloomingdale's and put it on the head of a pin and you will have left a universe in which the grand constellations move without the slightest danger of collision. (205)

In this scathing attack on Joyce, *Finnegan's Wake* is portrayed as a text incapable of restoring life in the next generation. Instead, the book is a complex maze of cryptic allusions and indecipherable language. As Miller writes, "Only, as the Bloomingdale experience goes to prove, this whole self, about which so much boasting has been done, falls apart very easily" (206). After this denouncement, he further develops his own conception of the crystal ego able to give vitality to the world.

Miller refers to this new ego-assemblage as the "happy rock," an appellation he continues to use throughout his books.[33] Immediately after the Joyce diatribe, he writes, "It is only after the third meal that the morning gifts, bequeathed by the phony alliance of the ancestors, begin to drop away and the true rock of the self, the happy rock sheers up out of the muck of the soul" (206). In juxtaposition to his take on Joyce, Miller encourages us to become independent, to break from past myths and literatures once their nourishment has provided strength. By reprising the Noah's Ark theme, he begins to introduce us to the "happy rock" concept, presenting himself as adrift on chaotic seas.

As we have seen in the passage where he shifts from a monster to a "dove," his vessel floating atop the chaos orders the surrounding disarray. He continues, "You live like a happy rock in the midst of the ocean: you are fixed while everything about you is in turbulent motion. You are fixed in a reality which permits the thought that nothing is fixed, that even the happiest and mightiest rock will one day be utterly dissolved and fluid as the ocean from which it was born" (331–32). As a sprawling mass of unfocused potential, the ocean should be seen in contrast with the river, an entity able to channel energy. The "happy rock" is the final refinement, as we move from sea to stream.[34] As he later writes, he transforms from "skater to a swimmer and the swimmer to a rock," a three-fold process in which one is above the waters of chaos, one is within, and then one crystallizes its power (332). Around this later passage, he describes becoming a "happy rock" in terms derived from Buddhism: "The rock is merely an image of the act which stops the futile rotation of the wheel and plunges the being into full consciousness" (332). In this passage, he suggests that the experience of becoming a "happy rock" is like the experience of nirvana, liberation from the wheel of samsara. This aware entity, we are then told, unites opposites within, antinomies such as light and darkness, sun and moon, and creative energy flowing within a stable shell.

Although nuanced by Eastern conceptions, Miller's "happy rock" has direct precedent in the Christian Bible. In canonized scripture, the image's forerunner can be found in 1 Corinthians, in which Paul identifies Christ as a rock from which the children of Israel imbibed: "for they *drank* from the *spiritual rock* that accompanied them, and that *rock was Christ*" (10.4, emphasis added). Naturally, this passage itself harkens Exodus, in which Moses brings water from rock.[35] Conveying spiritual replenishment, both scriptures preserve the tension between rock and water that resurfaces in Miller's metaphor of the salvific rock. His qualifier "happy," however, not only captures the Buddha's enlightened smile, but also supercedes rock associations from the Hebrew Bible, in which narratives, prophets, and psalms envision the "Rock of Ages" as a wrathful entity.

In addition to drawing upon traditional Christian texts, the metaphysics of Miller's "happy rock"—in which opposing pairs are united within the liberated self—are informed by esoteric texts addressing the concept of *coincidentia oppositorum*. Multiple mystics have been preoccupied by this idea, but Miller most likely encountered them through Meister Eckhart, Jacob Boehme, and various Rosicrucian sources, as we find allusions and

Tropic of Capricorn 81

references to these materials in *Tropic of Capricorn*.[36] Although he may not have known Eckhart's work directly, he was probably familiar with the basic concepts represented in Theosophical texts. Eckhart used the metaphor of fire to conceive the divine spark of consciousness, an image we also find in the "Land of Fuck" passage. He also discussed union with God as a "divine stillness" devoid of human desire, a concept we see recast in Miller's "happy rock" resting tranquilly. Boehme's ideas are even more integrated into the narrative and metaphysics of *Tropic of Capricorn*.[37] In the following passage, Miller indeed quotes him on the union of opposites: "All things are generated out of the grand mystery, and proceed out of one degree into another. Whatever goes forward in its degree, the same receives no abominate" (296). This citation attests to Miller's familiarity with his dialectic, in which rest is interrupted by one's desire for an opposite.[38] The mystic cobbler used this schematic to account for God's decision to assume human form, breaking rest to bring about motion that would itself resolve in rock-like stasis. We find a similar pattern replicated in his shift from "lying on a bed of ferroconcrete" to becoming a "happy rock" out of water. Similar takes on *coincidentia oppositorum* derived from Rosicrucian sources can be found in his notebooks, in which he recalls the three-fold process leading to "*vie unitive.*" This process is reinforced by many hermaphroditic symbols, including the reunion of Adam and Eve, Queen and King, and Christ and his ecclesiastical bride.

Forecasting himself as a unified "happy rock," Miller has traveled far from his position at the first of the narrative, in which he defines himself as "a contradiction in essence" (14). In fact, his journey towards the union of opposites is embedded in the very fabric of his narrative. Immediately following the "Land of Fuck" passage, for example, we find him as a young boy in front of the ocean at Far Rockaway. By choosing this location, he underscores his "far away" journey before becoming a "rock." He has to leave the firm foundation of the shore and drift in the oceans of desire before finding himself east in Paris, reborn as a liberated entity. Nevertheless, the artistic voyage begins at Far Rockaway. Between the tension of "everything and nothing," his liberating quest is set into motion in this passage (211). At the beginning of his writing career, in which the target of becoming a rock is sighted in the distance, he finds himself uttering the first Word, giving birth to the "dawn" of inner enlightenment.

When we examine the content of the novel closely, we find Miller's authorial quest dictates the book's narrative. In the final part of this chapter, I reorganize the events of *Tropic of Capricorn* into chronological order, interpreting the narrative as a quest for liberation. My analysis focuses on

82   *Henry Miller and Religion*

Miller's appropriation of astrological and Christian symbols. The story traces
his ascension to Golgotha, the solid basis of his so-called "rosy crucifixion"
that leads to resurrection as the "happy rock."

THE RISE OF THE SEA-GOAT

As we have seen, Miller begins his life caught in the waters of chaos, "a fluid
which enveloped me, which I breathed in through the gills" (9). Sometime
during his childhood, however, he found his way into the waters of freedom, the sacred *élan vital.* Although he hardly devotes space to detailing
this fleeting moment, we assume he was once free, since he writes of need-
ing to return to this state. Recalling adult years, in which devouring books
put him back on the path, he writes, "There could be no end, and there was
none, until inside me a bridge began to form which united me again with
the current of life from which as a child I had been separated" (61). In many
ways, his thoughts are derivative of Romanticism, but he supplements this
tradition through the sophisticated rock and water metaphors we have seen.

Miller relates a childhood event in which rock first became associated
with stasis. Near the ominous location of "Hell Gate," he and his friends,
all of whom were around eight or nine years old, become involved in a
rock fight with a rival gang. As he puts it, "We didn't know which side we
were fighting for but we were fighting in dead earnest amidst the rock pile
by the river bank" (124). By placing the rock pile next to the river bank, he
is again juxtaposing these two prime symbols, setting the stage for action.
In the fight, he throws a rock at a boy's head, striking his temple with a
blow that kills him. The boys all flee and are never caught. Miller and his
cousin Gene return to his Aunt Caroline's, whereupon they play marbles
with their friend Joey Kasselbaum. Miller recalls, "Gene and I allowed him
to win everything we had" (125). The implication here is that he has "lost
his marbles," meaning both that he consciously tries to get rid of the evidence—rocks—and also loses himself in the chaos of insanity. Years later,
he remains haunted by the traumatic event, even though the grown Gene
had forgotten his role in the event (though not the boy's death). We are
told that Gene now seems "more attached to the tropical fish which he was
collecting" (125). Gene, unlike Miller, was able to contain these exotic,
chaotic moments in bowls, as water is here a symbol of chaos. Miller, however, is left floundering in the aftermath of the event, drifting from job to
job without any real direction.

In his early adulthood, writing seemed a way to establish ground.
Reflecting upon this period, Miller writes, "One saw me bobbing up and

Tropic of Capricorn 83

down on the surface, rocking gently sometimes or else swinging backwards and forwards agitatedly. What held me down safely was the big pigeonholed desk which I put in the parlor" (282). This massive writing desk becomes a platform he holds onto in his bid to emerge out of the chaos. His attempts at writing, however, are equally chaotic. They were "titanic efforts [. . .] made to canalize the hot lava which was bubbling inside," but he was unable to harness these creative juices (283). He continues, "I didn't lack thoughts nor words nor the power of expression—I lacked something much more important: the lever which would shut off the juice. The bloody machine wouldn't stop, that was the difficulty. I was not only in the middle of the current but the current was running through me and I had no control over it whatever" (284). Not until Paris could he channel this chaos into form. His writing at this New York period, he claims, was particularly bad: "Everything I had written before was museum stuff, and most writing is still museum stuff and that's why it doesn't catch fire, doesn't inflame the world" (284). Sensing the discrete connection between museum and mausoleum, his writing was unable to resuscitate the living dead. There are, however, hints in this passage of future messianic abilities. In one part, he describes his writing desk as "antediluvian," suggesting that his work will be the Noah's Ark, restoring life to the next generation (289). We again find a connection to Christ, in this case his disciples, when he states, "certainly I didn't need twelve empty chairs placed around it in a semicircle; I needed only elbow room in which to write and a thirteenth chair which would take me out of the zodiac they were using and put me in a heaven beyond heaven" (289). In addition to proposing a movement from pagan astrology to Christianity, he also suggests he wanted to be more than a disciple; he wanted to be the messiah.

Later in his adulthood, Miller abandoned writing and clung to the solid terrains of family and career, the rocky shores from which he could remove himself from chaotic waters. With this in mind, we can see the astrological significance of "Capricorn." The sign not only refers to his late-December birth, but also designates stability, an earth sign in opposition to the watery Cancer. While Cancer is symbolized by the crab, Capricorn is represented by the sea-goat, a creature caught between land and ocean. As a sea-goat, we can see him in transition, pulling himself out of disorder and onto secure stations. Juxtaposing himself with his messenger employees, he writes, "I sat riveted to my desk and I traveled around the world at lightening speed" (32). His desk at the Cosmodemonic Telegraph Company is a profane perversion of the "antediluvian" writing desk that will truly bring him freedom. Seemingly grounded, he assumes he has arrived at a secure space. We will see, however, that this bedrock is illusory, itself composed of chaos. If he truly had power

84   *Henry Miller and Religion*

in the organization, he believes he "could have used the Cosmodemonic Telegraph Company of North America as a base to bring all humanity to God"
(27). Although unconnected power and prestige, this false foundation indeed
becomes his Golgotha, the rock upon which Christ was crucified. The "rosy
crucifixion" itself will not occur, however, until he confronts Mara.

Clinging to his Golgotha, Miller yearns to retreat into the waters out
of which he emerged. The twin hells of Brooklyn and Manhattan, where his
home and job are located, become linked to death and stagnation. Reflecting
on these moments, he writes:

> the remembrance of the past set in . . . remembrance of going back and
> forth over the bridge, going to a job which was death, returning to a
> home which was a morgue, memorizing *Faust* looking down into the
> cemetery, spitting into the cemetery from the elevated train, the same
> guard on the platform every morning, an imbecile, the other imbeciles
> reading their newspapers, new skyscrapers going up, new tombs to work
> in and die in. (50)

A modern Faust whose soul belongs to the Cosmodemonic Telegraph Company, Miller sees skyscrapers not as emblems of progress, but as immobile
tombs. He reemphasizes this association by writing, "the skyscrapers gleam-
ing like phosphorescent cadavers" (50). On the following page, we again
find skyscrapers twice called tombs, profane contrasts to the architecture
the Noah's Ark-like text.[39] Attached to his wife and job, he also sees himself
as impious:

> Just as the city itself had become a huge tomb in which men struggled
> to earn a decent death so my own life came to resemble a tomb which I
> was constructing out of my own death. I was walking around in a stone
> forest the center of which was chaos; sometimes in the dead center, in
> the very heart of chaos, I danced or drank myself silly, or I made love, or
> I befriended some one, or I planned a new life, but it was all chaos, all
> stone, and all hopeless and bewildering. (68–69)

Empty sex and reckless abandonment are vapid. Like the ride on the ovarian trolley, in which one remains grounded, these pursuits only signify the
illusion of movement. He wants to steer clear from these foolish endeavors,
as we see in the following passage: "I longed to be free of it all and yet I was
irresistibly attracted. I was violent and phlegmatic at the same time. I was
like the lighthouse itself—secure in the midst of the turbulent sea. Beneath

Tropic of Capricorn 85

ne was solid rock, the same shelf of rock on which the towering skyscrapers were reared. My foundations went deep into the earth and the armature of my body was made of steel riveted with hot bolts" (75–76). Although stable, Miller is far from being "happy" because he yearns for freedom. Furthermore, his ego is forged on the same soil that gives rise to skyscrapers. He continues his confession by claiming he wants his lighthouse self to crumble. It is a structure he associates with an "eye," itself a perversion of the true "I." The passage indeed begins with an allusion to Jesus' "Sermon on the Mount," in which he states, "If thy right eye offend thee, pluck it out":[40]

> If I longed for destruction it was merely that this eye might be extinguished. I longed for an earthquake, for some cataclysm of nature which would plunge the lighthouse into the sea. I wanted a metamorphosis, a change to fish, to leviathan, to destroyer. I wanted the earth to open up, to swallow everything in one engulfing yawn. I wanted to see the city buried fathoms deep in the bosom of the sea. I wanted to sit in a cave and read by candlelight. I wanted that eye extinguished so that I might have a chance to know my own body, my own desires. (76)

Wanting to be in touch with himself, he turns toward the feminine, emblemized in caves and bosoms. This functions as a prelude for the next section, in which Mara—his escape route—is mentioned for the first time. Turning to women was not an integral move, as without them he could have leaped off the ovarian trolley transporting him between twin hells. Crucifixion by Mara, however, appeared to be his only choice, as he writes, "I had already been crucified and marked by the cross; I had been born free of the need to suffer—and yet I knew no other way to struggle forward than to repeat the drama" (325). Too afraid to take the leap of faith that would send him on his divine authorial mission, he retreated into the womblike arms of another.

For Miller, women only offered the illusion of voyage or a fleeting glimpse of freedom. Nevertheless, uniting oneself with them represented a crumbling of the stodgy ego into the chaotic oceans of sensuality. During a rendezvous with his paramour Valeska, for example, sex rekindles childhood memories of freedom. First, an image of his grandfather working on a bench is renewed, as Miller recalls the aged man reading books aloud. He chronicles additional associations with freedom found in books, including images of Teddy Roosevelt and the Rough Riders. Nautical motifs are conjured, such as when the young Miller made battleships out of dominos. He recalls the Brooklyn Navy Yard and seamen famous during his boyhood, such as Admiral Dewey, Commodore Schley, and Admiral William T. Sampson of the USS

Brooklyn (60). The most poignant image comes when he writes, "I thought of the battleship 'Maine' that floated over my bed in the little room with the iron-barred window" (60). Taking flight with Valeska seems like a way out of the iron-barred cell of his marriage. In reality, however, such extramarital affairs keep him imprisoned.

Another moment in which the developing Miller feels that women may bring freedom comes when approaching the dance floor of the Roseland Ballroom. He describes the surface in aquatic terms, signaling that the floor is yet another ocean of chaos, writing: "On the sea floor the oysters are doing the St. Vitus dance" (107). In addition to associating female dancers with sea creatures, he also sees them as vessels sailing on the seas: "At the rail which fences off the floor I stand and watch them sailing around" (105). He also calls Paula, who he has identified as a "nymphomaniac," a "sea nymph" whose movements are "always ready to flow, [. . .] the flesh rippling like a lake furrowed by a breeze" (106). Watching her dance with his friend MacGregor, Miller writes that "they move like an octopus working up a rut" (107). While the dance floor provides a means of crumbing the platform onto which he has grounded his ego, it is only a temporary escape.

Before the dance floor, Miller begins to see the perversion behind buying a dance, the practice of "taxi dancing" observed at Roseland. The temperature drops: "So we dance, to an ice-cold frenzied rhythm" (121). Frozen and passionless, such interactions only promote a different variety of stagnation, in which *élan vital* cannot be freely exchanged. These cold exchanges lack the spark of fiery consciousness. Referring to them as "lunar," these women can only reflect enlightenment rather than being a true source of light (121). Describing himself as "a starfish swimming on the frozen dew of the moon," he draws a distinction between himself and the emptiness he sees in others around him, as light emanates from Miller, a star-fish that swims through energy (121). Curiously, he uses the concept of angel to compare himself with the others: "I am dancing the very sane and lovely dance of the angelic gorilla. These are my brothers and sisters who are insane and unangelic. We are dancing in the hollow of the cup of nothingness. We are of one flesh, but separated like stars" (121). Although he lacks "grace" in the form of a gorilla, and must undergo further evolution, there is the potential within him to become a holy entity, something he believes improbable for those around him. With wings, he is able to take flight, unlike the surrounding women who remain grounded.

Miller's revelation at the Roseland Ballroom continues as he discovers how to be liberated. The passage functions as a miniature outline of the abstruse "Land of Fuck" section to follow. Recalling his use of women as

Tropic of Capricorn

vessels in *Tropic of Cancer*, he begins to swim through the women into the "Land of Fuck," a voyage he describes by stating:

> I must shatter the walls and windows, the last shell of the lost body, if I am to rejoin the present. That is why I no longer look *into* the eyes or *through* the eyes, but by the legerdemain of will swim through the eyes, head and arms and legs, to explore the curve of vision. I see around myself as the mother who bore me once saw round the corners of time. I have broken the wall created by birth and the line of voyage is round and unbroken, even as the navel. No form, no image, no architecture, only concentric flights of sheer madness. I am the arrow of the dream's substantiality. I verify by flight. I nullify by dropping to earth. (122)

Although a plunge into the abyss, swimming in these waters allows him to smash his ego and rejoin chaos in order eventually to be reborn. Drowning in the fluids of his other—the female—he experiences what he calls "oceanic death," realizing he must resurface to become the "happy rock" (122). Describing this reemergence in a manner that again links him to Christ, he writes: "To raise my own individual life but a fraction of an inch above this sinking sea of death I must have a faith greater than Christ's, a wisdom deeper than that of the greatest seer" (122). Miller then understands how he must transform, stating: "My whole body must become a constant beam of light, moving with an ever greater rapidity, never arrested, never looking back, never dwindling. The city grows like a cancer; I must grow like a sun. [. . .] I am going to die as a city in order to become again a man. Therefore I close my ears, my eyes, my mouth" (123). In this last image, in which orifices are willed shut, he symbolizes a retreat from the desiring self, an organism dictated by the senses. While the entire assembly of women on the dance floor prompted his vision, one particular temptress—Mara—keeps him trapped in his aquatic state for years to come. His desire moves him to plunge into her arms, a leap off of his solid rock of Golgotha into what will become his "rosy crucifixion." This yearning for radical otherness nevertheless sets his quest in motion, giving rise to the dialectic that will result in the fused "happy rock."

Multiple times in the narrative, Miller confesses his need for an external force to break him away from his hellish domestic life and career. In one passage, referring to his current situation in a "mad stone forest," he writes, "Until the time when I would encounter a force strong enough to whirl me out of this mad stone forest no life would be possible for me nor could one page be written which would have meaning" (69). Only by being shoved into waters could he begin the journey that would lead him to become a true writer. The force, of course, was Mara. Later in the novel, he speaks of this moment with aquatic overtones, suggesting he had to be nudged: "Something had to happen, something big, something that would sweep me off my feet. All I needed was a push, but it had to be some force outside my world that could give me the right push" (279). Being "swept off his feet" also underscores Mara's beauty. Remembering this meeting and the hell that lead up to it, he writes, "Everything I endured was in the nature of a preparation for that moment when, putting on my hat one evening, I walked out of the office, out of my hitherto private life, and sought the woman who was to liberate me from a living death" (64). Towards the end of *Tropic of Capricorn*, he evokes angels when recollecting this event. Realizing that his choice to pursue Mara entailed leaving his wife and young child, he concedes:

> At such a moment what a man *does* is of no great importance, it's what he *is* that counts. It's at such a moment that a man becomes an angel. That is precisely what happened to me: *I became an angel.* It is not the purity of an angel which is so valuable, as the fact it can fly. An angel can break the pattern anywhere at any moment and find its heaven; it has the power to descend into the lowest matter and to extricate itself at will. The night in question I understood it perfectly. I was pure and inhuman, I was detached, I had wings. I was depossessed of the past and I had no concern about the future. I was beyond ecstasy. When I left the office I folded my wings and hid them beneath my coat. (339)

By making a conscious effort to change his life through reaching out to Mara, he was given wings, leading him on a journey to spiritual rebirth.

The same women we find in *Tropic of Cancer* under the name of "Mona." Mara, of course, like the other women on the dance floor, was herself not an angel. "Mara" signifies the demon of illusion, as we find in one of the Theosophical religious texts Miller knew well: Madame Blavatsky's *The Voice of the Silence* (1889). Containing many passages that inspired Miller, this brief text is devoted to teaching how must "slay thy lunar form at will," meaning one's desire, in order to be liberated (13). Her book posits additional ideas that resurface in *Tropic of Capricorn:* the presence of mystic fire within the individual; true hell is on earth; one has to return to one's childlike state; and we should all be prepared to sacrifice ourselves to liberate the masses. As one might expect, the enlightenment leading towards liberation is represented as a flowing stream: "If thou would'st have that stream of hard-earn'd knowledge, of Wisdom heaven-born, remain *sweet*

Tropic of Capricorn 89

running waters, thou should'st not leave it to become a *stagnant pond*" (72, emphasis added).

In his own copy of the text, Miller underlines many passages on these subjects, including the above quoted. Of these citations, the most striking pertain to Mara. Blavatsky's text states, "The unwary Soul that fails to grapple with the mocking demon of illusion, will return to earth the slave of Mara." Attached to this passage is a footnote also underscored by Miller: "*Mara* is in exoteric religions a demon, an Asura, but in *Esoteric Philosophy* it is *personified temptation* through men's vices, and translated literally means '*that which kills' the Soul*" (emphasis Miller's). We find almost identical words in the penultimate sentence of *Tropic of Capricorn*: "I take you as the personification of evil, as the destroyer of the soul, as the maharanee of the night" (348). Undoubtedly, he had this excerpt in mind when he transformed *Tropic of Cancer's* "Mona" into Mara. Reading through Blavatsky's text, we can see that Miller's autobiographical books in fact chronicle his journey away from vice rather than celebrating it. His Mara is, in fact, a demon in opposition to his angelic character.

Even without knowledge of this Theosophical work, Miller gives us clues that allow us to see Mona as a demonic figure. Since we find her on the "ocean" of the dance floor, in which he sees her "coming with sails spread," she's presented as a siren, one of those infernal figures in Homer's *Odyssey* whose seductive song brings men to their end. Referring to the effect of her words, he writes, "I have the feeling of being drowned in a deep mesh of words, of crawling painfully back to the top of the net, of looking into her eyes and trying to find there some reflection of the significance of her words—but I can find nothing, nothing except my own image wavering in a bottomless well" (343). Her song forces him to drown in illusion. Presenting himself as a man traversing the Tropics, he certainly identifies with Odysseus, the famous explorer who heard the siren's song. Furthermore, his texts are often in conversation with Joyce, who created the modern Odysseus—Leopold Bloom—in his *Ulysses.*

Miller additionally evokes classical mythology, namely the myth of Prometheus, when describing Mara.[41] After noting her ability to morph into different figures, he writes, "She had a way of swooping suddenly, as if she had spotted a ripe carcass, diving right into the bowels, pounding immediately on the tidbits—the heart, the liver, or the ovaries—and making off again in the twinkling of an eye" (235). In this sentence, he aligns Mara with the vulture ripping away Prometheus's liver, as he is imprisoned for bringing fire to the people. He also writes of their relationship, "How peaceful our little dove-and-vulture life in the dark!" (236). In this line, we find Miller as the Christ-like dove who, like Prometheus, undergoes pain and restrain for his gift to the world. When we consider that Prometheus's vulture was then associated with desire, due to Gide's revamping of the myth, we can see yet another reason why Miller associates Mara with the fiendish bird.

Miller makes even more immediate associations between Mara and wickedness. Describing her appearance, he writes, "She dressed in black almost exclusively, except for patches of purple now and then. She wore no underclothes, just a simple sheath of black velvet saturated with a diabolical perfume" (233). He underscores her devilishness again and again, writing: "She had the gift for transformation; almost as quick and subtle she was as the devil himself" (235). With little subtlety, he even calls her Lilith disguised as Venus (347). More strikingly, he also compares her to the Whore of Babylon that we find in Revelation, when he writes, "Tall, stately, full-bodied, self-possessed, she cuts the smoke and jazz and red-light glow like the queen mother of all the slippery Babylonian whores" (342).[42] Here he most likely had in mind Crowley's notion of the "Scarlet Whore," who helps men obtain salvation. The red glow reminds us that we remain in hell on earth, where illusion rules supreme.

We find another tie to the demonic through an allusion to Strindberg's piece, *There are Crimes and Crimes.* In this play, Henriette is an evil seductress who leads the playwright Maurice to his doom. In *Tropic of Capricorn,* Miller states that when first meeting Mara, they talked of Strindberg, in particular about "a character of his named Henriette" (341). He continues, "Henriette is me, my real self, she seemed to be saying. She wanted me to believe that Henriette was really the incarnation of evil" (341). In addition to underscoring Mara's infernal character, "Henriette" represents a mirroring of "Henry." Rather than becoming a truly liberated individual, in which the opposites of male and female are united in the "happy rock," this moment denotes profane bondage, a negative hermaphroditic union.

Miller develops this entrapment theme through additional metaphors. Highlighting his captivity while reminding us of her demonic nature, he writes, "What a blissful night of love! Saliva, sperm, succubation, sphincteritis all in one: the conjugal orgy in the Black Hole of Calcutta" (236). Besides obvious symbolism and its resonance with his metaphysics, the Black Hole of Calcutta likens their relationship to a prison, what he later again calls a "conjugal cell" (239). He also uses attachment metaphors to show his interdependence, even likening himself to a dog on a leash: "It is Sunday, the first Sunday of my new life, and I am wearing the dog collar you fastened around my neck" (347). As it takes place on Sunday, there is the suggestion that this "dog" can be reversed into "God." He continues to cultivate the

Tropic of Capricorn   *91*

captive motif by casting himself as a puppet controlled by Mara. The strings themselves suggest stigmata, as they are attached to the doll's hands and feet. The author chronicles his lack of will by writing, "I learned what to do just as though I were a part of her organism; I was better than a ventriloquist's dummy because I could act without being violently jerked by strings" (235). He expands this notion of interdependency by describing Mara and himself as "Siamese twins" (233). He then tells us that the relationship was so intertwined that they "interpenetrated, exchanged personalities, name, identity, religion, father, mother, brother" (237). Their relationship led to a complete meltdown of independent identity, the furthest cry from independence.

In the last pages of *Tropic of Capricorn*, Miller likens this co-dependence to stasis: "The world is in a womblike trance: the inner and the outer ego are in equilibrium. [. . .] My whole life is in the balance; I will enjoy the luxury of this for one day" (347). After this momentary rest, he forecasts, "Tomorrow I shall tip the scales. Tomorrow the equilibrium will be finished; if I ever find it again it will be in the blood and not in the stars" (347). He implies that the opposites will soon be set into motion, a process that will incorporate the stars' radiation. He uses this image to suggest that once the balance is turned, he will look for both sexes within: "Up to the present I traveled the opposite way of the sun; henceforth I travel two ways, as sun and as moon. Henceforth I take on two sexes, two hemispheres, two skies, two sets of everything. Henceforth I shall be double-jointed and double-sexed. Everything that happens will happen twice" (347–48). Rather than running away from enlightenment, he will journey towards the sun, morphing into a vessel that integrates opposites. Before this takes place, he elects to leap into the relationship with Mara. Ending *Tropic of Capricorn* with "Tack your womb up on my wall, so that I may remember you," we find confirmation of his perverse devotion to Mara and carnal sex (348). We are reminded of an earlier passage in which, after an early sexual experience with his piano teacher Lola, he tells us, "I hung her sporran over the bed and I prayed to it every night" (255). Once he connects with the flow of energy, however, he will become a great vessel like the Battleship Maine displayed over his bed during his childhood. Such liberation, however, remains far away.

CONCLUSION

In the final pages of *Tropic of Capricorn*, we also find Miller reflecting on his entire project. The book is presented as a failure, because he wanted to recount the entire story of his time with Mara. Symbolically, however, the work is a success, as it takes us to the abyss of his ocean, the rock of

Golgotha upon which he is to be crucified. It is as we find in *Tropic of Cancer;* he likens books to tombs. Presented from the perspective of the time chronicled, he writes, "Passing beneath the dance hall, thinking again of this book, I realized suddenly that our life had come to an end: I realized that the book I was planning was nothing more than a tomb in which to bury her—and the me which had belonged to her. That was some time ago, and ever since I have been trying to write it. Why is it so difficult? Why? Because the idea of an 'end' is intolerable to me" (334). Indeed, the work remains forever unfinished, as he was not even able to complete the work devoted to her: *The Rosy Crucifixion.*

Chapter Six

The Rosy Crucifixion

After the completion of *Tropic of Capricorn* in 1939, Henry Miller took Lawrence Durrell's invitation to live in Greece to avoid the imminent war. While staying with the Durrells, he continued to investigate Theosophical texts; Madame Blavatsky's *Secret Doctrine* was one of a few books he examined during his brief stay.[1] While such esoteric sources would continue to shape the themes and concerns of his texts, his writings radically changed when he returned to the United States a few months later. Beginning with his treatise *The World of Sex* (1941), he adopted a more accessible style. His books became straightforward memoirs, in which the real names of his companions were included for the first time. These texts, such as *The Colossus of Maroussi* (1941), also minimized both the confessional features and controversial language.

By examining these books within the era's political context, we can account, at least in part, for this dramatic shift in style and technique. With the European rise of fascism making freedom ever more precious, Miller's religion of personal self-liberation became more world-oriented. In short, he began to see religion as a public, political force. In this development, he was likely responding to criticisms from George Orwell (1940), who raised concerns about Miller's individualism and passivity during the troubling political climate of the 1930s.[2] Perhaps in light of the critique, his autobiographical writings unquestionably became less metaphorical, adopted a more transparent political edge, and were written in a coherent style in order to communicate clearly. Rather than chronicling a deeply personal and metaphorical inner reality, they aimed to present a more accurate depiction of our shared world. Furthermore, because they were purged of obscenities, these books were readily sold in places that formerly outlawed his prior works. Abandoning shock tactics, he hoped to heal his readers. These less provocative texts indeed presented the American author as a deeply religious man. Nevertheless, they did not gain a wide readership. For the remainder

93

of his writing career, only *The Rosy Crucifixion* trilogy (1949–60) and scattered pieces would revert to styles similar to the *Tropic* narratives of the 1930s.

THE ROSY CRUCIFIXION

Throughout his life, Henry Miller considered *The Rosy Crucifixion* (1949–60) the story he was destined to tell. On the same evening that Charles Lindbergh landed in Europe, Miller allegedly sketched his tumultuous affair with wife June Smerth, who took flight across the Atlantic with a lesbian friend days before. Although the Lindbergh coincidence could have been fabricated afterwards for symbolic flair, it appears that on some evening in May 1927, Miller was indeed outlining his magnum opus. Although he twice attempted to flesh out this work, resulting in *Tropic of Capricorn* (1939) and the posthumously published *Crazy Cock* (1991), not until he returned to the United States in the 1940s could he find the strength to chronicle the epic love affair.

Miller's massive endeavor shows another radical advance in his religiosity. The entire *Rosy Crucifixion* trilogy was likely conceived as an attempt to create an "energy double," a concept he developed from many sources. Passages in the trilogy suggest likely candidates. In *Nexus* (1960), for example, he mentions in conversation with Mona that he has seen her "astral body," demonstrating that he was familiar with the Theosophical concept as discussed in Madame Blavatsky's *Secret Doctrine* (10). Miller's own rendering, however, is mostly derived from an ancient Taoist text called *The Secret of the Golden Flower*. In fact, he even mentions a text entitled *The Golden Flower* in *Plexus* (1953).[3] Curiously, he consciously attributes the text to Wilhelm Reich, a pun on Richard Wilhelm, the first to bring this text to Western audiences in the early twentieth century.[4]

Many ideas in *The Secret of the Golden Flower* correspond to what we find in *The Rosy Crucifixion*. The Eastern work claims an energy double emerges out of the upward movement of life energy, a force spawned from the interaction of male and female opposites. Formed out of spirals, the "Golden Flower" is referred to as "the Elixir of Life"; consciousness and spirit merge in what is called the "Heavenly Heart." In addition to recasting these Taoist concepts in *The Rosy Crucifixion*, Miller also discusses nine forms of rebirth: "Sex is one of the nine reasons for reincarnation" (*Plexus* 465). However, the sections most in accord with his project pertain to the merging of masculine and feminine energies into the spiritual body or "energy double." As a creative work, *The Rosy Crucifixion* can be read as his double.

Judging from a letter penned when drafting *Sexus* (1949), Miller appears to have envisioned *The Rosy Crucifixion* as another experiment in "circular

The Rosy Crucifixion   *95*

or spiral form." Explaining this style to critic Herbert Muller, he writes, "I write circularly and spirally, if I could describe it. I want one to be [able to] open the book anywhere and read—as one does with the Bible." Without sufficient exposition, this circular/spiral form concept is misleading, since it connotes repetition. What it most successfully articulates, however, are the tensions between transcendence and immanence in his religious worldview, as the spiral indicates an upward progression that nevertheless travels back into familiar zones on a continuous plane. This tension can even be seen in his title *Black Spring,* meaning a horizontal flow ("spring" as in "small river") but also an upward leap—"spring"—all within the season of rebirth.

Although Miller had such experimental intentions, *The Rosy Crucifixion* departs from the more complicated narrative styles employed in *Tropic of Cancer* and *Tropic of Capricorn.* As with other books he authored after leaving Europe, the story is presented in a chronological narrative with only occasional moments of reflection upon the past events. From time to time, he will fast-forward or rewind to significant times, but such departures are clearly delineated and justified. In fact, the narrative of *The Rosy Crucifixion* seldom strays far from the notes he originally took in 1927.[5] The final product is primarily a straightforward account of his relationship with June Smerth, ending with his first visit to Europe.[6] His fidelity to the notes may have been brought on by a feeling that he had experienced divine illumination. Most likely, however, he was choosing communication over experimentation.

Even if his narrative is more linear than prior works, Miller nevertheless harnessed the story into an experimental framework guided by his metaphysics of flow. Throughout all three volumes of *The Rosy Crucifixion,* we find him refining his notion of a sacred current responsible for sexual desire and the creation of art and religion. In *The Rosy Crucifixion,* we again find the "happy rock," a hardened independent entity containing and formed out of liquid *élan vital,* as a symbol for the liberated individual. At the end of *Plexus,* for example, he includes a scene set in the afterlife where God asks him *"Who art thou?"* Miller replies "The Happy Rock!" (640). Although he does not elaborate at this point, he discusses the "happy rock" in more general terms in other parts of the trilogy. In one sentence from *Sexus,* he traces the entire journey that the liberated individual takes when he writes, "We must die as egos and be born again in the swarm, not separate and self-hypnotized, but individual and related" (337). In short, one must abandon the rock-like certainty of the established ego, lose oneself in life, and reemerge again as a free entity.

Miller's metaphors remain deliberately perplexing. As we have seen with the "happy rock," one has to suspend one's rock-like nature in order to become a rock again. Such transformations are crucial components of *The*

Rosy Crucifixion, in which many terms become alchemically translated from base meanings into higher ones. This technique accounts for the seemingly inconsistent way he uses "the current of life." One has to harness the inchoate mass of society that "goes with the flow" into a streaming artistic vision. Occasionally he differentiates, such as in *Sexus,* in which we find "the shuffle," "the common stream," and "primal flux" juxtaposed with "the blood of life" and "the current of life" (19). When he refers to "the current of life," a popular phrase in *The Rosy Crucifixion,* it refers to the divine energy we find described in all of his works. In these three books, he uses a greater variety of terms to describe it: "the great stream of life" (*Sexus* 127), "ebullience and *élan*" (*Sexus* 243), "flood of inspiration" (*Sexus* 244), "vital current" (*Sexus* 247), "clear stream" (*Sexus* 264), "elixir of life" (*Sexus* 265), "creative energy" (*Plexus* 51), "the flow" (*Plexus* 52), "life force" (*Plexus* 355), "the great Mind in which we swim" (*Nexus* 31), "healthy, dynamic force" (*Nexus* 35)," "quiet flow" (*Nexus* 75), and "the ocean of creation" (*Nexus* 131).[7] Considering all these examples, he finds multifarious ways to fuse the streams of sex, religion, and art into one potent cocktail.

Miller twice refers to this cosmic force in biblical terms through an allusion to Psalm 23 in which the restored soul sings, "my cup runneth over" (23.5). In the first example, he contemplates a being so full of creative energy that he either explodes or implodes. He writes, "When the cup is full it runs over. But when the cup and that which it contains are one substance, what then? There are moments when the elixir of life rises to such overbrimming splendor that the soul spills over" (*Sexus* 265). In the second instance, he describes Van Gogh in words that unmistakably come from the famous Psalm: "All flame and spirit, he overflows with creative energy. He is the cup which runneth over" (*Plexus* 84). He also refers to the Dutch painter as "a Christ," one of those "filled with the precious holy spirit" (*Plexus* 84–85). In this passage, he has clearly identified the *élan vital* saturating his entire opus with concepts and vocabulary taken directly from the Christian Bible.

Miller additionally accents his holy flow by specifically addressing blockages. While prior texts suggest he was aiming to promote the current of life within his readers, he never directly refers to blockages in concrete terms. Consider the following metaphorical phrase we find in *Sexus:* "If you persist in throttling your impulses you end by becoming a clot of phlegm" (205). He issues similar unhealthy renderings of stagnation through the image of the flounder. He writes, "To be sick, to be neurotic, if you like, is to ask for guarantees. The neurotic is the flounder that lies on the bed of the river, securely settled in the mud, waiting to be speared" (338). Since flounders are sea fish rather than river dwellers, he is certainly using the

The Rosy Crucifixion 97

creature for symbolic reasons. He chides the fish for being stationed on the ground, implying that one needs to travel towards transcendence. In other words, because the flounder is stagnant *and* close to the ground, the fish is not part of the holy flow *and* further removed from divine light. In *The Rosy Crucifixion,* the tension between transcendence and immanence—captured in the image of the grounded flounder at the bottom of a Heraclitian stream—becomes even more developed.

The tension between transcendence and immanence can even be seen in the trilogy's titles: *Sexus, Plexus,* and *Nexus.* A cross—the letter "x"—situated in the middle not only underscores the crucifixion motif central to the work, but serves as a focal point marking how the titles morph into one another. When we examine each title's meaning, we see a progression from the concrete to the abstract. Although "sexus" is not a well-defined word, it suggests sexual union. "Plexus" has both anatomical and abstract meanings. In the first definition, according to the Oxford English Dictionary (OED), it is "a network of fibres or vessels." The second meaning pertains to any network or web. Both, however, recall "solar plexus," which is probably what he had in mind. In this move from "sexus" to "plexus," we find the network rising from the sex organs through the body towards enlightenment (i.e., "solar"). "Nexus" designates an even more abstract network, referring both to legal bonds and language, since "nexus" can be defined as a "unit of words" (OED). In his schema, there is an ascent towards abstract ties and processes, such as writing. "Nexus" also reminds us of "new" and "next," as if *The Rosy Crucifixion* provides the scaffolding for the flight to Paris in which he becomes an artist. The tension between this upwards progression within the sequence of increasingly abstract networks is crucial to his religiosity. Furthermore, it puts into question traditional hierarchies in which sex is at the base and abstract pursuits are associated with the elevated mind. Here they are simply presented on different playing fields.

The stream of creative energy also dictates the form and content of each volume. Continuing from *Tropic of Capricorn,* the narrative begins with the crumbling of Miller's stony security in marriage and career: his Golgotha. Realizing he suffers from a profound lack, his desire for Mara sets the drama into motion. His trilogy tells the story of this "rosy crucifixion," taking us through the different stages of the cross. In the next section, I address narrative moments marking his cognizance of his authorial mission.

SEXUS: ROSY CRUCIFIXION I

Although the story focuses on his love affair with Mara-Mona, *Sexus* (1947)—the first volume of *The Rosy Crucifixion*—begins with Miller still

98   *Henry Miller and Religion*

grounded in bedrock, tied to his first wife—depicted as Maude—and his job at the Cosmodemonic Telegraph Company. As we have seen elsewhere, he symbolically represents restraint through images of imprisonment, weight, or entanglement. For example, he refers to his home as a "sepulcher," calling the kitchen his "comfortable prison cell," in which he "often sat alone late into the night planning [his] escape" (11). Indeed, the prisoner theme is rehearsed throughout the entire trilogy.

As we have already seen in *Tropic of Capricorn,* Miller develops connections between his job and hell by referring to "the Satanic Majesties of the Cosmodemoniacal Telegraph Company" and his relocation within the company by writing plainly, "They had relegated me to hell" (365–66). In the first few pages of the book, he relates a dream that captures many of these metaphors:

> My body is *heavy as lead* when I throw it into bed. I pass immediately into the *lowest depths* of dream. This body, which has become a *sarcophagus with stone handles,* lies perfectly *motionless;* the dreamer rises out of it, like a vapor, to circumnavigate the world. The dreamer seeks vainly to find a form and shape that will fit his ethereal essence. Like a celestial tailor, he tries on one body after another, but they are all misfits. Finally he is obliged to return to his own body, to reassume the *leaden mold,* to become *a prisoner of the flesh,* to carry on in torpor, pain and ennui. (8–9, emphasis added)

In addition to capturing these metaphors of death, stagnation, and imprisonment, this dream prophesizes his rise to the top.

Miller also uses webs as metaphors to describe many of his entrapments. Referring to the social needs of his family and friends, he writes, "What I secretly longed for was to disentangle myself from all those lives which had woven themselves into the pattern of my own life and were making my destiny a part of theirs. To shake myself free of these accumulating experiences which were mine only by force of inertia required a violent effort" (207). Regarding his job, he is more subtle with the entanglement metaphor, but refers to the equipment of telegraph technology—including cables—to suggest profane binding: "The officials of the cosmococcic telegraph world had lost faith in me and I had lost faith in the whole fantastic world which they were uniting with wires, cables, pulleys, buzzers and Christ only knows what" (15). He also writes about how the company would give out a pass "which entitled me to ride free of charge on all subway, elevated and streetcar lines of the city of Greater New York" (149). As in *Tropic of Capricorn,* this pass becomes a numbing agent providing the illusion of travel while one remains enslaved to corporate life.

As in prior works, Miller alludes to fellow modernists to provide a richer symbolic palate. We find this in passages, such as: "When finally I picked myself up and staggered off I was like a man under an anesthetic who has managed to slip away from the operating table" (6). This is an unmistakable allusion to T. S. Eliot's poem "The Love Song of J. Alfred Prufrock," which contains the iconic simile, "Like a patient etherized upon a table" (line 3). In *Sexus,* the allusion shows that Miller was before unable to be moved, a "pruf-rock" weighed down by obligations. Now, however, he has "managed to slip away," due to his desire for Mara. Although he finds himself "in a web of lies," Mara nevertheless prompts him to lead a more adventurous life (14). As the narrative progresses, however, he remains a "prisoner of the flesh," as portrayed in his prophetic dream (9).

Because he is lodged in this flesh-made cell, *The Rosy Crucifixion*'s first volume overflows with sex. Although the quasi-pornographic parts of the novel may not seem artfully executed, they represent Miller's consciousness in the novel's setting, not from his contemporary station. These scenes are confessions that do not unequivocally celebrate or even demonstrate his sexual prowess. He suggests this is a conscious literary ploy, when he writes about traditional African dance in a passage that could also refer to *Sexus.* Writing of a dancer imitating animals, he writes: "By his mimicry he demonstrates that he has made himself superior to the mere act of intercourse" (480). Considering this observation, we can read *Sexus* as his triumph over the Rosicrucian "desire body."

In some passages, Miller even explicitly decries his behavior. Reflecting on how poorly he treated his wife, he calls himself "a worthless son of a bitch" (23). He also praises a married couple who are publicly proclaiming their love, saying that the husband is "on the way to becoming an evangelist" and even indirectly comparing him to the Buddha and St. Francis of Assisi (126–28). This scene indicates the married man was a positive influence on Miller, who had just left his wife for Mara. Relating how social barriers were broken as people began to dance, he finds a living example of what he hopes to accomplish through literature. In his books, he wants to infect us with a St. Vitus dance, leading us to liberation.

Miller's frank sexual encounters also relate to his liquid metaphysics, since during the period chronicled in *Sexus,* he was unable to channel his sacred energy into creative enterprises. Instead, he squandered himself in sexual misadventures with Maude, Mara, and anyone available. While his attention wanders from woman to woman, Mara is frequently the focal point of his libido. Choosing the appellation "Mara" for his lover, he confesses his devotion to illusion, rather than channeling energy into loftier pursuits. Nevertheless, her presence compels him to change. During the time captured in *The Rosy Crucifixion,* he indeed abandons stasis, but he is again entrapped by the third volume, due to his fateful union with illusion incarnate.

In addition to representing misspent energy, the copious sex with Mara symbolizes the seeds giving rise to Miller's artistic career. Not only did she provide material for his epic crucifixion, but she also encouraged him to become a writer, as we find at the beginning of *Sexus.* Recounting her words, he pens: "'*Why don't you try to write?*' That was the phrase which had stuck in my crop all day" (17). "Crop" itself suggests sowing a seed that will give rise to his books. Also, the word choice—"crop"—connotes an organic writing style, one able to replenish modernity's wasteland.

After Mara encourages him to devote all his time to writing, Miller begins to envision the writing process in explicitly religious terms. As he writes, "The act of writing puts a stop to one kind of activity in order to release another. When a monk, prayerfully meditating, walks slowly and silently down the hall of a temple, and thus walking sets in motion one prayer wheel after another, he gives a living illustration of the act of sitting down to write" (214–215). We recall the opening of *Tropic of Cancer,* in which he conceives writing as a performance, a literature of action. His life, chronicled in *The Rosy Crucifixion,* is meant to be seen as his own personal example that will inspire others.[8]

In *Sexus,* Roy Hamilton reminds us of literature's performative function. A mentor figure in *Tropic of Capricorn,* Hamilton again serves as a role model in Miller's identity formation. Speaking of the way Hamilton devours books, Miller writes, "He thought and lived his way through a book, emerging from the experience a new and glorified being. He was the very opposite of the scholar whose stature diminishes with each book he reads. Books for him were what Yoga is to the earnest seeker after truth: they helped him unite with God" (316). This passage conveys that books are more than merely words; rather, they can be portals to the divine.

For Miller, writing is a way to author one's life. In one section he candidly writes, "You are the author, director and actor all in one: the drama is always going to be your own life, not someone else's" (340). Art again is rendered as a channel promoting the flow of *élan vital,* as he writes when contemplating the prospect of writing: "What I want is to open up. I want to know what's inside me. I want everybody to open up" (397). At this point in the narrative, the books he aims to create will accomplish this task; by "authorizing" himself, he wants to inspire others to take charge.

The Rosy Crucifixion 101

These themes are most preciously fused when Miller has a vision leading him closer to becoming a writer. Coming out of the Lorimer Street station on the way to see a burlesque show, he becomes overwhelmed. He writes, "I was caught in the fiery flux, fixed there just as definitely as I had been speared by a fisherman. All those currents I had let loose were swirling about me, engulfing me, sucking me down into the whirlpool" (246). After this moment that recalls biblical prophetic visions, the Miller-fish begins to harness what he has seen, becoming intoxicated and moved instead of paralyzed. As if the instant had just occurred, he reflects, "A moment ago I had forgotten absolutely who I was: I had spread myself over the whole earth. Had it been more intense perhaps I would have passed over that thin line which separates the sane from the insane. I might have achieved depersonalization, drowned myself in the ocean of immensity" (246). Here we find a strong allusion to Whitman, who also spreads across the earth and becomes "afoot with vision." At this moment in narrative time, however, he is unable to channel his vision, becoming instead an unfocused "ocean."

Once inside the burlesque show, where Miller had aimed to go before being struck with vision, he is presented with a lifeless display. Writing of the theater's performers, he states, "they seemed made of the same substance, a gray slag infused with a low voltage of the vital current" (247). Soon afterwards he calls them "*clay,* common clay" (247). These descriptions conjure Genesis, as Adam was "common clay" before receiving the breath of life, which Miller interprets here in his Bergsonian language of "vital current." Outside of the theatre, he reflects on his own artistic mission, questioning his abilities by asking, "Would I be able, on a sheet of paper, to exfoliate in all directions at once? Was it the purpose of art to stagger from fit to fit, leaving a bloody hemorrhage in one's wake? Was one merely to report the 'dictation'—like a faithful chela obeying the telepathic behest of his Master?" (248). "Chela," which means "crab claw," refers to the free figure of the crab, able to travel in all directions.[9] In the paragraph that follows, we find Miller fully cognizant of the literary mission he would fulfill through *Tropic of Cancer:* "My task was to develop a mnemonic index to my inspirational atlas. Even the hardiest adventurer scarcely deludes himself that he will be able to cover every square foot of earth on this mysterious globe. Indeed, the true adventurer must come to realize, long before he has come to the end of his wanderings, that there is something stupid about the mere accumulation of wonderful experiences" (248). In the lines of his texts, the strata of longitude and latitude traversing experience, he would ultimately show his ability to triumph over his "mere accumulation of wonderful experiences"—namely, his sexual exploits—and become a man united with God. But at this point

102   *Henry Miller and Religion*

in the narrative, his writing career had scarcely begun. In *Plexus,* he begins to
take up his own challenges.

PLEXUS: THE ROSY CRUCIFIXION II

Plexus (1953) begins with Miller abandoning his job with the Cosmodemonic Telegraph Company, a decision that leads him to many misadventures,
drifting between apartments and aimless jobs, including selling scribblings,
hocking candy, opening a speakeasy, and pursuing real estate in the South.
Relief of his obligations and a greater understanding of his literary mission
lead to a misguided, albeit lighter Miller. It is therefore fitting that the book
opens with many symbols attesting to his elevation. On the very first page,
we discover that the season is spring, suggesting not only rebirth but an
upward movement, a "springing" (7). We are told that he and Mara, now
called Mona, are looking for an apartment in "Brooklyn Heights," a location
whose name signals climbing, though in the trite social sphere. He also states
they were starting a *"vita nuova,"* a phrase that underscores his ongoing identification with Dante (7). These opening moments demonstrate that he has
risen from the sex-laden state of *Sexus* to the skyward plateau of *Plexus.* The
dearth of sex scenes and questionable language reaffirm this ascension.

The bulk of *Plexus* attempts to document Miller's rise into his communion of saints, namely, writers who guided the American author's career.
As he reflects early on the book, when describing his reading habits, "Ah,
what dialogues I conducted with kindred, ghostly spirits! [. . .] They were
carried on in a language that does not exist, a language so simple, so direct,
so transparent, that words were useless. It was not a silent language either,
as is often used in communication with 'higher beings.' It was a language of
clamor and tumult—the heart's clamor, the heart's tumult" (151). We find
the language of community and elevation, even if height is called into question to underscore their accessibility. One of the most emblematic moments
of this ascension through communication comes when he, along with Mona
and a couple with whom they are forced to live, plays with a Ouija board.
Recalling the event, he writes, "As usual it was I who summoned the eccentric figures—Jacob Boehme, Swedenborg, Paracelsus, Nostradamus, Claude
Saint-Martin, Ignatius Loyola, the Marquis de Sade and such like" (341).
This playful passage nevertheless symbolizes a deeper accord that he develops with such figures. His sincerity is perceived in an earlier passage, in
which he discusses the relationship he and his friend Stanley, whom we
first met in *Tropic of Capricorn,* have with such authors: "We were, without
knowing it, members of that traditional underground which vomits forth

The Rosy Crucifixion 103

at suitable intervals those writers who will later be called Romantics, mystics, visionaries or diabolists. It was for such as us—then mere embryonic beings—that certain 'outlandish' passages were written. It is we who keep alive these books which are constantly threatening to fall back into oblivion" (319). In this excerpt, he conveys the urgent potency of these books while assembling an election of spirits, the "inhuman artists" stemming back to *Tropic of Cancer*.

These issues become more intensified when we consider Miller's relationship to Fyodor Dostoyevsky in *Plexus*. Early in the novel, when he first mentions his conversations with "kindred, ghostly spirits," the first summoned was Dostoyevsky. He elaborates, "If it were Dostoevski whom I summoned, it was 'the complete Dostoevski,' that is to say, the man who wrote the novels, diaries and letters we know, *plus* the man we also know by what he left unsaid, unwritten" (151). His dialogue with his Russian mentor is ongoing, eventually resulting in strange passages in which his own life folds into Dostoyevsky's. Exiting the subway, he recalls, "Whenever I had no set destination I would get out automatically at Times Square. There I always came upon the *rambla*, the Nevsky Prospekt, the souks and bazaars of the damned" (574). When he again reminds us he is still on the Nevsky Prospekt, Saint Petersburg's main thoroughfare and Dostoyevsky's former address, we are given the impression that books not only portal us to new places, but also generate a means by which one's identity can become merged with another.

Miller's relationship with Dostoyevsky becomes increasingly complicated towards the end of the novel, in which the Russian author is found seated beside him, with "Emperor Anathema" to his left (610). In this scene, he echoes Christ's notion that God is present when "two or three are gathered together in my name" (Matthew 18:20). His revision of the biblical passage follows: "That we are together and privileged to discuss the existence of God, this in itself is conclusive evidence for me that we are basking in the sunshine of His presence. I do not speak 'as if' He were present, I speak 'because' He is present" (610–11). Miller continues by addressing both Dostoyevsky and Emperor Anathema from the viewpoint of a Christian solider: "We have not come together to settle an absurd problem. We are here, comrades, because outside this room, *in the world,* as they call it, there is no place in which to mention the Holy Name. We are the chosen ones, and we are united ecumenically" (611). Miller's membership among his community of saintly artists can be seen in contrast with Jewish notions of election, especially when he writes "united ecumenically," words associated with Christianity. He follows with the mission of his neo-Christian trio:

The resurrection of man will be ushered in with our aid; the dead will rise from their graves clothed in radiant flesh and sinew, and we shall have communion, real everlasting communion, with all who once were: with those who made history and with those who had no history. Instead of myth and fable we shall have everlasting reality. [. . .] Though we are assembled here as men, we are bound through the divine spirit. When we take leave of one another we shall return to the world of chaos, to the realm of space which no amount of activity can exhaust. We are not of this world, nor are we yet of the world to come, except in thought and spirit. Our place is on the threshold of eternity; our function is that of prime movers. It is our *privilege* to be crucified in the name of freedom. [. . .] The quick and the dead will soon be separated. Life eternal is rushing back to fill the empty cup of sorrow. Man will rise from his bed of ignorance and suffering with a song on his lips. He will stand forth in all the radiance of his godhood. (612–13)

In this sermon, he rehearses many doctrines purveying his philosophy. In the form of "life eternal," spirit is presented in liquid form. Strong distinctions are made between those who are living—those filled with *élan vital*—and the dead—those who live a standard sort of existence. He also reminds us that his community of artists will bring forth this sacred energy in those who witness their work. He also uses the word "crucified" to represent the artist's struggle, but chooses the word "resurrection" to signify the results that will appear by those who receive the message.

Many of these ideas represent an internalization of what Miller was told earlier by Mona's friend Claude, who allegedly had a profound influence. This mysterious figure functions as a prophet, one who intuits that Miller is a Capricorn and will soon be taking an "important voyage," anticipating his first trip to Paris in 1928 (566). Claude calls him a "man of great faith" and encourages him to pursue his dreams, assuring him he is protected (588). Claude most clearly voices the words that Miller will again use in the above remarks, as the prophet is able to see the two as a band apart: "It isn't age which makes us wise. [. . .] It's the quickness of spirit. *The quick and the dead*. . . . You, of all people, should know what I mean. There are only two classes in this world—*and in every world*—the quick and the dead. For those who cultivate the spirit nothing is impossible" (571). Claude goes on to say,

There will come a time when man will no longer distinguish between man and god. When the human being is raised to his full powers he will be divine—his human consciousness will have fallen away. What is

The Rosy Crucifixion   105

called death will have disappeared. [. . .] Man will be free, that's what
I mean. Once he becomes the god which he is, he will have realized
his destiny—which is freedom. Freedom includes everything. Freedom
converts everything to its basic nature, which is perfection. [. . .] There
is only the one thing, *spirit*. It's all, everything, and when you realize it
you're it. (571–72)

In this passage, we can clearly see a source for Miller's liberation theology, in
which we are to elevate ourselves to God's level through the cultivation of
spirit. By the end of their talk, Claude will implore Miller to liberate himself,
a task he aims to accomplish through his art.

When Miller tries to write, however, he finds himself unable to focus his
energy, even if his creative juices are no longer aimed at procreating. Towards
the first of *Plexus*, he frankly discusses his shortcomings: "My creative energy
suddenly released, I spilled over in all directions at once" (51–52). He continues to develop the fluid metaphor when he follows with, "It was impossible for me to sit down quietly and just turn on the flow; I was dancing
inside. [. . .] But I had no order, no discipline, no set goal. I was completely
at the mercy of my impulses, my whims, my desires. My frenzy to live the
life of the writer was so great that I overlooked the vast reservoir of material
which had accumulated during the years leading up to this moment" (52).
Forced to become merely an absorber by his own inability to remain still, he
continues to struggle with his writing throughout the novel, relegated to collecting impressions for future attempts.

Miller's failure to express himself and "tap" into his unique vision is
reflected in a stylistic device he employs toward the end of the novel. Just
as he would fuse his personality with Dostoyevsky's, he infuses vast blocks
of quotations from writers he admires, thereby demonstrating how it was
possible to elevate his own voice from the community of artistic saints surrounding him. In one case, he includes the final paragraph of Joyce's short
story "The Dead." (513–14). Just as he did with *Finnegan's Wake* in *Tropic of
Cancer*, Miller does not acknowledge the source, though he alludes to Joyce
by saying his friend Ulric could recite the passage "like a born Dubliner"
(513). In the final pages of *Plexus*, we are also confronted with a few key
passages from Dostoyevsky's *Brothers Karamazov* and a cumbersome amount
of material from Oswald Spengler's *Decline of the West*, most of which is
included without any qualification save enthusiastic words of praise. As presented, these moments in *Plexus* are unbearable to read. However awkward,
these pages transmit his difficulty of getting beyond authors who profoundly
affected him. His claim that Dostoyevsky and Spengler, along with Friedrich

106   *Henry Miller and Religion*

Nietzsche and Elie Faure, are the "four horsemen of my own private Apocalypse!" assures us that *Plexus* ends on the cusp of "revelation," as the final volume of the trilogy presents his first honest efforts toward becoming a self-proclaimed divine author.

NEXUS: ROSY CRUCIFIXION III

The narrative of *Nexus* (1960) continues to chronicle Miller's quest for self-expression and his deteriorating relationship with Mona. The conflict increases due to the presence of her friend Anastasia, who moves in with the couple. Presented as Mona's lesbian lover, Anastasia is often called Stasia, perhaps to connote "stasis" given her constant presence. Eventually, Mona and Stasia leave for Paris without Miller, a gesture that wounds him dramatically. The moment of their departure comes only halfway through *Nexus;* the final half is devoted to his time alone, Mona's return from Paris (without Stasia), and the construction of his first novel, a work commission by a patron simply named "Pop" under the guise that it was written by his wife. *Nexus* ends with Miller and Mona departing for a six-month vacation to Europe, financed by Pop's cash. He hoped to finish *The Rosy Crucifixion* with a second part of *Nexus* that would bridge this moment to his solo arrival in Paris in 1930. For whatever reason, the follow-up was never completed in his lifetime.[10]

As with other volumes of *The Rosy Crucifixion, Nexus* is guided by significant encounters that forever have an impact on the burgeoning author. Toward the beginning, we find Miller in conversation with a lawyer named John Stymer. In the course of their talk, which continues far into the night, Stymer chastises him for his stagnation and even offers him a position recording the lawyer's thoughts while traveling. The barrister repeats many ideas now familiar to careful Miller readers, rendering some in Christological terms, such as when he says that "man was not made to live by mind alone. Man was meant to live with his whole being" (31).[11] We find the familiar rhetoric of *élan vital:* "To live dangerously, as Nietzsche put it, is to live naked and unashamed. It means putting one's trust in the life-force and ceasing to battle with a phantom called death, a phantom called disease, a phantom called sin, a phantom called fear, and so on" (32). And putting words into Stymer's mouth about Dostoyevsky, Miller could have just as easily been writing about himself. In the following lengthy passage, Christ is plainly discussed, albeit characteristically tempered with Miller's own notion of "life force":

> You know, I suppose, that the advent of Christ was of the greatest importance to Dostoevski. [. . .] The only sin, or crime, that man

The Rosy Crucifixion   107

could commit, in the eyes of Jesus, was to sin against the Holy Ghost.
To deny the spirit, or the life force, if you will. [. . .] we've got to
come to grips with the demonic power which rules us. We've got to
convert it into a healthy, dynamic force which will liberate not us
alone—*we* are not so important!—but the life-force which is dammed
up in us. Only then will we begin to live. And to live means eternal
life, nothing less. (35)

In this passage, Miller uses Stymer's voice to clarify his own vision of Christ,
a modified conception of the freedom-giving Christ of Dostoyevsky's "Grand
Inquisitor." By including these ideas at this point of the narrative, they serve
as a prelude to Miller's own personal realizations, marking crucial points in
his life, in which literature and the "living books" around him helped bring
the author closer to God.

While Stymer's words and his open apartment give him a taste of freedom, his domestic life renders Miller imprisoned. Instead of being captured
by Maude and the Cosmodemonic Telegraph Company, Mona and Stasia
provide new sources of pain. In a few sentences, he describes his situation
as being in a "vice" and a "straitjacket," ultimately leading him to wonder,
"Was it love that kept me chained?" (37). Writing of his feelings about the
outside world from the confines of his apartment, he calls it "a Siberia of
the mind," connoting in this powerful image entrapment and the lack of
vital flow through the location's association with freezing temperatures.[12] He
tells of attempting to commemorate his sufferings by hanging the following
above Stasia's bed: "ET HAEC OLIM MEMINISSE IUVABIT," a passage
from Virgil's *Aeneid* that he roughly translates as *"One day it will be pleasant
to remember these things"* (43, 46). All these details underscore his feelings of
entrapment and futility.

Summating his own situation, Miller mentions a play by Edouard
Bourdet called *The Captive* (1926), which itself alludes to Marcel Proust's
La prisonnière. This scandalous play tells the story of a love triangle between
Irène de Montcel, her husband Jacques Virieu, and her lesbian lover Madame
D'Aiguines. Even after Virieu learns of his wife's illicit affair with D'Aiguines,
he remains married. In *Nexus,* Mona and Stasia see the play, which they rec-
ommend to Miller upon returning. As he recounts, the lesbian lovers thought
the play would make him more open-minded. Unbeknownst to Mona and
Stasia, he had already seen it.

Miller's decision to mention *The Captive* at this particular point of *The
Rosy Crucifixion* is significant on multiple levels. First, it attests to the intertwined relationship between art and life, a common theme in his work. In

108 *Henry Miller and Religion*

this case, Mona and Stasia act out this play with Miller. Second, the production's title, along with its story, captures Miller's own feelings of imprisonment. Third, the play's narrative so closely matches the story presented in *Nexus,* we are made to question the veracity of Miller's own account. The dates of the production certainly match the time in which this portion of *The Rosy Crucifixion* is set, and it is likely the events in his narrative are true, but the gesture makes us call authorship into question. Fourth, when he tells of writing attempts shortly after this event, we find that he is writing a play. He writes, "It was to be in three acts and for three players only. Needless to say who they were, these strolling players" (73).

While said in passing, the fleeting portrait underscores how he remains "captive" to the styles of others, still under the sphere of influence and unable to find his authentic voice. He later conveys his experience of hearing criticism from his friend Stanley, a moment that critically impacts him: "Reduced to ashes by Stanley's heartless words, I had come face to face with the source, with authorship itself, one might say. And how utterly different this was, this quiet flow from the source, than the strident act of creation which is writing!" (75). From this moment on, Miller will arise out of his Phoenix-ashes and come that much closer to channeling his own *élan vital,* his unique voice into words, rather than imitating the art around him.

In the meantime, Miller tries to find the mysterious liquid source of creativity by examining the biographies of other writers and artists. Bringing him to the library for research, he writes,

> What I wanted to lay hold of [. . .] was that crucial point in the evolution of a genius when the hard dry rock suddenly yields water. As the heavenly vapors are eventually collected in vast watersheds and there converted into streams and rivers, so in the mind and soul, I felt, there must ever exist this reservoir waiting to be transformed into words, sentences, books, to be drowned again in the ocean of thought. (129)

Once again, we find that he rehearses the familiar alchemical motif elsewhere, though here fused to the tangible process of creating books out of *élan vital*'s flow. In this passage, he specifically refers to Moses's demonstrates of God's power and mercy by making water appear from rock.[13] As we continue to scan this scene, he wonders, "Were the creative ones tormented beings who found salvation only through wrestling with the media of art?" (129). His own answer, though only implied, seems to be affirmative. Once establishing his conversation in this religious language, he continues to flow from his own Bergsonian conception of divinity to traditional

The Rosy Crucifixion 109

Christian language, writing of falling upon "the stream which would lead me into the open" to referring to artists who discover vision on the cross (130–31). After a long list of artists, writers, and mystics that includes William Blake and Dante, he asks, "And I, was I to add my name to this host of illustrious martyrs?" (131). The scene suggests his own self-election to this group, while it also foreshadows his ability to see more precisely his literary mission in religious terms.

Before this is to happen, however, Miller has to reach a point of agony on his metaphorical cross. While he does not strictly conform his narrative to the unfolding stages of the Passion, there are two pivotal moments that function as a consummation of suffering. First, he meets with Mona's brother and discovers she has completely fabricated her biography, including her last name. The second and most critical moment comes when Mona and Stasia leave for Paris. When he returns from errands to discover they are gone, he smashes the entire apartment into bits. In the next few days, he begins to read the Bible again, moves back with his parents at the age of thirty-five, and prepares the notes for what would become *The Rosy Crucifixion.*

In the next significant part of the narrative, Miller is visited by a guardian angel after reverting back to his habit of visiting dance halls. Before the angelic encounter, the club scene functions as a moment of temptation: "I merely craved to become like any ordinary mortal, a jellyfish, if you like, in the ocean of drift. I asked for nothing more than to be swished and sloshed about in an eddying pool of fragrant flesh under a subaqueous rainbow of subdued and intoxicating lights" (169). Rather than channeling the chaos he knew into art, he wants to lose himself in the sprawling waters of sensuality. After yet another night at the dance hall, he retreats to Central Park where he falls asleep broken and frustrated. In his dream, he finds he can do anything he wants, even flying. Then an angel appears: "Someone was at my side, like a shadow, moving with the same ease and assurance as myself. My guardian angel, most likely" (175–76).

The dream signifies that Miller is undergoing crucifixion, as he writes, "Slowly I became aware that I was bleeding, that indeed I was a mass of wounds, from head to foot. It was then that, seized with fright, I swooned away. When at last I opened my eyes I saw to my astonishment that the Being who had accompanied me was tenderly bathing my wounds, anointing my body with oil" (176). Although the wounds are generic, the image of bathing his body with oil reminds us of the biblical passage in which Christ's feet are anointed with oil (Luke 7.37–50, John 12.3) and the legion of Mary, Mary Magdalene and Salome who come to care for the body of Christ after crucifixion (Mark 16.1). The angel completely restores Miller, except for his heart.

He then awakens to another dream, in which he confesses his heart had completely shriveled due to overprotection: "I saw that it never had been broken, as I imagined, but that, paralyzed by fear, it had shrunk almost to nothingness. I saw that the grievous wounds which had brought me low had all been received in a senseless effort to prevent this shriveled heart from breaking. The heart itself had never been touched; it had dwindled from disuse" (176). In the next paragraph, he tells us his heart was taken "by the Angel of Mercy" (177). He continues, "I had been healed and restored so that I might live on in death as I had never lived in life. Vulnerable no longer, what need was there for a heart?" (177). Then the Angel reappears and restores his heart, "In her hands, cupped like a chalice, she held the poor, shrunken semblance of a heart which was mine. Bestowing upon me a look of the utmost compassion, she blew upon this dead-looking ember until it swelled and filled with blood, until it palpitated between her fingers like a live, human heart" (177). He continues, "Restoring it to its place, her lips moved as if pronouncing the benediction, but no sound issued forth. My transgressions had been forgiven; I was free to sin again, free to burn with the flame of the spirit. But in that moment I knew, and would never, nevermore forget, that it is the heart which rules, the heart which binds and protects" (177).

Drawing upon the early parts of Dante's *Vita Nuova,* this narrative moment marks a significant rebirth, in which Miller is able to reenter the world with a new vitality. Using the language of the Psalmist David and using water metaphors, he announces his heart was "cleansed of its iniquities, had lost all fear," suggesting that Miller will march forward with the strength to accomplish his mission (177).[14] He ends the passage by exclaiming "Take heart, O brothers and sisters! Take heart!," words that strongly echo Christ (178).[15] He is simultaneously cleansed of sin *and* is closer to being an entity that can take away the world's problems.

This visit from the guardian angel or "Angel of Mercy" functions as a critical point in which Miller is now able truly to begin his writing career. Upon Mona's return from Europe, a plan is hatched in which a patron named Pop will pay for a novel, which will appear to have been written by June. Although the book—posthumously published as *Moloch: This Gentile World* (1992)—was not an inspired effort, the novel is presented in *Nexus* to show him becoming increasingly inspired by religious materials. The title alone refers to the pagan god—Moloch—we find in the Christian Bible.[16] But Miller also presents himself as one who combs the Bible to search for inspiration. He writes, "In the Bible were slips of paper to indicate where gems were to be found. The Bible was a veritable diamond mine. Every time I looked up a passage I become intoxicated" (192). He

The Rosy Crucifixion

also describes borrowing religious language from different traditions, such as follows: "And then, as when the hurricane abates, it would flow like a song—quietly, evenly, with the steady luster of magnesium. As if hymning the *Bhagavad Gita*. A monk in a saffron robe extolling the work of the Omniscient One. No longer a writer. A saint. A saint from the Sanhedrin sent. God bless the author! (Have we a David here?)" (196–97). In these few words, he uses motifs from his own Bergsonian conception of spirit ("flow"), Hinduism ("*Bhagavad Gita*"), Tibetan Buddhism ("monk in a saffron robe"), Christianity ("saint"), and Judaism ("David"). The excerpt demonstrates how his religious practice of writing conjoins with both traditional religious practices and his own metaphysical flow.

As the narrative progresses, Miller uses Judeo-Christian language to articulate his undertaking. To cast away the anxiety of influence, he must depart from authors that so pivotally shaped him. He specifically evokes the language of sacrifice, as in the following passage:

> All my idols—and I possessed a veritable pantheon—I would offer up as sacrifices. What powers of utterance they had given me I would use to curse and blaspheme. Had not the prophets of old promised destruction? Had they ever hesitated to befoul their speech, in order to awaken the dead? [. . .] Of what use the poems of death, the maxims and counsels of the sage ones, the codes and tablets of the lawgivers, of what use leaders, thinkers, men of art, if the very elements that made up the fabric of life were incapable of being transformed? (248)

In his imagination, sacrificing "secular" prophets, along with canonized holy literature, imitates the rebellious Christ who fails to observe Jewish Law. Their work provides the scaffolding upon which his vision stands, a structure he would abandon after taking the leap of faith.

Miller also uses the language of the Judeo-Christian tradition to express the literature he seeks to create. As Christ with the Pharisees, we find him in debate with Jews he encountered through Mara. With increased inspiration, he states he will write in "the language of our fathers, [. . .] Abraham, Issac, Ezekiel, Nehemiah. . . ." whereupon the names of David, Solomon, Ruth, and Esther are added by Mr. Elfenbein (231). This Jewish character also instructs him by saying, "Drink of the spirit. Like Moses. From the rock gushes water, from the bottle only foolishness" (233). Writing of his desire to use such ideas in fulfilling his literary mission, he states, "If I craved magical powers it was not to rear new structures, not to add to the Tower of Babel, but to destroy, to undermine" (247). By drawing on the biblical reference, he

112   *Henry Miller and Religion*

simultaneously captures that he does not want to create nonsense while also stressing a literature that resists verticality. As he plainly expresses, "Then to hell with literature! *The book of life,* that's what I would write" (218). When he goes on to say that he would sign this work as simply "*The Creator's*" (218), we perceive a complete synthesis between Miller the artist-creator and man-god. He goes on to develop this idea of "the book of life," writing: "The thought of one day tackling such a book—*the book of life*—kept me tossing all night. [. . .] Nevertheless, I was certain of one thing—it would flow once I began it. It wouldn't be a matter of squeezing out drops and trickles" (218). Again we find this "book of life" to be full of *élan vital,* a pure gift transmitted from the inspired author. Rather than selling encyclopedias—books that claim to encompass all of life—as we find in *Sexus,* he dares to create them in *Nexus.*

THE ROSY CRUCIFIXION AS MILLER'S NEW TESTAMENT

Although Miller's use of language from the Jewish and Christian traditions peaks in *Nexus,* a glance over all three volumes demonstrates religious rhetoric has been used throughout. We have already seen numerous examples, but there are a few more that should be noted. For example, as we have come to expect, he refers to many non-Christian religions in his Christocentric narrative. Although not pivotal to his work, figures and ideas related to Hinduism are also mentioned, including Swami Vivekananda of the Vedanta Society.[17] There are multiple references to Taoism, particularly the *Tao te Ching,* in the trilogy.[18] There are even more citations of Buddhist scriptures, particularly materials related to the branch of Mahayana Buddhism popularly known as Zen.[19] We may also find scattered references to fringe religious movements and quasi-religious organizations popular in New York during the time his narrative is set. Among these are the evangelist Benjamin Fay Mills, Theosophy, New Thought, Ethical Culture, and the Rand School of Social Science, which was founded by Christian Socialists.[20] With the exception of Taoism, he does not appear to deeply engage any of these listed traditions. Nevertheless, they pivotally function as models, allowing him to create his own mix-and-match religiosity that focuses on merging religion and politics.

Miller frequently frames his own experience within the tools given to him by Christianity. During an early part of the trilogy, he writes in reference to Christianity, "I don't care about the religion," but such an opinion reflects a less mature incarnation of his religious development (*Sexus* 425).[21] When we examine the text itself, it is difficult to see how he could be so aloof about a tradition with which he was so obviously engaged. Often we find him mentioning

The Rosy Crucifixion

an exuberant amount of important figures from the Christian tradition, such as we find in the following passage, in which mystics are mentioned along with other ancients: "Pythagoras, Heraclitus, Longinus, Virgil, Hermes Trimegistus, Apollonius of Tyana, Montezuma, Xenophon, Jan van Ruysbroeck, Nicolaus of Cusa, Meister Eckhart, St. Bernard of Clairvaux, Asoka, St. François de Sales, Fénelon, Chuang Tzu, Nostradamus, Saladin, the Pope Joanna, St. Vincent de Paul, Paracelsus, Malatesta, Origen, together with a coterie of women saints" (*Plexus* 342–43). In addition to these, we find elsewhere in the trilogy mention of Augustine, Boehme, Swedenborg, and Saint Jerome.[22]

As in *Tropic of Capricorn,* Miller refers to Dante and the famous pair of lovers alluded to in his *Divine Comedy,* Abelard and Heloise. The reference to Dante comes at the beginning of *Nexus,* in which he tells us on the first page, "I am in Dante's fifth heaven" (7).[23] Miller suggests we enter higher into Paradiso when we go further into his narrative. Since this is the third volume of his *Rosy Crucifixion,* positing relations between *Paradiso* and *Nexus* seems natural. Out of the three times that Abelard and Heloise are mentioned in the trilogy, Miller twice suggests an affinity between his own project and Abelard's.[24] After drafting the notes that would become *The Rosy Crucifixion,* he refers to them as "the story of my misfortunes" and mentions Abelard twice afterwards (*Nexus* 166). We find a similar passage later in *Nexus,* in which he refers to his work from the third-person perspective as "your terrible *historia de calamitatis*" (302). Although Abelard is not cited, the Latin certainly indicates the Christian's work. In both cases, the references remind us that sex-filled narratives can lead to a higher understanding.

There are additional non-canonical sources that refer to Christianity. Two moments in *Plexus* interweave American folk songs that treat the subject of Jesus's crucifixion. The first is John Jacob Niles's "I Wonder as I Wander" and the second is called "The Seven Great Joys."[25] Their inclusion implies that Miller himself uses a folk idiom to present an American version of Christ. Additional traditional materials are used to convey his religiosity, such as when he quotes renditions of the Catholic "Novena": "*Lead on, O kindly light!*" (*Nexus* 308). We return to the singing motif when he incorporates the following line from Shakespeare's *Cymbeline,* the famous paean to the sun: "*Hark, hark the lark at heaven's gate sings!*" (*Nexus* 9).[26] He continues his celebration of the sun and holy light when he harkens St. Francis of Assisi's "Canticle of the Sun." After writing, "every cell in my body was shouting Hosanna," connoting a sort of liberation from his "cells," he says he heard "a delirious muezzin sending forth canticles to the sun" (*Nexus* 305). Referring to the piece indicates Miller's affinity towards the vernacular, as St. Francis's is reportedly the first piece of literature written in Italian.

114   *Henry Miller and Religion*

On the following pages, we find him continuing with the music motif, fusing St. Francis's work with that of the great Psalmist:

> As from a tree shaking off its wintry slumber, the butterflies warmed from my noggin crying Hosanna, Hosanna to the Highest! Jacob I blessed and Ezekiel, and in turn Rachel, Sarah, Ruth and Esther. [. . .] Praise be to the Lord! Glory to King David! And to Solomon resplendent in his wisdom! The sea opens before us, the eagles point the way. Yet another note, beloved cantor . . . a high and piercing one! Let it shatter the breastplate of the High Priest! Let it drown the screams of the damned! *And he did it,* my wonderful, wonderful cantor *cantatibus.* Bless you, O son of Israel! Bless you! (*Nexus* 305–06)

Situated near the end of his trilogy, the words suggest he has found his own voice, one that merges with the great tradition.

There are dozens of references to the Bible, all used to frame and give depth to Miller's experience. Occasionally we find him comparing living women to those in scripture.[27] In one curious passage, he quotes the Book of Ruth to lend significance to Mara's name, noting that she "had been afflicted by the Lord" (41). Coupled with the Sanskrit interpretation, we can read Mara as the total embodiment of emptiness and bitter illusion.

Other biblical allusions are rarely elaborated on, such as references to King Solomon and the story of Daniel and the lions.[28] In the former case, it could be a reminder of the dangers of the polytheism Miller comes short of espousing, but it seems clear that Daniel is evoked in a moment of identification, as Miller is himself trapped in a perilous situation. At other times, he identifies with Moses, such as when he writes, "I feel as if I had come down from Mt. Sinai by parachute. All about me are my brothers, *humanity,* as they say, still marching on all fours" (*Plexus* 578). Later on, he follows Moses's footsteps when he announces, "Carried away by the thought, I had a picture of myself as another Moses, leading my people out of the wilderness. To stem the tide, reverse the process, start a grand march backward, back toward the source!" (*Nexus* 101). In this passage, he fuses Hebrew scripture with his own liquid salvation. He also identifies his own suffering with Job's through allusion, such as we find during *Nexus*'s opening: "Issac Dust, born of the dust and returning to dust" (8). Furthermore, we are later told that he likes reading from the wisdom book.[29]

The Epistles of St. Paul are also mentioned by a friend suggestively named Luther.[30] His friend wishes to look them up, but Miller discourages him. The incident ends in Luther telling him to have faith, whereupon the

The Rosy Crucifixion 115

man then tries to sell him insurance. The moment signals not only Luther's hypocrisy, but Miller's inability to open himself up to scripture at this point in the narrative. A few pages later, Miller destroys his Bible, a gesture symbolizing his rage and inability to accept the word.[31] After this passage, however, his words occasionally merge with biblical passages. In the following excerpt, we find him echoing the words of Psalm 51, as he expresses his guilt about abandoning his child: "I kept on with head down, the rain running down my back. I wanted to be soaked through and through. I wanted to be cleansed of all iniquity. Yes, that's how I put it to myself—*cleansed of all iniquity*" (*Plexus* 392).[32] The passage is particularly poignant when considering the Psalm was allegedly written after David committed adultery. In another part, he echoes Paul's Epistle to the Philippians: "Alone in it I experienced a strange sort of peace. It was not the 'peace that passeth understanding.' Ah no! It was an intermittent sort, the augur of a greater, a more enduring peace. It was the peace of a man who was able to reconcile himself with the condition of the world *in thought*" (*Plexus* 633).[33] Later, in *Nexus*, he recalls the Epistle of James by writing, "*Be still, and wait the coming of the Lord!*" (243).[34] Finally, towards the end of *The Rosy Crucifixion*, he fittingly uses John 3.16 to summate his own mission: "For God so loved the world that He gave his only begotten Son. . . ." (*Nexus* 300).

Miller also recasts Hebrew prophetic visions. We have already seen this in *Sexus's* Lorimer Street hallucination, in which he is caught in a "fiery flux," but there are additional ones (246). When he begins to understand his creative mission in *Nexus*, he has a vision similar to Ezekiel's, who saw fiery wheels in the sky with angels in between.[35] Looking at Mona and Stasia, he writes: "I saw the walls of the room recede and the city beyond it melt to nothingness; I saw fields ploughed to infinity, lakes, seas, oceans melt into space, a space studded with fiery orbs, and in the pure unfading limitless light there whirred before my eyes radiant hosts of godlike creatures, angels, archangels, seraphim, cherubim" (*Nexus* 75). A similar apparition occurs later in which he relates to Mona and Stasia: "'Everything at once,' I said. 'Past, present, future; earth, air, fire and water. A motionless wheel. A wheel of light, I feel like saying. And the light revolving, not the wheel'" (*Nexus* 77). Here he also associates himself with Elijah when he writes of Mona and Stasia: "They were so terribly eager to satisfy my least whim . . . it was almost as if an Elijah had appeared to them from out of the sky" (*Nexus* 76). The error is conscious, as the coming of Elijah signifies the coming of the apocalypse.

An apocalyptic visionary, Miller naturally incorporates the Book of Revelation into his texts. While the figure of the "whore of Babylon" is fleetingly

116   *Henry Miller and Religion*

mentioned in relation to a burlesque house, most references to Revelation come at the beginning of *Plexus*.[36] In this episode, which recalls W. B. Yeats' "Crazy Jane Visits the Bishop," a man from his youth named "Crazy George," begins to preach to Mona and Miller from the Book of Revelation. First, he speaks of "The Lamb which is in the midst of the Throne shall feed them, and shall lead them unto living fountains of waters," a direct quote from Revelation 7.17 whose water metaphor resonated with Miller (*Plexus* 33). George continues with Revelation 17.15–16: "The waters which thou sawest, where the whore sitteth, are peoples, and multitudes, and nations, and tongues. And the ten horns . . ." (*Plexus* 33–34). After he leaves, the Bible is left behind. Again harkening water metaphors and paraphrasing the Bible, Miller writes, "I had asked for the Bible and I had received it. 'Seek and ye shall find. Ask and it shall be given unto you. Knock and it shall be opened.' I began spouting a bit myself. The Scriptures are headier than the strongest wines" (*Plexus* 34).[37] Then he relates the following from Revelation 17.5–8:

> I opened the Book at random and it fell open to one of my favorite passages:
>
> > 'And upon her forehead was a name written, MYSTERY, BABYLON THE GREAT, THE MOTHER OF HARLOTS AND ABOMINATIONS OF THE EARTH.
> >
> > 'And I saw the woman drunken with the blood of the saints, and with the blood of the martyrs of Jesus; and when I saw her, I wondered with great admiration.
> >
> > 'And the angel said unto me, Wherefore didst thou marvel? I will tell thee the mystery of the woman, and of the beast that carrieth her, which hath the seven heads and ten horns.
> >
> > 'The beast that thou sawest was, and is not; and shall ascend out of the bottomless pit, and go into perdition: and they that dwell on earth shall wonder, whose names were not yet written in the Book of Life from the foundation of the world, when they behold the beast that was, and is not, and yet is.' (*Plexus* 34)

Calling upon the Gnostic Mass of the Ordo Templi Orientis (OTO), in which the union of Beast and the "Scarlet Whore" lead towards salvation, the long quotation suggests that both Mona and Miller are the beast and the Whore of Babylon in their unholy union. This sets the stage for his quest towards purity, an ascension to a spiritual union unprofaned. These references help demark his own "revelation" and ability to subsume his religious vision into Christian terms via Rosicrucianism.

The Rosy Crucifixion

Attempting to encompass Omega *and* Alpha, Miller also fits his life into the framework of creation, as set forth in the traditional Genesis narrative. Twice, he acknowledges his lineage to "Adam Cadmus," a fusion of Adam and the Greek god Cadmus, who was the grandfather of Dionysus and father to Semele.[38] Early in the trilogy, he acknowledges that Mona had "nourished" the story of the Garden of Eden:

> In some quiet part of me there was a legend which she had nourished. It was of a tree, just as in the Bible, and beneath it stood the woman called Eve with an apple in her hand. Here it ran like a clear stream, all that really constituted my life. Here there was feeling, from bank to bank. What was I getting at—*here where the subterranean stream ran clear?* Why that image of the Tree of Life? Why was it so exhilarating to retaste the poisonous apple, to kneel in supplication at the feet of a woman in the Bible? (*Sexus* 264)

Then he relates the experience of seeing her smile at the dance hall when they first met. The passage suggests that she not only made him think of the Genesis narrative but together they to some degree reenacted it:

> It was the seraphic smile of peace and benediction. It was given in a public place wherein we found ourselves alone. It was a sacrament, and the hour, the day, the place were recorded in letters of gold in the book of the legend which lay at the foot of the Tree of Life.•[. . .] For a few timeless moments we had stood at the gates of Paradise—then we were driven forth and that starry effulgence was shattered. (*Sexus* 265)[39]

Although each of these positions reinforces his connection to "Adam Cadmus," they appear to be in contradiction with latter passages, in which he casts Mona as the Whore of Babylon and himself as the Beast. These excerpts from *Sexus*, however, attest that he was disillusioned with Mona earlier in the narrative while, at the same time, suggest the birth of the creative process by recasting the creation myth.

MILLER AS CHRIST

Miller's self professed link to Adam additionally underscores his association with Christ—the new Adam.[40] From the very first page of *The Rosy Crucifixion*, he suggests affinities with the Christian messiah: "I was approaching my thirty-third year, the age of Christ crucified" (*Sexus* 5). He directly and

118   *Henry Miller and Religion*

indirectly reminds us of this number throughout *The Rosy Crucifixion,* such as when he writes that Christmas dinner will take place at "three-thirty," an inverse thirty-three (85).[41] At this event, Mona also says that he will "never die," intimating his immortality (*Nexus* 91). He also assembles two configurations of twelve disciples: 1) the twelve messengers also mentioned in *Tropic of Capricorn* and 2) the Xerxes society, his boyhood "club of twelve" (*Sexus* 203). In *Sexus,* he even tells us that his first book was ironically criticized by someone "who had written a highly successful book about Jesus-the-carpenter" (25). And as he prepares for Paris at the trilogy's end, he records hearing a radio advertising "'Last Supper' tablecloths," a pun on his own "last supper" and a slight critique of commercializing religion (*Nexus* 310). The connection between himself and Christ is strengthened when he explicitly mentions carrying "the iron cross of ignominious servitude" in the opening of *Sexus* (10). As the narrative progresses, he additionally refers to crucifixion, such as when his friend MacGregor flags him for mispronouncing apotheosis.[42] The most poignant moment, however, comes at the end of *Plexus,* when Miller meets God and announces, "My life was one long rosy crucifixion" (639). Considering these details and the overarching title of the trilogy, he undoubtedly built upon the "Christ complex" first mentioned in *Tropic of Capricorn.*

Miller demonstrates his identification with Christ in more subtle ways. For example, when sitting down to write, he tells himself "Now you can play God again," a comment suggesting that *The Rosy Crucifixion* is his way of being God (*Nexus* 300). He also uses Christ symbolism through the image of the dove. In one section, for example, his first wife Maude, we are told, "stoops to stroke the head of a dove," the bird functioning as a euphemism for his phallus (*Sexus* 84). He continues, "Like a merciful angel she spreads her legs apart: the dove flutters between her legs, the wings brush lightly against the marble arch. The little dove is fluttering madly; she must squeeze his soft little head between her legs" (*Sexus* 85). Coupling dove with angel gives the potentially secular metaphor definite religious overtones. Considering its early placement in the narrative, the image signifies his potential elevation that will come through sex.

In addition to such symbolic associations, we also find Miller echoing Christ's words, appropriating them as his own. Speaking of the artist, he writes, "It is only in the measure that he is aware of more life, the life abundant, that he may be said to live in his work" (*Sexus* 212). This passage borrows language from John 10.10, in which we find, "I am come that they might have life, and that they might have it more abundantly." He also quotes from another famous passage from the Gospel of John: "In my

The Rosy Crucifixion   *119*

Father's house are many mansions . . ." (*Plexus* 509).[43] These passages aim to convey that his message comes from the same source of divine inspiration.

The most profound appropriation of the life of Christ comes when Miller reworks the biblical story of the wedding at Cana, where Christ transforms water into wine.[44] He recasts the story in various guises throughout the trilogy, but the most noteworthy variation comes towards the end of *Sexus*. He becomes intoxicated with water, as if he has been able to transform water into wine. Before the scene, he sets the stage by referencing his father's alcoholism: "While he was drinking with his cronies I was feeding from the bottle of creative life" (209). With this textual setup, we then find Miller becoming drunk on water, as he sits with his friend Ned. He says somewhat jokingly, "Water is the elixir of life, my dear Ned. If I were running the world I'd give the creative people a bread and water diet" (461). In the scene, he goes on to take bites out of one of Ned's paintings, reminding us of Ezekiel eating the scroll.[45] When Mona and Marcelle—Ned's wife—enter, Ned attempts to explain Miller's actions: "He doesn't mean ordinary hunger—he means spiritual hunger" (462). The passage alludes to Christ's response to Satan during Jesus's time of temptation: "Man shall not live by bread alone, but by every word that proceedeth out of the mouth of God" (Matthew 4.4); the allusion obviously puts the woman in a dangerous role as temptresses. After identifying water as "the elixir of life," Miller goes on to tell Marcelle that she needs "cosmic juices," yet another variation of *élan vital* (463). When she asks how to receive them, he simply says, "you pray for them. Didn't you ever hear of the manna that fell from the sky?," a passage that not only refers to God giving Israelites manna, but Jesus's own reinterpolation of the passage, in which he announces himself as heavily bread, "the bread of life" (464; John 6.35).[46] Miller's own episode ends with him confirming his divinity, saying he is "going to live forever" (466). Later he becomes intoxicated with books, including the Bible and Spengler's *Decline of the West*.[47] But the prior translation of water into wine attests to his self-proclaimed divinity.

Alchemical transformation indeed remains an important theme in Miller's work. Although somewhat trite, one of the guiding themes is the transition from "dog" to "God." Since "God" refers to a liberated individual in his schema, it is fitting that we find tension between liberation and "dogs" on the very first page of *The Rosy Crucifixion:* "To make the fatal step, to throw everything to the dogs, is in itself an emancipation: the thought of consequences never entered my head" (*Sexus* 5). In this case, "to throw everything to the dogs" hints of sloughing off the chains that bind one's self. This interpretation is confirmed when, at the end of *Sexus*, he flashes forward to future events. In reference to Mona and Stasia, he writes: "I wait for her night after night, like a prisoner chained to the floor of his cell. There is a woman with her whom she calls her friend. They have conspired to betray me and defeat me. They leave me without food, without heat, without light" (489). He elaborates on his imprisonment, in which he feels treated like an animal. He even begins to imitate a dog, describing a walk back to his apartment: "I could crawl in like a dog with his tail between his legs" (494). The grand fantasy ending the book continues the canine theme, as he finds himself in a dog show, in which he is called a "dirty dog" (504–506). The horrible vision ends with Miller-as-puppy clutched by a composite female figure, a synthesis of Mona and his mother.

After establishing himself as "dog" in *Sexus*, we find Miller transforming himself into "God" in *Plexus*. At the end of the book, he again forecasts the final installment, claiming he "shall even take to howling like a dog" (639). Even after he announces that his has been a "rosy crucifixion," he writes, "As to the meaning of this, if it is not already clear, it shall be elucidated. If I fail then am I but a dog in the manger" (639). Playing on the tradition that Christ was born in a manger, he posits an undeniable connection between "dog" and "God." As we have been promised, the opening words of *Nexus* give us canine Miller: "Woof! Woof woof! *Woof! Woof!*" (7). In the narrative, he reflects upon his forfeited working life, presenting workers as "trained poodles" and recalling his managerial position as "a dog baying at the moon" (70–71). Even when he discusses his newfound freedom at the end of the book, he writes, "There was nothing to keep me chained indoors any longer. The novel was finished, the money was in the bank, the trunk was packed, the passports were in order, the Angel of Mercy was guarding the tomb" (308). Through angels and the motif of liberation, God is again posited as the opposite of a chained dog.

In strange symmetry, god-dog is part of the predominate concern with union. Miller aspires towards unification, such as in the following passage: "I fell back in to the vacuum (where God is all) with the most delicious sense of relief. I could see it all clearly—my earthly evolution, from the larval stage to the present, and even beyond the present. What was the struggle for or toward? Toward union" (301). Situated toward the end of *Nexus,* this passage demarks his journey from mundane sexual conjunction to a loftier, abstract union. He discusses this amalgamation in increasingly abstract terms, mostly through the web metaphor. Earlier in the trilogy, he has used the symbol in passages such as the following on the dreamer: "He sees without seeing, to be exact. Vision without sight, a fluid grasp of intangibles: the merging of sight and sound: the heart of the web. Here stream the distant personalities which evade the crude contact of the senses; here the overtones of recognition

The Rosy Crucifixion 121

discreetly lap against one another in bright, vibrant harmonies. There is no language employed, no outlines delineated" (*Sexus* 208). In this excerpt, we find a fusion of fluid, sonic, and luminescent metaphors. Toward the end of the trilogy, he has a final vision that again employs this net image:

> A picture now obtruded. A picture of the world as a web of magnetic forces. Studding this web like nuclei were the burning spirits of the earth about whom the various orders of humanity spun like constellations. Due to the hierarchical distribution of powers and aptitudes a sublime harmony reigned. No discord was possible. All the conflict, all the disturbance, all the confusion and disorder to which man vainly endeavored to adjust was meaningless. The intelligence which invested the universe recognized it not. The murderous, the suicidal, the maniacal activity of earthly beings, yea, even their benevolent, their worshipful, their all too humane activities, were illusory. In the magnetic web motion itself was nil. Nothing to go toward, nothing to retreat from, nothing to reach up to. The vast, unending field of force was like a suspended thought, a suspended note. Aeons from now—and what was *now?*—another thought might replace it. (*Nexus* 302)

In this hallucination, which strongly parallels the amphitheatre of Dante's *Paradiso,* he performs an alchemical inversion similar to the shift from dog to God. Here he shifts from a web of entrapment and imprisonment—his jobs and marriages—to total connection with the universe.

Miller's abstract rendering of union is tied to a commingling of male and female. Describing a metaphysical union with what he deems to be feminine, he writes, "In this sort of union, which is really a marriage of spirit with spirit, a man comes face to face with the meaning of creation" (*Sexus* 345). As a source of creation, this marriage is also discussed in Gnostic sources, such as the Valentius school writings and Rosicrucian sources. He suggests familiarity with these writings by having Mona call him "Val" throughout the trilogy.[48] In writings attributed to Valentinus and others familiar with his thought, God is conceived as a mixture of male and female forces.[49] Similar ideas saturate *The Rosy Crucifixion,* in which we have already seen him use the particular term "Aeons."[50] Throughout the books, he indeed renders Mara as a feminine force that sets his world into motion, leading him on his divine mission.

In *The Rosy Crucifixion,* Miller even recasts Sophia, a mystical figure central to Gnosticism.[51] Prefiguring in Christian mysticism, Sophia in union with Adam represents the male and female tendencies united in the holy

122   *Henry Miller and Religion*

Androgyne: Christ. Although Mona moves Miller to creation, his path is further steered through a dramatic encounter with a woman named "Sylvia," whose name echoes the mystical figure. He meets her at his friend Ulric's apartment; relating his impressions upon meeting her, Miller writes, "I knew that this was the preliminary to some strange adventure" (*Sexus* 37). The woman convinces him that he is protected but maintains he needs to be freed. As she says, "It isn't a woman you need—it is an instrument to liberate yourself. You crave a more adventurous life, you want to break your chains" (39). Looking at her, he later states, "To look into your eyes is like looking into a dark mirror," an utterance that suggests some identification, an intimation of male and female union (40). She then accuses him of "sucking the life out of a woman," telling him: "Art can transform the hideous into the beautiful. Better a monstrous book than a monstrous life. Art is painful, tedious, softening. If you don't die in the attempt, your work may transform you into a sociable, charitable human being" (42). In these few words, we find his message of transformation through books rehearsed again. She continues, "You have all the feminine virtues, but you are ashamed to acknowledge them to yourself. You think because you are strong sexually that you are a virile man, but you are more of a woman than a man. Your sexual virility is the only sign of a greater power which you haven't begun to use" (42). As the personification of wisdom, Sylvia announces that Miller needs to cultivate the feminine within, unlocking his artistic powers through blending male virility and female creativity. The woman's mythological status is confirmed the next day, when Ulric will not accept this encounter happened. It appears the drama transpired within his imagination.

Throughout the trilogy, Miller tries to achieve physical union, rather than spiritual, through Mona. Suggesting he lives below the glass ceiling separating the carnal from the celestial, he writes of his misguided relationship with Mona, "Like mandragoras under a glass roof, Mona and I lay rooted in our own bed, which was a strictly human bed, and fertilized the egg of hermaphroditic love" (*Sexus* 347).

By *Nexus*, Miller realizes his union with Mona was profane; true hermaphroditic integration only occurs through spiritual pursuits, using art as the vehicle. Questioning his relationship with illusion incarnate, he asks himself, "Was it the faith with which she inspired me? (The faith in myself, I mean.) Or was it that we were joined like Siamese twins?" (37). Later he adds, "The thin membrane of skin which separated us served as a magnetic coat of armor through which the mightiest current was powerless to operate" (42). Both examples suggest that *élan vital* or creative "faith" did not indeed flow

The Rosy Crucifixion   *123*

between them. He discovers the feminine comes from within, not through literal union with a woman. In opposition to the spiritual, the ridiculousness of concretized conjunction is imaged in the hermaphroditic robot he hears of in *Plexus,* a symbol of ill-conceived, mechanistic coupling.[52]

Miller's encounter with Stasia marks another increase in his hermaphroditic knowledge. Because of her masculine appearance, even Mona questions her sex, saying: "There's some added quality in her which is beyond sexual distinction. Sometimes she reminds me of an angel, except that there's nothing ethereal or remote about her" (*Plexus* 588). In *Nexus,* their friend Dr. Kronski even "inspected" Stasia, only to pronounce her "normal" (49–50). As someone between Miller and Mona, a blend of masculine and feminine, Stasia functions as Miller's androgynous role model, albeit on a metaphysical and, therefore, artistic level.

When demonstrating his creativity, Miller indeed describes himself in feminine terms. The most moving example comes when he writes about resuming his work: "As I sat there I realized that the room was impregnated with my spirit" (*Plexus* 284). In other passages, he even discusses his femininity in more concrete terms, such as when he describes himself as pregnant with book, a carryover from *Tropic of Cancer.*[53] In *Nexus,* he even refers to his initial scribbling as a "miscarriage" (218). Although a comical admission of servitude to his patron, he states the following of the writing process: "Every time I sat down to write a page for him I readjusted my skirt, primped my hairdo and powdered my nose" (*Nexus* 249).

Nevertheless, the position of blending his own voice with Mona's, the condition of his ghostwriting contract, anticipates the purer blending of masculine and feminine that will occur through *Tropic of Cancer.*[54] He even uses increasingly biological metaphors when he writes, "*I began to menstruate. I menstruated from every hole in my body*" (*Sexus* 498). In this scene of spiritual awakening, he not only underscores becoming woman, but also increases his identification with the crucified Christ, who "menstruates" out of his wounds. Elaborating on another mystical moment, we again find him situating himself between genders: "Between Adam and Eve I lay, surrounded by a thousand reindeer" (*Plexus* 514). Calling on the Bible, he situations himself between male and female, the point of origin for all pure artistic creation.

Containing both male and female sexual organs, flowers also have a crucial role in the trilogy, demarcating Miller's transition from profane conjunction to divine unity. The persistent metaphor harkens the Taoist text *The Secret of the Golden Flower,* in which readers are encouraged to link masculine "animus" with feminine "anima." More than just a flower, the rose is

124   Henry Miller and Religion

even present in the trilogy's title. While *The Rosy Crucifixion* is an obvious play on "Rosicrucianism," it also alludes to the thirteenth century French poem, *Le Roman de la rose* by Guillaume de Lorris and Jean de Meun. A pivotal influence on Dante, the sprawling verse poem begins as a dream vision of love. The protaganist becomes enamored by a rosebud, which he wants to imprison. The poem's first part, penned by Guillaume, ends with Jealousy building a tower around the rose. While the poem certainly has thematic affinities with Miller's work, it also contains similar formal elements, especially in relation to the second section by Jean de Meun. Like Miller in *Plexus*, de Meun incorporated copious quotations from other works of literature. Furthermore, the poem instructs readers on sundry matters, including philosophical, religious, and amorous concerns. De Meun's section dramatically ends with the protagonist breaking into the tower, thereby uniting male and female through liberation, the American author's own persistent theme.

Miller is also using the rose image or, in some cases, a generic flower, to trace a journey to salvation that begins in excrement. The most explicit passage can be found in *Sexus*, when he asks, "Where are the beasts of the field, the crops, the manure, the roses that flower in the midst of corruption?" (9–10). This prefatory remark in the trilogy traces his own blooming quest. He repeats the flower motif often in *Sexus*, such as the following problematic passage: "The irresistible creature of the other sex is a monster in process of becoming a flower. Feminine beauty is a ceaseless creation, a ceaseless revolution about a defect (often imaginary) which causes the whole being to gyrate heavenward" (252). Informed by the *Golden Flower* text and Valentinian theology, we can see his travels as an infinite spiraling that encompasses the feminine. At the end of *Plexus*, he poignantly returns with the representation of the rose, writing of his own suffering: "The great open wound which was draining the blood of life closes up, the organism blossoms like a rose" (640). The moment forecasts his healing from suffering brought about by Mona.

His use of flower imagery movingly charts the transition from Miller's profane love of sex to the more divine spiritual unity, from sexual "passion" to the true "passion" of Christ. While divorcing his first wife Maude, he has a picnic with the family he will soon leave. He almost forces Maude to have sex while the child is playing nearby, a gesture that makes his wife disgusted and saddened to tears. Before the ordeal, their daughter was "running about gathering flowers" (*Sexus* 370). He, conversely, "de-flowers" his wife by forcing his finger inside her vagina. His daughter is championed as keeper of the true way, in opposition to his vulgarity

The Rosy Crucifixion   *125*

The scene vividly contrasts the end of *The Rosy Crucifixion*, in which Miller addresses a citation from Diderot that claims "my ideas are my whores" (*Nexus* 250). Miller responds:

> No, my ideas were a garden of delights. An absentminded gardener I was, who, though tender and observing, did not attach too much importance to the presence of weeds, thorns, nettles, but craved only the joy of frequenting this place apart, this intimate domain people with shrubs, blossoms, flowers, bees, birds, bugs of every variety. I never walked the garden as a pimp, nor even in a fornicating frame of mind. [. . .] The look of a flower was enough, or its perfume. How did the flower come to be? How did *anything* come to be? If I questioned, it was to ask—'*Are you there, little friend? Are the dewdrops still clinging to your petals?*
>
> "What could be more considerate—better manners!—than to treat thoughts, ideas, inspirational flashes, as flowers of delight? (*Nexus* 250)

The journey from the rape of his wife to his identification of his work with flowers shows a massive transition integrally tied to the triumph of innocent love over carnal lust.

Although considered his most scandalous work, *The Rosy Crucifixion* was conceived as writings on the higher theme of love. We find this sentiment expressed in an unpublished letter to Herbert Muller: "The next volume of Capricorn is called 'The Rosy Crucifixion' and literally deals with my crucifixion and resurrection, through love. I had to learn the meaning of love, as we get it in Balzac's '*Seraphita.*' I no longer have any attachments. I love, that's all" (3). This theme made itself into *The Rosy Crucifixion*, such as in this passage from its final volume: "'In pure love (which no doubt does not exist at all except in our imagination),' says one I admire, 'the giver is not aware that he gives nor of what he gives, nor to whom he gives, still less of whether it is appreciated by the recipient or not.' [. . .] To be free of the bondage of love, to burn down like a candle, to melt in love, melt *with* love—what bliss!" (*Nexus* 39). This passage is the ultimate conclusion of his work. Art should be a pure labor of love, elevating one to spiritual liberation, rather than illusionary pursuits through profane lust. The melting metaphor, of course, further resonates with his liquid notion of divinity, an idea further developed on the following page:

> If energy is imperishable, how much more so is love! Like energy, which is still a complete enigma, love is always there, always on tap. Man has never created an ounce of energy, nor did he create love. Love and energy have always been, always will be. Perhaps in essence they are one

and the same. Why not? Perhaps this mysterious energy which is identified with the life of the universe, which is God in action, as someone has said, perhaps this secret, all-invasive force is but the manifestation of love. What is even more awesome to consider is that, if there be nothing in our universe which is not informed with this unseizable force, then what of love? (*Nexus* 40)

This "someone" is Bergson, who in *Two Sources of Morality and Religion* identified *élan vital* with love. In this final message, Miller shows he has fully accepted the message of Bergson, testifying that love and the sacred energy discussed throughout his work are one. He has fully accepted the essential Christian doctrine: "God is love."

Chapter Seven

Conclusion

Throughout his literary career, Henry Miller constructed a religious universe in which self-liberation remained his ultimate goal. Building upon the traditions of Christian writers such as William Blake, Miller saw religion, art, and sex as three kindred vehicles to achieve emancipation. The sexual dimensions of his oeuvre should be seen within this greater project, a schematic that intended to be religious in nature, given the contexts in which it was originally forged. By releasing everything pent-up inside, he attempted to purify himself, letting the "smut" collect in books, only to be used, in turn, as catalysts for the reader's inner awakenings. While anyone might esteem his works simply for their linguistic bravado, doing so distorts the richer world that comes to light once the deep religious architecture is uncovered.

Henry Miller and Religion does not attempt to be a comprehensive study of Miller's engagement with religion. To offer close readings of all his major works would have stretched this study beyond a single volume. I hope that future scholars will create a more complete picture of his self-constructed universe by attempting to uncover the religious motivations in all of his "non-fiction" and "fiction," as I distinguished these genres in the opening chapter. It would also be helpful to determine how the religious concerns of the non-fiction works, along with their different literary styles, should be understood in relationship to his fiction.

By focusing on what is truly unique about his work—his ongoing preoccupation with religion—I hope that scholars will value Miller as a major literary voice of the twentieth century, a pivotal writer engaged with Modernist concerns. Other Modernists certainly shared his preoccupation with religion: D. H. Lawrence erected a similar primal religion; W. B. Yeats also assembled a choate order out of the era's wild esoterica. What distinguishes Miller, however, is his alleged self-apotheosis or, to be blunt, his self-obsession. He assembles a religious world in which the self is God.

Miller's American style of religiosity further distinguishes him from his European brethren. In addition to creating an experiential personal religion that samples from dozens of established traditions, his self-worship takes American religiosity to its extreme, pushing self-reliance to its irresponsible limits. Freedom is to be achieved at all costs, tearing social bonds between family and friends.

Surveying Miller's life, however, shows he employed his philosophy of self-liberation only when convenient, as he depended heavily upon the generosity of acquaintances. Although not angelic, June Smerth, whom he demonized as illusion personified, found money that freed him to try his hand at writing. When she left, Anaïs Nin took over this task, taking out an apartment in her name, allowing him to live and work alone. Miller was by no means a solitary walker. How ironic, then, that he promoted a religion of radical independence.

Miller ultimately could not fulfill his own grandiose expectations; he never became the truly liberated individual advertised in his books. In the end, his name can be added to the lengthy register of religious figures who fall short of glory. Nevertheless, his works remain inspirational to countless individuals, prompting readers to begin their own journeys toward self-emancipation. Although neither saintly nor divine, Henry Miller today remains an important writer and American religious figure.

Notes

NOTES TO CHAPTER ONE

1. In the widely distributed revised version of 1959, he removes some of the agency from this position: "Perhaps, without knowing it, I have always been a religious person" (13). Nevertheless, the sentiment remains unchanged.
2. For two examples of his tendency to provide Whitmanesque lists of holy figures, see *Plexus* 342–43 and *Nexus* 35.
3. For more information on the Emmanuel Movement, see Gifford.
4. For more on the establishment of Theosophy in the United States, see Prothero.
5. On Theosophy's warm reception among artists of the 1920s, see Oja.
6. The OTO was founded by Carl Kellner, developed by Theodor Reuss, and eventually overtaken by Aleister Crowley, formerly of the Hermetic Order of the Golden Dawn, which itself also included W. B. Yeats among its brethren.
7. For more about her relationship with Gurdjieff, see Anderson.
8. As a publisher of Mansfield, Pound, George Bernard Shaw and other important authors of the early twentieth century, Orage's role in Modernism, particularly as a proselytizer of Gurdjieff, has yet to be sufficiently examined. Years before he studied Gurdjieff, Orage had informal contact with members of the Hermetic Order of the Golden Dawn. In 1896, the year in which he married Theosophist Jean Walker, he became a member of the Theosophical Society and even published articles in the *Theosophical Review* between 1905–07. During this time, he also spearheaded a group called the Leeds Art Club (founded 1902), which included Yeats and Shaw among its members. Although a comprehensive biography does not exist, his story can be pieced together from a few sources; see Conford, Munson, Paul Taylor, and Welch.
9. She then becomes "Mona" later in *The Rosy Crucifixion* to provide consistency with *Tropic of Cancer.*

10. This is suggested by multiple items housed in the Henry Miller Papers at UCLA, including a poster-sized outline that features the corresponding colors in the left-hand margin.
11. A version of this manuscript has since appeared in French translation. No English edition is yet available.
12. For an overview of this recent movement in literary studies, see Gallagher and Greenblatt.
13. See Viscomi.
14. See Thompson.
15. See McGann.
16. Paul R. Jackson's essay "Henry Miller, Emerson, and the Divided Self" is an example of how one can easily be led astray. While an insightful piece, the essay begins by arguing that Miller must have been thoroughly familiar with Emerson's journals, as he includes two obscure quotes from them in *Tropic of Cancer*. With Miller's acquaintanceship apparently established, Jackson goes on to argue that an Indian character in *The Rosy Crucifixion* named Osmanli is Miller's double, a parallel of Emerson's fictional self, Osman. Miller's notebooks reveal, however, that he lifted the quote from Lewisohn's study of American literature, *Expression in America* (1932), proving that he was far from conversant with Emerson's journals.
17. See *Theory of Religion* and *The Accursed Share*.
18. Although Miller never mentions Bataille, we know he was thoroughly familiar with Breton's second *Manifesto of Surrealism*, in which the final few pages are devoted to a diatribe against Bataille. I have not been able to locate concrete evidence indicating that they knew one another, but they certainly operated within the same circles, sharing important French intellectuals and writers as friends, including Raymond Queneau. Another acquaintance of Miller's, the astrologer Conrad Moricand, also spent an extensive amount of time copying esoteric religious materials out of rare books at the Bibliothèque Nationale where Bataille worked as an important librarian. Moricand may have gone through Bataille to gain access to these materials. Judging from the manuscript, which was given to Miller in 1938, Bataille and Moricand certainly had overlapping interests, which could have resulted in friendship between the two. For more on Miller and Bataille, see Mayné.
19. Finn Jensen's "Cancer and Nomads: Miller, Brassaï, and a Touch of Deleuze" rightly suggests that Deleuze's philosophy could be inspirational to future Miller scholars. He does little else, however, than to point us in the Deleuzian direction by introducing his most basic concepts and stating that *Marcel Proust et les signes* offers readings of *Remembrance of Things Past* that could be applied to Miller's works.
20. A recent collection entitled *Deleuze and Religion* is beginning to rectify this problem. See Bryden.

Notes to Chapter Two 131

21. For these three criteria, see *Kafka* 16–17.

NOTES TO CHAPTER TWO

1. This review was not published until Gottesman's collection of Henry Miller essays and the date is uncertain, but the editor argues 1935. Similar sentiments are also expressed in a letter quoted and paraphrased by Martin (304).
2. See Miller and Fraenkel, Dearborn 178.
3. See Martin 413.
4. For specific accounts, see *Big Sur.*
5. For example, see the sundry articles published in San Francisco after the sordid affair with Conrad Moricand, who stayed with Miller in the 1940s. Miller's response is preserved in the "Paradise Lost" section of *Big Sur.*
6. See Miller and Gertz, Hutchinson.
7. For more information about the gallery, see Winslow. Ironically, excerpts from Miller's letters featured in his book show his lack of enthusiasm towards the studio, sometimes to the point of outright embarrassment (262). Winslow's book also provides a window into his gold-digging activities before the American publication of *Tropic of Cancer* brought him riches. The fanatic ways he asks her to sell his watercolors, special addition books, and other miscellanea lend great insight into his character, especially his duplicitous take on capitalism and the American way.
8. See Mailer.
9. See "Female Sexuality."
10. Although less notorious and noteworthy, Claude Chabrol's *Jours tranquilles à Clichy* (1990) was another film adaptation of *Quiet Days in Clichy,* released twenty years later.
11. The relationship between the two appears to be complicated, as Snyder brought out his own book that uses similar footage entitled, *This is Henry, Henry Miller from Brooklyn* (1974). Many tried to cash in on Miller during his final years, though Snyder has thankfully preserved Miller's image on film, supplementing the scant audio recordings available.
12. Since then, she has gone on to publish titles such as *Secrets of Seduction: How to be the Best Lover Your Woman Ever Had* (1993) and its follow-up *Secrets of Seduction for Women* (1996).
13. *Mailer: A Biography* was published in 1999.
14. See Gilbert and Gubar 1:48, 116.
15. Two pop songs in the mid-1990s presented Miller in a jovial, neutral light, though each had limited exposure: Dan Bern's "Marilyn" (1993) and Jewel's "Morning Song" (1995).
16. See Davis.

NOTES TO CHAPTER THREE

1. See *Capricorn.*
2. This became the posthumously published *Moloch.*
3. Burke's translation, in which he called Spengler's text "The Downfall of Western Civilization," appeared in three issues. Like many writers, Miller most likely first encountered Spengler through *The Dial.* In the October 1924 issue, another one of Miller's pivotal influences found his way into *The Dial,* as an essay by Elie Faure was included along with a review, written by Thomas Craven.
4. See Jones.
5. See Nikhilananda.
6. For Miller's final recounting of this story, see *Book of Friends* (135).
7. Challacombe reappears in *Tropic of Capricorn* as Roy Hamilton.
8. See Miller and Schnellock 31.
9. This title, along with A. P. Sinnett's *Esoteric Buddhism,* is listed in Miller's list entitled "The Hundred Books that Influenced me Most," which can be found as an appendix in *The Books of My Life* (317).
10. Both works were published by the Theosophical Society.
11. See Koenig.
12. See Henry Miller Papers, UCLA.
13. During multiple visits to the Bibliothèque Nationale, Moricand copied a wide variety of texts from rare books, eventually forming this manuscript comprised of hundreds of handwritten pages. He presented this two volume manuscript to Miller as a gift in 1938, the year in that saw the completion of *Tropic of Capricorn.* Why Moricand would hand over such a labor to his friend is uncertain, but the gesture certainly underscores Miller's thirst for such materials.
14. See Ferguson 225–26.
15. In an October 1932 letter to Nin, Miller asks her to return this specific book to him (*Letters* 68). He also takes extensive notes on the text in his Lawrence notebooks. See Henry Miller Papers, UCLA.
16. Miller often mentions this text and the ideas within it, particularly in a letter to Nin penned on 7 March 1933 after visiting Rank (*Letters* 82).
17. In a letter dated 14 March 1949 to fellow writer and close friend Lawrence Durrell, Miller lists his main influences in order to aid Durrell in a study he is writing on the American author himself. Miller writes, "Bergson belongs to my 'youth' (tailor shop days). How much he influenced me is imponderable" (229). "Tailor shop days," in which he helped his father with his small business, refers to Miller's own twenty-something years, times chronicled in both *Black Spring* and *Tropic of Capricorn.* In both of these books, Bergson's *Creative Evolution,* his most famous and influential piece, is specifically mentioned as a work that he was trying to understand during the 1910s, as were many of his contemporaries.

Notes to Chapter Three 133

18. Always eager to acknowledge his influences, Miller often included Faure in his pantheon, such as in the following passage from *Plexus:* "Nietzsche, Dostoevski, Elie Faure, Spengler [. . .] The four horseman of my own private Apocalypse!" (639). Faure's *History of Art* is also mentioned in *Tropic of Cancer* (62).

19. See the opening chapter of *The Spirit of the Forms*, the fifth volume of *The History of Art*, for Faure's explanation of the "great rhythm."

20. See Henry Miller Papers, UCLA.

21. See Henry Miller Papers, UCLA.

22. For one account, see Martin 285–86.

23. An authorized version of *The World of Lawrence* appeared after Miller's death in 1980. This version consciously preserves the bulk of his material, as it loosely arranges some of the manuscript under one of his proposed schema. The result, however, does not reflect the careful argument he had tried in vain to develop.

24. These excerpts from the Lawrence study can be found in various essay collections. See "The Universe of Death," "Creative Death," "Into the Future," and "Shadowy Monomania." For the "Inhuman" designation, see *Tropic of Cancer* (233–34).

25. "Avant-garde" is a French military term used to designate the military guard ("garde") that comes before ("avant"). The term was used this way for centuries before it became associated with the arts in the early twentieth century.

26. The impact of Spengler on Miller's work is admittedly massive, although he has perhaps overplayed this influence in his writings. Nevertheless, he was certainly guided by concepts in his philosophy. To gauge his enthusiasm for the German philosopher, consider the end of *Plexus,* in which he includes pages of block quotations from *Decline of the West.* Spengler is mentioned throughout his writings, including *Tropic of Cancer* (27) and *Tropic of Capricorn* (195).

27. Compare W. B. Yeats's "The Second Coming."

28. Miller's was familiar with Nietzsche well before he began writing *Tropic of Cancer.* He would often tell the story of how his first piece of writing was an essay on Nietzsche's *Anti-Christ,* which he wrote in his early twenties. For one example, see *My Life and Times.* Jay Martin tells us more about his youthful interest in Nietzsche and German philosophy: "Even the German salesman from Fisher & Company called Henry *ein echter Philosoph von Geburt* and begged Heinrich [Miller's father] to free him for the serious study of philosophy" (34). Unfortunately, his parents did not have enough money to send him to Cornell, where he wanted to study. He continued to read Nietzsche, however, through his Paris years. A May 1932 letter to Nin assigns her various works by Nietzsche, suggesting that he piqued her interest through conversation (*Letters* 48).

29. See Henry Miller Papers, UCLA.

134   *Notes to Chapter Four*

30. Miller's conception of Prometheus may have been slightly nuanced by the updated version told by André Gide, *Le Prométhée mal enchaîné* (1899). In this version, the vultures that torture him are passions, and he is only freed once he consumes the vulture. Prometheus's ordeal is similar to what we find in *Tropic of Cancer,* as Miller is freed only when he forsakes his passion for Mona. Gide's text, which is now out of print, was reissued in the 1920s along with illustrations by Pierre Bonnard, an artist Miller intensely admired. Most likely, he was familiar with the text, as he lists one of Gide's texts, a study of Dostoyevsky, as a text that dramatically influenced him (*Books* 317).

31. In an October 1932 letter to Nin, Miller asks her for anything on the subject of Orphic myths, adding that "*Birth of Tragedy* gives it better than anything" (*Letters* 70). His notebooks include articles from the Encyclopedia Britannica on these subjects, along with passages from *The Hymns of Orpheus* and Salomon Reinach's *Orpheus: A History of Religions.*

32. See Henry Miller Papers, UCLA.

33. See *Orpheus.*

34. See Henry Miller Papers, UCLA.

35. In a letter to Nin dated 28 September 1932, Miller mentions Lewisohn's study and, in particular, his treatment of Emerson. He writes, "I wanted to raise Waldo Emerson to the skies, just to prove to the world that once there had been a great American—but more than that, because I once had been greatly influenced by him, he was bound up with a whole side of me that I consider my better side" (*Letters* 58).

36. These notes were sent to Richard Osborn and now reside in the Henry Miller Papers, UCLA.

37. See Henry Miller Papers, UCLA.

38. See Henry Miller Papers, UCLA.

39. See Henry Miller Papers, UCLA.

40. See *The World of Lawrence* (241) for one example of his allusion to Luke 17.20–21. In *Reflections,* a collection of Miller's final conversations edited by his caretaker Twinka Thiebaud, he is quoted as saying, "The truly enlightened teachers don't talk so much of finding God as developing the Self. [. . .] As a final word, I'd say that until you know yourself, no amount of searching or seeking will bring you closer to God. God is within *you*" (123).

NOTES TO CHAPTER FOUR

1. Miller would note this a few years later in *The World of Sex,* "Liberally dosed with a sexual content as was that book the problem of the author was never one of sex, nor even of religion, but of self-liberation." His quest for self-liberation, however, is his personal religion, in opposition to more popular ways of worship.

Notes to Chapter Four   *135*

2. See *Inferno* 1.1.

3. This transition from death into life is in keeping with the astrological significance of the Cancer sign as a house of birth and death.

4. Multiple places in Blake's early tractate discuss energy in relation to restraint (for example, see plate 4). Like Blake, Miller is interested in striking a balance between the traditional dichotomies of the transcendental and the immanent, which Blake divides into reason and energy. In his writings, Miller admits the influence of Blake, especially through secondary literature on the British poet. In one of his last essays, entitled "Reflections on the Maurizius Case," Miller writes, "I have pondered over *The Maurizius Case* more than over any book I have ever read, I guess, unless it be *William Blake's Circle of Destiny*" (*Sextet* 142).

5. See Exodus 3.14, John 8.58 (KJV). While one may think this reference is a bit of a stretch, the connection is bolstered when Miller refers to God as "The Great I AM" later in the text (91). The fact that he mentions "I AM" in relationship to the religious practices of a Hindu acquaintance does not lessen the impact, as the philosophy of Emerson presented him with a correspondence between the Hindu conception of God as "Brahma" and the God worshipped by the people of the Book, in which both were united in the divine within.

6. This sentiment is also expressed earlier in relation to what Miller calls "The Last Book." He writes, "We have no need for genius—genius is dead. We have need for strong hands, for spirits who are willing to give up the ghost and put on flesh . . ." (44).

7. See the final pages of chapter 12 and the opening of chapter 13 in *Tropic of Cancer*.

8. Miller's use of the river symbol may have been inspired by Jung's *Two Essays on Analytical Psychology*, a text he often mentions in unpublished notes and correspondence. In this study, Jung relates a woman's dream in which she tries to cross a river but is confronted by a crab that holds her captive, an image replicated on the first Obelisk Press editions of *Tropic of Cancer*. Naturally, this dream resonates with many other symbols and themes in Miller's text: travel, captivity, and crab/cancer. But Jung's exegesis of the woman's dream provides additional correspondences, as Jung identifies the crab with untamed libido and the dual figure of the woman's female friend and her mother. This finds correspondence in Miller as he is trying to tame his libido to move beyond Mona and his mother. Although the symbols are used in different ways, the themes certainly are similar.

9. In the second journal devoted to notes on D. H. Lawrence, now housed at UCLA, Miller also writes the following about Joyce, suggesting once again a correspondence between women and water: "The three great mother images are water, wood and earth, and how great a part these play in Joyce's compositions is needless to stress. The mother is also often represented as

a murderess, a devourer of men, as in Grimm's Fairy Tales, Hansel and Gretel, for example. Woman, the mother, is also symbolized by City, as in the biblical stories, in Revelation particularly, the great whore of Babylon, and crowds or throngs symbolizes mystery." By associating the crowd and the metropolis with the feminine, we may also see the bulk of *Tropic of Cancer*'s narrative as devoted to exploring his feminine side, as Miller wonders the streets of Paris.

10. Also at this time, Miller included information about hermaphrodites in his notebooks. While the interpretation I just offered may seem far fetched, we see these hermaphroditic tendencies throughout his work. Erica Jong recognizes this to some degree when she writes: "Shall we burn Miller? Better to emulate him. Better to follow his path from sexual madness to spiritual serenity, from bleeding maleness to an androgyny that fills the heart with light" (212). In this surprising passage, she acknowledges that it was at least Miller's goal to refine his sexist impurities into a pure soul unchained to antiquated notions of gender. Even if this was his aim, we cannot say that his published work is a testament of one who has reached such heights. Nevertheless, the Androgyne represented the highest form of spiritual union, ideas he most likely derived from Aleister Crowley's Ordo Templi Orientis (OTO).

11. Admittedly, there is a section to be found in between, in which Miller admits prejudice against such heights. He writes, "I want to make a detour of those lofty arid mountain ranges where one dies of thirst and cold, that 'extra-temporal' history, that absolute of time and space where there exists neither man, beast, nor vegetation, where one goes crazy with loneliness, with language that is mere words, where everything is unhooked, ungeared, out of joint with the times" (235). Because this is found in a paean to flow, it stands to reason, at least within this context, that he would be adverse to mountains.

12. Also, the goat is associated with the astrological sign "Capricorn," an earth sign related to stasis.

13. Miller could have been additionally driven by Paul's Epistle to the Galatians, but I have not uncovered enough evidence to confirm his familiarity with the biblical text.

14. Miller quotes this "Parable of Hell" from *The Marriage of Heaven and Hell* in an essay entitled "On Turning Eighty" (*Sextet* 13).

15. See Exodus 3.2.

16. See Ferguson 262.

17. See Emerson.

18. In *The Books in My Life*, Miller acknowledges the influence of "Greek Myths and Legends," though he does not cite specific sources (317). Biographers and the author himself often talk about the "Xerxes Society" he formed during his youth, so Ellis and Horne's work is representative of the type of text

Notes to Chapter Four   137

that would influence youths at this time. As an aside, Miller's attraction to Xerxes is in itself interesting, as the Persian ruler tried to harness the sea, first by having his men whip it like a slave, then throwing a set of fetters into it.

19. It is possible that Miller has in mind here Crowley's idea of the "Scarlet Whore," which was used in the OTO's Gnostic Mass in order for the male initiate (Beast) to obtain salvation. Most likely, however, he was not conversant with Crowley's particular readings of Rosicrucianism via the OTO until after *Tropic of Cancer* was published.

20. Miller uses this metaphor more explicitly later in the novel: "Going back in a flash over the women I've known. It's like a chain which I've forged out of my own misery. Each one bound to the other" (259).

21. The crab is also emblematic of Miller's superficial toughness and inward tenderness.

22. This method of using women to obtain transcendence resonates with Crowley's Gnostic Mass.

23. A valuable study could arise out of a comparison of Strindberg's *Inferno* and *Tropic of Cancer*, as there are many similarities, too numerous to chronicle in this study. Its impact on Miller must have been tremendous, as there are seven pages of notes on the text in one of his notebooks housed in the Henry Miller Papers, UCLA. Strindberg is also mentioned in *Plexus* and *Nexus*.

24. This one-man-revolution interpretation is further enforced by the following: "At the very hub of this wheel which is falling apart, is Matisse. [. . .] Even as the world falls apart the Paris that belongs to Matisse shudders with bright, gasping orgasms, the air itself is steady with a stagnant sperm, the trees tangled like hair. [. . .] The wheel is falling apart, but the revolution is intact . . ." (159–60).

25. In addition to being a response to Eliot's poem, Miller's use of the rock/water dichotomy is also in conversation with many passages from the Bible. The most famous of these comes in the twentieth chapter of Numbers, in which Moses strikes rock with his rod in order to make water flow. In an unpublished piece of what would become *Black Spring*, Miller writes of his own liberation in similar terms: "When therefore I congratulate myself upon my deliverance, *when from this hard rock that was me there spurts an uninterrupted stream,* [. . .] I cry aloud in my new-found freedom" (emphasis added). We also read this image typologically in the New Testament parable of the wine flasks.

26. This new type of literature is also in line with what Bergson writes about in his *Two Sources of Morality and Religion*. In this study, he identifies two types of writing that correspond to static and dynamic religion. The first and more traditional method of composition, which is implicitly linked to static religion, relies on established norms. The second technique is predictably more

138   *Notes to Chapter Five*

experimental and attempts to communicate and evoke the flow of *élan vital.* After establishing his claim that this second style comes from an inner impetus to create, he describes this writing as "revert[ing] to the simple emotion [. . .] driven to strain the words, to do violence to speech" (253–54). This is a probable source that prompted Miller to revert back to the primitive language of the street.

NOTES TO CHAPTER FIVE

1. See the "Paradise Lost" section of *Big Sur* for more about Moricand.
2. In a document related to *Black Spring* titled "Scheme and Significance," Miller attempts to put the different people in his life under types, and even provides a tedious "Character Chart" on Benjamin Fay Mills, the evangelist who had a great impact on him during his youth. He places the most influential people in his life into different groups, using titles obvious inspired by astrology: Earthy, Uranian, Dead Planets, and many others. He assigns a symbol to each group, some of which are facsimiles of astrological signs. At the end of his list, he indicates that the types should be divided into stars and planets, put into positions either on the northern or southern hemisphere, and each individual person is to be assigned a certain size and color based on how significant of a role they played in his life. This system, it seems, would be used to orchestrate the form of the book. As with many of the grandiose ideas originally conceived for *Black Spring,* few made the final cut. Nevertheless, this gesture shows how he increasingly tried to envision his entire work in spiritual terms.
3. The plan consists of two sketches. In the first one, we find people and events related to Miller's pre-Paris life linked with five different planets: Mars, Venus, Saturn, Uranus, and Neptune. Around Mars, Miller includes Nietzsche, Dostoievski, Religion, Bergson, Books/Music, Emma Goldman, Challocombe, and Dewer. In Saturn we find Bill Dewer, self-sacrifice, suicide, George-consumption, Stanley, father-drunkered, and no work. Surrounding Neptune, we again find religion, Challacombe, Benjamin Fay Mills, and Lou Jacobs. In Uranus, we see Beatrice, Dewar, Writing, Music. And lastly, around Venus, we discover Cora, Pauline, and Mother. These five houses are arranged to form a large X pattern, in which Venus is in the middle, Mars and Saturn are at the top, and Uranus and Neptune are situated at the bottom. A horizon, which supposedly splits them between northern and southern hemispheres, runs between Venus and the bottom two houses. Also included on the graphic are the following words crowned with a question mark: "(Phrenology) *What am I destined for?*" As a sort of title for the entire graphic, we find "*IDEA = Escape*" placed at the top. The second graphic, which is much rougher than the first one, attempts to map certain locations on a chessboard cartoon. Startlingly, we find the

Notes to Chapter Five   *139*

word "RIVER" sketched in the very middle of the board in bold letters, a
position that underscores the image's centrality. These two drawings, which
could have been made simply in a whim of inspiration, are similar to the
proposed plan of *Black Spring*, as they attempt to divide different characters
and even activities into astrological houses.

4. See Luke 2.49.
5. Compare Luke 22.19.
6. Although prior scholars have ventured connections between Miller's oeuvre
   and Dante's *Divine Comedy*, few have been systematic in showing how the
   American author adopts such a schematic. For most it is simply a convenient
   trope to elevate his work. Bertrand Mathieu's article "Henry Miller's Divine
   Comedy" is an exception, although he presents *Tropic of Cancer* as *Inferno*,
   The Colossus of Maroussi as *Purgatorio*, and *Big Sur and the Oranges of Hieronymus Bosch* as *Paradiso*. Despite Mathieu's claims, *Tropic of Capricorn* is the
   only novel in which Miller deeply converses with Dante's work, even though
   the figure of Dante does reappear, as Mathieu notes, in *Big Sur* (156).
7. Compare *Inferno* 6.14–33.
8. Compare *Inferno* 3.9.
9. Without a doubt, "On the Ovarian Trolley" was an important idea to
   Miller, so central that he wanted it to at least be the subtitle of *Tropic of
   Capricorn*. Sundry correspondence and other unpublished material confirm
   that Miller intended this to be the subtitle or perhaps wanted this book to
   be called "On the Ovarian Trolley" with "Tropic of Capricorn" being an
   umbrella title for his novels concerned with his love affair with June Smerth,
   fictionalized as Mara-Mona. He would eventually call these novels *The Rosy
   Crucifixion* and leave *Tropic of Capricorn* as the title of this first volume.
10. Miller writes, "With *Creative Evolution* under my arm I board the elevated
    line at the Brooklyn Bridge after work and I commence the journey home-
    ward toward the cemetery" (222).
11. For the suicide, see lines 17–20. While one may think that suggesting such
    an allusion here is a stretch, there are unmistakable similarities between
    Miller's language and Crane's. To Miller's "corkscrew," we have Crane's
    seagulls who are "shedding white rings of tumult" (line 3), itself an allu-
    sion to Whitman's "slow-wheeling circles" in "Crossing Brooklyn Ferry."
    One should also consider that Miller's friend Walter Lowenfels published
    an elegy to Crane shortly after the American poet plunged forever into the
    Gulf of Mexico.
12. See *Inferno* 19.19–21.
13. See *Inferno* 33–34.
14. As an aside, Miller's first wife happened to be named Beatrice. Although
    this marriage is associated with hell in his mind, this detail provides addi-
    tional proof that he was most likely heavily contemplating Dante's world
    during his years in New York City and later in Paris. A more positive parallel

140   *Notes to Chapter Five*

between Dante's Beatrice and Miller's loves would be Cora Seward, someone he loved deeply as a child. Although nameless, she is discussed in *Tropic of Capricorn* (337–38) and she is the subject of his essay "First Love."

15. See *Paradiso* 30–32.

16. See *Inferno* 5.

17. Even if the Abelard epigraph is excised in American editions of *Tropic of Capricorn*, Abelard is still mentioned in the text (131).

18. The confessional motif is somewhat underscored by Miller's ruminations on writing his first book, where he tells us, "I was itching to get the thing off my chest" and then again "just wait until I get it off my chest" (30). Although trivial, these moments convey that he wants us to see even his early attempts at writing as confessions.

19. This first section runs from page 9 to "An Interlude" on page 176.

20. This passage begins on page 176 and ends on 208.

21. The section runs from page 208 to 348.

22. See the opening page of the section in *Tropic of Capricorn* (208).

23. See Koenig.

24. See Koenig.

25. Hart Crane also associates the river with Logos in the conclusion of his poem "The River."

26. In the essay "Walking Up and Down in China" from *Black Spring*, we also find Miller connecting Paris with China, the "Far East." He writes, "In Paris, out of Paris, leaving Paris or coming back to Paris, it's always Paris and Paris is France and France is China" (187). At this time, he was also developing in his notebooks and unpublished writings his mythical conception of China. In his Lawrence notes, for example, we find him writing such things as, "China, an imaginary realm, to which I the artist have miraculously escaped." From this quote, we can see it as a land of pure liberation, located at the opposite pole of the confinement experienced in New York City.

27. See Judges 16 for the account of Samson's last days.

28. This should be seen in light of an earlier passage when Miller is discussing his unliberated self as: "Boiled alive, the lobsters swim in ice, giving no quarter and asking no quarter, simply motionless and unmotivated in the ice-watered ennui of death, life drifting by the show window muffled in desolation, a sorrowful scurvy eaten away by ptomaine, the frozen glass of the window cutting like a jackknife, clean and no remainder" (100).

29. See Matthew 17.20 and its less famous variant in Luke 17.6 in which mountain is replaced with mulberry bush.

30. See Matthew 13.31, Mark 4.31, and Luke 13.19.

31. For other moments in which the Ark narrative is mentioned, see pages 185, 205, and 331. The first reference should be seen in light of the general movement of the text's second part, where Miller attempts to represent the self traveling from uncertain knowledge to wisdom.

Notes to Chapter Five   141

32. In Miller's copy of Sinnett's *Esoteric Buddhism,* he underlined the following passage that goes on to discuss how this small group that gives birth to the next generation is like Noah's ark: *"Even during obscuration a small colony of humanity clings to each planet,* and the monads associated with these small colonies following different laws of evolution, and beyond the reach of those attractions which govern the main vortex of humanity in the planet occupied by the great tide-wave, *pass on from world to world along what may be called the inner round of evolution, far ahead of the race at large"* (146–47, emphasis Miller). In the margin, Miller writes: "All this is amazing—in that I just wrote it this afternoon in connection with myself as an artist. Henry Miller Paris 8/17/38 P.S. Even down to the Ark!!" (147). He also recalls "going daffy over" this book in *The Air-Conditioned Nightmare* (244).

33. Although it is dangerous to speculate how Miller arrived at this modified conception of stability, a probable influence could be the preface by Edwin Björkman to an English translation of August Strindberg's play, *There are Crimes and Crimes.* In this piece, Björkman quotes Strindberg's own words about Strindberg's religious experience in Paris, describing it as a feeling of "full, rock-firm Certitude." In describing the religious journey related in Strindberg's play, he uses water metaphors strikingly similar to Miller's: "The play, seen in this light, pictures a deep-reaching spiritual change, leading us step by step from the soul adrift on the waters of life to the state where it is definitely oriented and impelled." He also uses Strindberg's "rock-firm Certitude" phrase two additional times to describe the end of religious journeys, which he refers as "currents," again reviving aquatic images. Miller was certainly familiar with *There are Crimes and Crimes,* as Mona at the end of *Tropic of Capricorn* refers to herself as Strindberg's Henriette, the temptress of his comedy. Since Miller would have had to read the work in translation, he probably consulted the edition prefaced and translated by Björkman instead of opting for a French translation.

34. Ocean is understood in *Tropic of Capricorn* to be a chaotic entity rather than a reservoir of creative energy like we see in *Tropic of Cancer,* in which Miller refers to wells of creative energy as oceans, particularly Dante and Shakespeare, in his paean to flow (*Cancer* 235). One exception in *Tropic of Capricorn* is when he refers to the work of Elie Faure, a source of inspiration: "I had almost reached the shore of that great French ocean which goes by the name of Elie Faure, an ocean which the French themselves had hardly navigated and which they had mistaken, it seems, for an inland sea" (299). Besides this moment, ocean is a consistent symbol for unbridled energy.

35. See Exodus 17.6.

36. Although Boehme's name is not found in the text, Miller refers to him as "the mad cobbler" (296). He directly mentions Meister Eckhart, however, when he writes, "Standing knee deep in the garbage I said one day what Meister Eckhart is reported to have said long ago: 'I truly have need of God,

142   *Notes to Chapter Six*

but God has need of me too'" (297). There are also references to other Christian mystics, such as an allusion to St. John of the Cross: "We were locked in throughout the long *dark night of the soul,* a period of incommensurable time which began and ended in the manner of an eclipse" (233, emphasis added). He also lists him, along with St. Hildegarde and St. Bridget, when writing, "All the compositions I had created in my head, all these private and artistic auditions which were permitted me, thanks to St. Hildegarde or St. Bridget, or John of the Cross, or God knows whom, were written for an age to come, an age with less instruments and stronger antennae, stronger eardrums too" (250).

37. We know that Miller encountered Boehme's thought through the Moricand holograph, *Pages curieuses des grande occulistes.*

38. In *Remember to Remember,* published eight years after *Tropic of Capricorn,* Miller mentions Nicolaus Cusanus, who inspired Boehme, and "the coincidence of opposites" (108). He may have known about Nicholas of Cusa at this time as well, but his understanding of dialectics seems more Boehmean, albeit tempered by the early illuminated works of William Blake.

39. In this same passage, Miller confusingly refers to his own writing as a skyscraper but attempts to distinguish it by writing, "This is a skyscraper, as I said, but it is *different* from the usual skyscraper à l'américaine" (57). This architecture is more crisply conceived in the Ark image.

40. See Matthew 5.29 (KJV). Compare Mark 9.47.

41. Miller also mentions Percy Bysshe Shelley's *Prometheus Unbound* in *Nexus.*

42. Compare Revelation 17–18.

NOTES TO CHAPTER SIX

1. See *Colossus* 22.

2. See "Inside."

3. See 431.

4. Miller was also indebted to Wilhelm Reich at this time, who had just published his book on Orgone Energy, yet another tool in Miller's religious workshop. But Richard Wilhelm's "Golden Flower" text was introduced to English speaking audiences with a "European Commentary" by C. G. Jung.

5. I have not been able to locate the original notes, but a copy housed at Dartmouth College begins with the prefatory note: "Originally compiled in space of 24 hours handrunning at the office of the Park Commissioner, Queen's County in 1927 while June was in Europe with her friend Jean Kronski. Copy of original given to Berthe Schrank when in Paris, 1932 or 1933." Comprised of 23 single-spaced pages, the Dartmouth notes are most likely faithful to the original 1927 document, though Miller occasionally

Notes to Chapter Six 143

refers to things pertaining to his time in France, such as Place Clichy, the Dordogne, and *Tropic of Cancer*. Also, the notes end with June Smerth's departure, not where the narrative in its realized form ends.

6. In the narrative, Miller leaves it unsettled whether the European departure is his main flight to Paris without June Smerth or the brief vacation they enjoyed together. Chronically, it should be the latter, but Miller may have fused the two, knowing that he would not bridge the small gap of time between the end of *Nexus*, the third volume, and *Tropic of Cancer*. In his correspondence, Miller occasionally mentions a second volume of *Nexus* and a capstone to the project in a form of a mystical book called *Draco and the Ecliptic*, but neither was fully realized.

7. Some of these, especially "life force" and "the current of life," are found numerous times in the trilogy. The page numbers included refer to the first instance they were mentioned.

8. Miller echoes similar sentiments in *Plexus* when he writes the following about artists whom he calls "men of spirit": "They indicate, and usually illustrate by their lives, how we may convert seeming catastrophe to divine ends. That is to say, they show us, those of us who are ready and aware, how to adapt and attune ourselves to a reality which is permanent and indestructible" (350).

9. Miller earlier refers to his thoughts as "running crabwise" (230).

10. The 100+ page rough manuscript was published recently in French translation. See *Nexus 2*.

11. Compare with Matthew 4.4 and Luke 6.4.

12. The phrase is also a poignant reversal of the "Coney Island of the mind" Miller described in "Into the Night Life" from *Black Spring* (149).

13. See Exodus 17.6.

14. See Psalms 51. Miller also uses the language of Ezekiel, saying that he "had come through the valley of the shadow of death" (177).

15. See New International Version (NIV) translation of Matthew 9.2 and 9.22. Similar language can be found in the Psalms, such as 27.14 and 31.24.

16. See Acts 7.43 and Amos 5.26.

17. See *Plexus* 33, 463; *Nexus* 266, 292, 294.

18. For examples, see *Sexus* 64; *Plexus* 575, 628. There is also the Bohemian character of "Dr. Tao," whom Miller first mentions on *Sexus* 55.

19. For references to Buddhism and the sources of Miller's knowledge of the tradition, see *Plexus* 65, 574, 628, 630, 634; *Nexus* 38. In addition to these more interesting references, he frequently mentions the figure of the Buddha.

20. Benjamin Fay Mills is mentioned in *Plexus* (574–75). A reference to Theosophy can be found in *Nexus* (292). New Thought is brought up in *Plexus* (460–62). Ethical Culture is mentioned in *Nexus* (227). And, lastly, the Rand School is mentioned in *Nexus* (268–70).

21. This remark is also indicative of Miller's radical Christianity, in which he views it as a religion that is constantly in revolt.

144   *Notes to Chapter Six*

22. Augustine and Jerome are mentioned in *Plexus,* in which Miller reveals that he identifies himself more with Augustine (633). Swedenborg is referred to in *Nexus* (18); there are multiple references to Boehme, just as there are with Blake, throughout the trilogy, such as in *Plexus* (575).

23. Dante is also mentioned in *Nexus* (243).

24. For the passing reference, see *Sexus* 320.

25. The entire first stanza of the John Jacob Niles song is includes in *Plexus:* "I wonder as I wander out under the sky / How Jesus our Saviour did come for to die / For poor orn'ry people like you and like I / I wonder as I wander out under the sky" (458). Multiple stanzas from "The Seven Great Joys" are included sporadically in a passage relating Miller's own time in the "wilderness" of North Carolina. They can be found on 532–48.

26. See *Cymbeline* ii.3.

27. See *Sexus* 163, when Miller figures a woman he encounters must be named "Ruth or Esther. Or perhaps Miriam."

28. For references to King Solomon, see *Plexus* 49, 66; *Nexus* 38. The Daniel citation can be found in *Plexus* (39).

29. See *Nexus* 164.

30. See *Plexus* 281–83.

31. See *Plexus* 301.

32. Compare Psalms 51.2.

33. Compare Philippians 4.7.

34. Compare James 5.7.

35. See Ezekiel 1, 3, 10.

36. See *Sexus* 476.

37. Compare Matthew 7.7.

38. See *Plexus* 313; *Nexus* 151.

39. The "tree of life" is also mentioned in the last sentence of Plexus (640).

40. Christ was also a descendent from Adam, since the Bible tells us that Christ was of Abraham's lineage. See Luke 1.1.

41. For a more direct reference, see *Plexus* 46.

42. See *Plexus* 480.

43. See John 14.2.

44. See John 2.

45. See Ezekiel 3.3.

46. See Exodus 16.

47. See *Plexus* 32, 34, 629.

48. For the first time Miller is called "Val," see *Sexus* 166. Miller was certainly familiar with Gnostic ideas through his association with Moricand and David Edger. Also in the trilogy, we find Miller referring to his writing as guided by "archons," which are traditional the angels responsible for creation in Gnostic beliefs (*Nexus* 131).

49. See Brons.

Notes to Chapter Six 145

50. See *Nexus* 302.
51. See Brons.
52. See 407.
53. For example, see *Sexus* 451.
54. As before, Miller equates women with water, writing: "Like water, woman always finds her own level. And like water also, she mirrors faithfully all that passes in the soul of man" (*Sexus* 345).

Bibliography

Abelard, Peter. *Historia Calamitatum: The Story of My Misfortunes.* Trans. Henry Adams Bellows. Saint Paul, MN: T. A. Boyd, 1922.

American Pie. Dir. Paul Weitz. Universal, 1999.

Anderson, Margaret. *The Unknowable Gurdjieff.* London: Routledge and Kegan Paul, 1956.

Artaud, Antonin. Letter to Jean Paulhan. 25 Jan. 1936. 10 Nov. 2004 <http://homepages.tesco.net/~theatre/tezzaland/webstuff/ArtaudPres.html>.

———. *The Theater and its Double.* Trans. Mary Caroline Richards. New York: Grove, 1958.

Assisi, Saint Francis of. "The Canticle of the Sun." Trans. Bill Barrett. 18 Oct. 2004. <http://whitman.webster.edu/~barrettb/canticle.htm>.

Augustine, Saint. *Confessions.* Trans. Edward B. Pusey. New York: Modern Library, 1949.

Balzac, Honore de. *Seraphita.* Philadelphia: Avil, 1901.

Bataille, Georges. *The Accursed Share: An Essay on General Economy.* 3 vols. Trans. Robert Hurley. New York: Zone, 1988–91.

———. *Theory of Religion.* Trans. Robert Hurley. New York: Zone, 1989.

"The Beat Friar." *Time.* 25 May 1959: 60–61.

Bergson, Henri. *Creative Evolution.* Trans. Arthur Mitchell. New York: Modern Library, 1944.

———. *The Two Sources of Morality and Religion.* Trans. R. Ashley Audra and Cloudesley Brereton. London: Macmillan, 1935.

Bern, Dan. "Marilyn." *Dan Bern.* Sony, 1993.

Berthoff, Warner. *A Literature Without Qualities: American Writing Since 1945.* Berkeley: U of California P, 1979.

Bhagavad Gita. Trans. Ann Stanford. New York: Herder and Herder, 1970.

Bible. *New International Version. The Bible Gateway.* 29 Oct. 2004 <http://www.biblegateway.com/>.

Björkman, Edwin. Introduction. *There are Crimes and Crimes.* By August Strindberg.

147

Bibliography

Blake, William. *The Marriage of Heaven and Hell*. Coral Gables, FL: U of Miami P, 1963.

Blavatsky, H. P. *The Secret Doctrine*. Los Angeles: The Theosophy Company, 1982.

[————?]. *The Voice of the Silence: Chosen Fragments from the "Book of the Golden Precepts" for the Daily Use of Lanoos (Disciples)*. London and New York, [1889?].

Bourdet, Edouard. *The Captive*. Trans. Arthur Hornblow, Jr. New York: Brentano's, 1926.

Brady, Mildred Edie. "The New Cult of Sex and Anarchy." *Harper's*. April 1947. 312–22

Breton, André. *Manifestes du surréalisme*. Paris: J. J. Pauvert, 1962.

Brons, David. "A Brief Summary of Valentinian Theology." *The Gnosis Archive*. 19 Nov. 2004 <http://www.gnosis.org/library/valentinus/Brief_Summary_Theology.htm>.

————. "Valentinian Theology." *The Gnosis Archive*. 19 Nov. 2004. <http://www.gnosis.org/library/valentinus/Valentinian_Theology.htm>.

Bryden, Mary, ed. *Deleuze and Religion*. London: Routledge, 2001.

Cape Fear. Dir. Martin Scorsese. Universal, 1991.

Cendrars, Blaise. "Un écrivain américain nous est né: Henry Miller, auteur de *Tropic of Cancer*." *Orbes* (Summer 1935): 9.

Conford, Philip. "Unsung Hero of an Ephemeral Art." *The Times Higher Education Supplement* 16 Nov 1984: 15.

Cornelius, J. Edward. "Henry Miller." *Red Flame: A Thelemic Research Group*. 19 Nov. 2004 <http://www.redflame93.com/Miller.html>.

Crane, Hart. *The Bridge*. Paris: Black Sun, 1930.

————. "Proem: To Brooklyn Bridge." *The Bridge*.

————. "The River." *The Bridge*.

Craven, Thomas. Rev. of *History of Art*, by Elie Faure. *The Dial*. 77.4 (Oct. 1924): 342–45.

Dante. *The Divine Comedy*. Trans. Frederick Pollack. London, 1854.

————. *Inferno*. *The Divine Comedy*.

————. *Paradiso*. *The Divine Comedy*.

————. *Purgatorio*. *The Divine Comedy*.

————. *Vita Nuova*. Trans. Theodore Martin. London, 1862.

Davis, Patti. "From Henry Miller to Howard Stern." *Newsweek*. 9 March 2004 <www.msnbc.msn.com/id/4489463/>.

Dearborn, Mary V. *The Happiest Man Alive: A Biography of Henry Miller*. New York: Simon and Schuster, 1991.

Deleuze, Gilles. *Marcel Proust et les signes*. Paris: Presses Universitaires de France, 1964.

Deleuze, Gilles, and Felix Guattari. *Anti-Oedipus: Capitalism and Schizophrenia*. Trans. Robert Hurley, Mark Seem, and Helen R. Lane. Minneapolis: University of Minnesota, 1985.

————. *Kafka: Toward a Minor Literature*. Trans. Dana Polan. Minneapolis: University of Minnesota, 1986.

Bibliography 149

———. *A Thousand Plateaus: Capitalism and Schizophrenia.* Trans. Brian Mussumi. Minneapolis: University of Minnesota, 1987.

DeSalvo, Louise. Introduction. *Tropic of Cancer.* vii-xx.

Dostoyevsky, Fyodor. *The Brothers Karamazov.* Trans. Constance Garnett. New York: Modern Library, 1929.

Eliade, Mircea. *Yoga: Essai sur l'origine de la mystique indienne.* Paris: P. Geuthner, 1936.

Eliot, T. S. *Complete Poems and Plays, 1909–1950.* New York: Harcourt, Brace, 1958.

———. "The Love Song of J. Alfred Prufrock." *Complete Poems and Plays, 1909–1950.*

———. "The Waste Land." *Complete Poems and Plays, 1909–1950.* New York: Harcourt, Brace, 1958.

Ellis, Edward and Charles F. Horne. *The Story of the World's Greatest Nations and the World's Famous Events.* Vol. 1. 1913. 16 Nov. 2004 <http://www.public-bookshelf.com/public_html/The_Story_of_the_Greatest_Nations_and_the_Worlds_Famous_Events_Vol_1/ancienti_bdc>.

Emerson, Ralph Waldo. *Nature.* Boston, 1876.

Faure, Elie. *The Dial.* 77.4 (Oct. 1924): 330–35.

———. *History of Art.* 5 vols. Garden City, NY: Garden City, 1937.

Ferguson, Robert. *Henry Miller: A Life.* London: Hutchinson, 1991.

Fishbein, Leslie. "The Culture of Contradiction: The Greenwich Village Rebellion." *Greenwich Village: Culture and Counterculture.* Ed. Rick Beard and Leslie Cohen Berlowitz. New Brunswick, NJ: Rutgers UP, 1993.

Gallagher, Catherine and Stephen Greenblatt. *Practicing New Historicism.* Chicago: University of Chicago Press, 2000.

Geddes, Alexander. *Prospectus of a New Translation of the Holy Bible.* London, 1786.

Gide, André. *Le Prométhée mal enchaîné.* Paris, 1899.

Gifford, Sanford. *The Emmanuel Movement: The Origins of Group Treatment and the Assault on Lay Psychotherapy.* Boston: Harvard UP, 1998.

Gilbert, Sandra M. and Susan Gubar. *No Man's Land.* 3 vols. New Haven: Yale UP, 1988–94.

Goethe, Johann Wolfgang von, and Johann Peter Eckermann. *Conversations with Goethe in the Last Years of His Life.* Trans. S. M. Fuller. Boston, 1839.

Gottesman, Ronald, ed. *Critical Essays on Henry Miller.* New York: G. K. Hall, 1992.

Guillaume, de Lorris and Jean de Meun. *Le Roman de la rose.* Paris, 1814.

Heindel, Max. *The Rosicrucian Cosmo-Conception.* London: L. N. Fowler, 1929.

Henry and June. Dir. Philip Kaufman. Universal, 1990.

Henry Miller: Asleep and Awake. Dir. Tom Schiller. Kultur, 1975.

The Henry Miller Odyssey. Dir. Robert Snyder. Mystic Fire, 1974.

Homer. *Odyssey.* Trans. S. H. Butcher and A. Lang. New York: Modern Library, 1950.

Bibliography

Humphrey, Robert. *Children of Fantasy: The First Rebels of Greenwich Village.* New York: Wiley, 1978.

Hutchinson, E. R. *Tropic of Cancer on Trial.* New York: Grove, 1968.

The Hymns of Orpheus. Trans. Thomas Taylor. London, 1792.

Jackson, Paul. R. "Henry Miller, Emerson, and the Divided Self." *Critical Essays on Henry Miller.* Ed. Ronald Gottesman. 223–31.

Jensen, Finn. "Cancer and Nomads: Milier, Brassaï, and a Touch of Deleuze." *Nexus: The International Journal of Henry Miller.* 1.1 (2004).

Jewel. "Morning Song." *Pieces of You.* Atlantic, 1995.

Jones, Llewellyn. "The Meaning of Bergsonism." *The Little Review.* 1.1 (March 1914): 38–41.

Jong, Erica. *The Devil at Large.* New York: Random House, 1993.

———. *Fear of Flying.* New York: Rinehart and Winston, 1973.

Jours tranquilles à Clichy. Dir. Claude Chabrol. 1990.

Joyce, James. "The Dead." *Dubliners.* London: J. Cape, 1944.

———. *Finnegan's Wake.* New York: Viking, 1939.

———. *Ulysses.* Paris: Shakespeare and Company, 1922.

Jung, C. G. *Two Essays on Analytical Psychology.* Trans. H. G. and C. F. Baynes. London: Baillière, Tindall and Cox, 1928.

Kahn, Albert E. *The Daily Worker.* 15 Jan. 1945: 11.

Kerouac, Jack. *The Dharma Bums.* New York: Viking, 1958.

———. *The Subterraneans.* New York: Avon, 1959.

Koenig, P. R. "Ordo Templi Orientis: Spermo-Gnosis." *The Ordo Templi Orientis Phenomenon.* 15 Nov. 2004 <http://user.cyberlink.ch/~koenig/spermo.htm>.

Das Lächeln am Fuße der Leiter. By Antonio Bibalo. Libretto by Henry Miller. Staatsoper, Hamburg. 6 Apr. 1965.

Laozi. *Tao te Ching.* Trans. Gia-fu Feng and Jane English. New York: Knopf, 1972.

Lawrence, D. H. *Lady Chatterley's Lover.* London: William Faro, 1932.

Lewisohn, Ludwig. *Expression in America.* New York and London: Harper, 1932.

"The Library." *Seinfeld.* NBC. 16 October 1991.

Lolita. Dir. Stanley Kubrick. Warner, 1962.

Mailer, Norman. *The Prisoner of Sex.* Boston: Little, Brown & Co., 1971.

Martin, Jay. *Always Merry and Bright: The Life of Henry Miller: An Unauthorized Biography.* Santa Barbara, CA: Capra, 1978.

Mathieu, Bertrand. "Henry Miller's Divine Comedy." *Temenos.* 7 (May 1986): 125–57.

———. *Orpheus in Brooklyn: Orphism, Rimbaud, and Henry Miller.* The Hague: Mouton, 1976.

McGann, Jerome J. "The Idea of the Indeterminate Text: Blake's Bible of Hell and Dr. Alexander Geddes." *Studies in Romanticism* 25 (Fall 1986): 303–324.

Mensch ohne Namen. Dir. Gustav Ucicky. 1932.

Miller, Henry. *The Air-Conditioned Nightmare.* New York: New Directions, 1945.

———. *Aller Retour New York.* New York: New Directions, 1991.

———. "Autobiographical Note." *The Cosmological Eye.* 365–71.

Bibliography

———. *Big Sur and the Oranges of Hieronymus Bosch.* New York: New Directions, 1957.

———. *Black Spring.* New York: Grove, 1963.

———. *The Books in My Life.* New York: New Directions, 1952.

———. *The Colossus of Maroussi.* New York: New Directions, 1941.

———. *The Complete Book of Friends.* London: Allison & Busby, 1988.

———. *The Cosmological Eye.* New York: New Directions, 1939.

———. *Crazy Cock.* New York: Grove, 1991.

———. "Creative Death." *The Wisdom of the Heart.* 1–12.

———. *Dear, Dear Brenda: The Love Letters of Henry Miller to Brenda Venus.* New York: W. Morrow, 1986.

———. "Female Sexuality: What it is—and Isn't." *Mademoiselle.* July 1971. 108–17.

———. "First Love." *Stand Still Like the Hummingbird.* 46–49.

———. "Into the Future." *The Wisdom of the Heart.* 159–72.

———. "Into the Night Life." *Black Spring.* 149–81.

———. *Just Wild About Harry.* New York: New Directions, 1963.

———. Letter to Herbert Muller. 2 July 1941. Ts. Herbert Muller Papers, Indiana University. Courtesy Lilly Library, Indiana University, Bloomington, IN.

———. "Mademoiselle Claude." *The Wisdom of the Heart.* 140–50.

———. *The Mezzotints.* Ann Arbor: Roger Jackson, 1993.

———. *Moloch, or This Gentile World.* New York: Grove, 1992.

———. "Murder the Murderer." Berkeley: Porter, 1944.

———. *My Life and Times.* Chicago: Playboy, 1971.

———. *Nexus 2. Vacances à l'étranger.* Trans. Christian Séruzier. Paris: Autrement, 2004.

———. *Notebooks.* Ts. and ms. Henry Miller Papers (Collection 110). Department of Special Collections, Charles E. Young Research Library, UCLA.

———. "On Turning Eighty." *Sextet.*

———. *Opus Pistorum.* New York: Grove, 1983.

———. *Quiet Days in Clichy.* New York: Grove, 1965.

———. Preface. *Boyhood with Gurdjieff.* By Fritz Peters.

———. Preface. *The Subterraneans.* By Jack Kerouac.

———. *Reflections.* Ed. Twinka Thiebaud. Santa Barbara, CA: Capra, 1981.

———. "Reflections on the Maurizius Case." *Sextet.*

———. *Remember to Remember.* New York: New Directions, 1947.

———. *The Rosy Crucifixion Book One: Sexus.* New York: Grove, 1965.

———. *The Rosy Crucifixion Book Three: Nexus.* New York: Grove, 1965.

———. *The Rosy Crucifixion Book Two: Plexus.* New York: Grove, 1965.

———. Rosy Crucifixion Notes. Herbert Faulkner West Papers, Dartmouth College. Courtesy of Dartmouth College Library.

———. "Scheme and Significance." Ts. Henry Miller Papers (Collection 110). Department of Special Collections, Charles E. Young Research Library, UCLA.

———. *Sextet*. Santa Barbara, CA: Capra, 1977.

———. "Shadowy Monomania." *Sunday After the War*. 232–75.

———. *The Smile at the Foot of the Ladder*. New York: New Directions, 1958.

———. *Stand Still Like the Hummingbird*. New York: New Directions, 1962.

———. *Sunday After the War*. New York: New Directions, 1944.

———. *This is Henry, Henry Miller from Brooklyn*. Los Angeles: Nash, 1974.

———. *The Time of the Assassins: A Study of Rimbaud*. New York: New Directions, 1962.

———. *Tropic of Cancer*. New York: Signet, 1995.

———. *Tropic of Capricorn*. New York: Grove, 1962.

———. "The Universe of Death." *The Cosmological Eye*. 107–34.

———. "Walking Up and Down in China." *Black Spring*. 183–211.

———. *The Wisdom of the Heart*. New York: New Directions, 1941.

———. *The World of Lawrence: A Passionate Appreciation*. Santa Barbara, CA: Capra, 1980.

———. *The World of Sex*. Ts. Henry Miller Papers, Rare Book and Manuscript Library, Columbia University.

———. *The World of Sex*. Rev. ed. New York: Grove, 1959.

Miller, Henry and Lawrence Durrell. *Lawrence Durrell and Henry Miller: A Private Correspondence*. New York: E. P. Dutton, 1963.

Miller, Henry, and Michael Fraenkel. *Hamlet : Volume I & Volume II*. London: Edition du Laurier; Carrefour, 1962.

Miller, Henry, and Elmer Gertz. *Henry Miller: Years of Trial and Triumph, 1962–1964: The Correspondence of Henry Miller and Elmer Gertz*. Carbondale: Southern Illinois UP, 1978.

Miller, Henry, and Anaïs Nin. *Letters to Anaïs Nin*. New York: G. P. Putnam's Sons, 1965.

Miller, Henry, and Emil Schnellock. *Letters to Emil*. New York: New Directions, 1989.

Millett, Kate. *Sexual Politics*. Garden City, NY: Doubleday, 1970.

Milton, John. "Lycidas." 1638. *Poems*. London, 1645. Facsim. ed. Oxford: Clarendon, 1924. 57–65.

———. *Paradise Lost*. 2nd ed. London, 1674.

Moricand, Conrad, ed. *Pages curieuses des grandes occultistes*. Ms. Henry Miller Papers (Collection 110). Department of Special Collections, Charles E. Young Research Library, UCLA.

Mosher, Clint. "Emma Goldman Inspired Carmel Hate Cult Chief: Anarchist Eulogized by Henry Miller, Escapest [sic] Doctrines Spread Here." *San Francisco Examiner* 5 May 1947.

———. "Group Establishes Cult of Hatred in Carmel Mountains." *San Francisco Examiner* 4 May 1947.

Munson, Gorham Bert. *The Awakening Twenties: A Memoir-History of a Literary Period*. Baton Rouge: Louisiana State UP, 1985.

Neagoe, Peter, ed. *Americans Abroad*. The Hague: Servire, 1932.

Bibliography

"Nexus." *Oxford English Dictionary.* 24 Nov. 2004 <http://dictionary.oed.com/>.

Nietzsche, Friedrich. *Anti-Christ.* Trans. H. L. Mencken. Tucson, AZ: Sharp, 1999.

———. *The Birth of Tragedy.* Trans. Clifton P. Fadiman. New York: Modern Library, 1927.

Nikhilananda, Swami. *Vivekananda: A Biography.* 1953. 18 Nov. 2004 <http://www.ramakrishnavivekananda.info/vivekananda_biography/vivekananda_biography.htm>.

Nin, Anaïs. *Henry and June.* San Diego: Harcourt Brace Jovanovich, 1986.

Omarr, Sydney. *Henry Miller: His World of Urania.* London: Villiers, 1960.

Oja, Carol J. "Dane Rudhyar's Vision of American Dissonance." *American Music* Summer (1999). 1 Dec. 2004 <http://www.findarticles.com/p/articles/mi_m2298/is_2_17/ai_61551810/pg_2>.

"One Hundred Best Novels of the Twentieth Century List." *New York Times.* 20 July 1998.

Orwell, George. *"An Age Like This: 1920–1940" The Collected Essays, Journalism and Letters of George Orwell.* Vol. 1. Ed. Sonia Orwell and Ian Angus. New York: Harcourt, Brace and World, 1968.

———. "Inside the Whale." *"An Age Like This: 1920–1940."* 493–527.

———. Rev. of *Black Spring. "An Age Like This: 1920–1940."* 230–32.

———. Rev. of *Tropic of Cancer. "An Age Like This: 1920–1940."* 154–56.

Peters, Fritz. *Boyhood with Gurdjieff.* Oregon House, CA: Bardic, 2005.

"Plexus." *Oxford English Dictionary.* 24 Nov. 2004 <http://dictionary.oed.com/>.

Porter, Bern, ed. *The Happy Rock: A Book About Henry Miller.* Berkeley: Porter, 1945.

Prothero, Stephen R. *The White Buddhist: The Asian Odyssey of Henry Steel Olcott.* Religion in North America. Bloomington, IN: Indiana UP, 1996.

Pound, Ezra. Rev. of Tropic of Cancer. *Critical Essays on Henry Miller.* Ed. Ronald Gottesman.

Proust, Marcel. *La prisonnière.* Paris: Gallimard, 1954.

———. *Remembrance of Things Past.* 2 vols. Trans. C. K. Scott-Moncrieff. New York: Random House, 1934.

Rank, Otto. *Art and Artist: Creative Urge and Personality Development.* New York: Agathon, 1975.

Reds. Dir. Warren Beatty. Paramount, 1981.

Reinach, Salomon. *Orpheus: A History of Religions.* Trans. Florence Simmonds. New York: Horace Liveright, 1930.

Rushdie, Salman. "Outside the Whale." *Imaginary Homelands.* Granta, London: 1991. 87–101.

The Secret of the Golden Flower. Trans. Walter Picca. 1964. 18 Nov. 2004 <http://www.alchemylab.com/golden_flower.htm>.

Shakespeare, William. *Cymbeline.* London, 1777.

Shapiro, Karl. "The Greatest Living Author." *Tropic of Cancer.* By Henry Miller. New York: Grove, 1961.

Bibliography

Shelley, Percy Bysshe. *Prometheus Unbound*. Boston, 1892.

Sinnett, A. P. *Esoteric Buddhism*. Boston, 1887.

Spengler, Oswald. *The Decline of the West*. New York: Knopf, 1932.

———. "The Downfall of Western Civilization." Trans. Kenneth Burke. *The Dial* 77.5 (Nov. 1924): 361–78; 77.6 (Dec. 1924): 482–504; 78.1 (Jan. 1925): 9–26.

Stille dage i Clichy. Dir. Jens Jørgen Thorsen. Blue Underground, 1970.

Strindberg, August. *Inferno*. Stockholm: Norstedts, 1994.

———. *There are Crimes and Crimes*. New York: C. Scribner's, 1912.

Taylor, Paul Beekman. *Gurdjieff and Orage*. Weiser, 2001.

Thompson, E. P. *Witness Against the Beast: William Blake and the Moral Law*. New York: New Press, 1993.

Tropic of Cancer. Dir. Joseph Strick. Paramount, 1970.

The Unbearable Lightness of Being. Dir. Philip Kaufman. Home Vision Entertainment, 1988.

Venus, Brenda. *Secrets of Seduction: How to be the Best Lover Your Woman Ever Had*. Dutton Adult, New York: 1993.

———. *Secrets of Seduction for Women*. Dutton Adult, New York: 1996.

Virgil. *Aeneid*. Trans. Robert Fitzgerald. New York: Vintage, 1990.

Viscomi, Joseph. "The Caves of Heaven and Hell: Swedenborg and Printmaking in Blake's *Marriage*." *Blake in the Nineties*. Ed. David Worrall and Steve Clark. London: Macmillan, 1999. 27–60.

Welch, Louise. *Orage with Gurdjieff in America*. Boston: Routledge and Kegan Paul, 1982.

Whitman, Walt. "Crossing Brooklyn Ferry." *Leaves of Grass*.

———. *Leaves of Grass*. New York: W.W. Norton, 1973.

Winslow, Kathryn. *Henry Miller: Full of Life*. Los Angeles: J. P. Tarcher, 1986.

Yeats, W. B. *Collected Poems*. New York: Macmillan, 1951.

———. "Crazy Jane Visits the Bishop." *Collected Poems*.

———. "The Second Coming." *Collected Poems*.

Index

A

Abelard, Peter, 71, 113, 140
Abraham (Biblical figure), 44, 111, 144
Absalom (Biblical figure), 76
Abuse, sexual, 22
Adam (Biblical figure), 81, 101, 117, 121, 123, 144
Adonis, 5
Aeneid (Virgil), 107
Air-Conditioned Nightmare (Miller), 7, 16, 141
Aller Retour New York (Miller), 6
American Communist Party, 16
American Pie (film), 25
Americans Abroad *(Neagoe), 14*
Anarchism, 17; *see also* Goldman
Anastasia (character), 106–109, 115, 119, 123; *see also* Kronski, Jean
Ancient and Mystical Order Rosae Crucis, 4
Anderson, Margaret, 4, 29, 129
Androgyny, 10, 122–123, 136; *see also* Hermaphroditic union
Angels, as symbol, 55, 66, 74, 86, 88, 89, 109–110, 115, 116, 118, 120, 123, 144
Anti-Christ (Nietzsche), 9, 133
Anti-Oedipus (Deleuze), 9–10
Anti-Semitism, 16, 21–22, 51
Antinomianism, 8
Antoninus, Brother, 1
Apis, 76
Apollo, 35
Apollonius of Tyana, 113

Archetypes, 32, 48; *see also* Jung
Archons, *see* Angels
Ark, *see* Noah's
Art and Artist (Rank), 32
Artaud, Antonin, 31, 32
Asoka, 113
Astral body, 94
Astrology, 3, 55, 56, 63, 76, 78, 82, 83, 135, 136, 138, 139; *see also* Cancer; Capricorn; Moricand; Omarr
Augustine, *see* Saint
"Autobiographical Note" (Miller), 6
Autobiographies, 5–6, 41–42, 56, 63, 66, 70, 89, 93; *see also* Confessions; Hagiographies; Testaments

B

Babel, Tower of, 74, 111
Bahá'i, 3, 29
Balzac, Honoré de, 125
Bataille, Georges, 9, 10, 13, 130
Beatrice (Dante), 70, 139–140
Bennett, Arnold, 14
Bergson, Henri, 9, 10, 28, 32, 33, 38, 51, 64, 69, 72, 76, 126, 132, 137, 138; *see also* Elan vital
Bern, Dan, 131
Berthoff, Warner, 20
Besant, Annie, 3
Bhagavad Gita, 111
Bibalo, Antonio, 13
Bible, 24, 73, 95, 109, 110, 114–117, 119, 123, 137, 144

155

156   Index

Christian Bible, 78, 80, 96, 110, 112, 114, 137
  Acts of the Apostles, 143
  Corinthians, First Epistle to the, 80
  Galatians, Epistle to the, 136
  Luke, Gospel of, 109, 134, 139, 140, 143, 144
  James, Epistle of, 115, 144
  John, Gospel of, 44, 51, 73–74, 109, 115, 118, 119, 135, 144
  Mark, Gospel of, 109, 140, 142
  Matthew, Gospel of, 103, 119, 140, 142, 143, 144
  Philippians, Epistle to the, 115, 144
  Revelation, Book of, 54, 90, 115, 116, 136, 142
Hebrew Bible, 10, 52, 76, 80, 111, 114, 115
  Amos, Book of, 143
  Exodus, Book of, 44, 52, 80, 135, 136, 141, 143, 144
  Ezekiel, Book of, 144
  Genesis, Book of, 73, 79, 101, 117
  Judges, Book of, 140
  Numbers, Book of, 137
  Psalms, Book of, 96, 110, 114, 115, 143, 144
  Ruth, Book of, 114
Bibliothèque Nationale, 130, 132
Big Sur and the Oranges of Hieronymous Bosch (Miller), 7, 64, 131, 138, 139
Birth of Tragedy (Nietzsche), 35–36, 134
Björkman, Edwin, 141
Black Spring (Miller), 6, 14, 15, 63, 95, 132, 137, 138, 139, 140, 143
Blake, William, 8, 42, 52, 109, 127, 135, 142, 144
Blavatsky, H. P., 3, 30, 48, 88–89, 93, 94
Boehme, Jacob, 31, 80, 81, 102, 113, 141, 142, 144
Bonnard, Pierre, 134
Book of Friends (Miller), 7, 22, 132
Books in My Life (Miller), 7, 132, 134
Bourdet, Edouard, 107
Boyhood with Gurdjieff (Peters), 29
Boys Brigade, 22

Brady, Mildred Edie, 17
Breton, André, 130
Brooklyn Bridge, as symbol, 68–69, 74, 76
Brothers Karamazov (Dostoyevsky), 105
Buddha, 2, 30, 80, 99, 143
Buddhism, 80, 143
  Tibetan, 111
  Zen, 2, 20, 112
Buñuel, Luis, 29
Burke, Kenneth, 28, 132

C

Camus, Albert, 13
Cancer (sign), 48, 55, 78, 83; *see also* Astrology; Crabs
Cannes Film Festival, 13
"Canticle of the Sun," 113
Cape Fear, 24
Capitalism, 79, 131
Capricorn (sign), 48, 76, 78, 82–83, 104, 136; *see also* Astrology
Captive, The (play), 107
Cendrars, Blaise, 13, 20
Chabrol, Claude, 131
Challacombe, Robert Hamilton, 19, 132, 138; *see also* Hamilton
Children of Fantasy (Humphrey), 27
China, as symbol, 140
Chouteau, Pauline, 138
Christ, Jesus (Biblical figure), 2, 5, 30, 32, 34, 38, 44, 48, 50–51, 58, 60, 63–66, 73–78, 80, 81, 83, 84, 85, 87, 90, 96, 98, 103, 106–107, 109–110, 111, 113, 116, 117–124, 144
Christian Science, 3, 29
Christianity, 2–5, 8, 9–10, 24, 36, 38, 45, 51, 60, 63, 64–67, 70, 72, 74, 76, 80, 82, 83, 103, 109, 111–113, 116, 117, 121, 126, 127
Chuang Tzu, 113
Citizens for Decent Literature, 18
"Clipped Wings" (Miller), 66
Coincidentia oppositorum, 80–81, 142; *see also* Nicolaus of Cusa
Colossus of Maroussi (Miller), 5, 7, 15, 93, 139, 142

Index

157

Communism, 16, 17
Confessions, 5, 11, 41, 71–72, 85, 99, 140;
    see also Autobiographies; Hagi-
    ographies; Testaments
Confessions (Augustine), 5
Conversations with Goethe, 57
Cornelius, J. Edward, 31
Cosmodemonic Telegraph Company, 66,
    68, 70, 72, 83–84, 98, 102,
    107; *see also* Western
Cosmological Eye (Miller), 7, 15
Cowley, Malcolm, 15
Cowly, Herbert, 4
Crabs, 101, 135, 137; *see also* Cancer
Crane, Hart, 4, 69, 139, 140
Craven, Thomas, 132
Crazy Cock (Miller), 6, 21, 94
"Crazy Jane Visits the Bishop" (Yeats), 116
"Creative Death" (Miller), 34–35, 63, 133
Creative Evolution (Bergson), 64, 69, 72,
    132, 139
Criterion, 15
Critical Essays on Henry Miller (Gottesman),
    21, 131
Crosby, Bing, 20
"Crossing Brooklyn Ferry" (Whitman), 139
Crowley, Aleister, 31, 73, 90, 129, 136, 137;
    see also Ordo
Crucifixions, as symbol, 36, 38, 48, 58, 66–
    67, 85, 87, 92, 97, 100, 104,
    109, 118–120, 123, 125
Cusa, Nicholaus of; *see* Nicholaus
Cymbeline (Shakespeare), 113, 144

D

Daily Worker, 16
Daniel (Biblical figure), 114, 144
Dante, 41, 42, 45, 47, 57, 67–71, 72, 102,
    109, 110, 113, 121, 124, 139–
    140, 141, 144
David, King (Biblical figure), 110, 111, 114,
    115
"Dead" (Joyce), 105
Dear, Dear Brenda (Miller), 21
Dearborn, Mary, 21–23, 131
Decline of the West (Spengler), 28, 105, 119,
    132, 133

Deleuze, Gilles, 9–11, 130
Delilah (Biblical figure), 76
DeSalvo, Louise, 23–24
Desire body, 30, 99
Devil at Large (Jong), 1, 5, 22
Devils, as symbol, 68, 90
Dewer, Bill, 138
Dewey, George, 65, 85
Dharma Bums (Kerouac), 2
Dial, 28, 132
Diderot, Denis, 125
Dido, 53
"Dionysian artists," 34–36
Dionysus, 35–36, 117
Divine Comedy (Dante), 41, 42, 67, 70, 113,
    139
Dogs, as symbol, 68, 90, 119–121
Dos Passos, John, 16
Dostoyevsky, Fyodor, 34, 103, 105, 106,
    107, 133, 134, 138
Draco and the Ecliptic (Miller), 6–7, 143
DuBois, W. E. B., 29
Durrell, Lawrence, 7, 16, 20, 93, 132

E

Eckermann, J. P., 57
Eckhart, Meister, 80–81, 113, 141
Edger, David, 30, 144
Elan vital, 29, 32–33, 52–53, 60, 64, 69–
    70, 74, 76, 78, 82, 86, 95–96,
    100, 104, 106–108, 112, 119,
    122, 126, 138; *see also* Bergson
Eliade, Mircea, 31
Elijah (Biblical figure), 115
Eliot, T. S., 2, 3, 14–15, 20, 30, 58–59, 99,
    137
Ellis, Edward, 53, 136
Ellis, Havelock, 51
Emmanuel Movement, 3, 129
Emerson, Ralph Waldo, 3, 5, 37, 53, 57,
    130, 134, 135, 136
Esoteric Buddhism (Sinnett), 30, 132, 141
Esther (Biblical figure), 111, 114, 144
Ethical Culture, 29, 112, 143
Eve (Biblical figure), 81, 117, 123
Evergreen Review, 19
Everson, Bill, *see* Antoninus

158   Index

Expression in America (Lewisohn), 37, 130
Ezekiel (Biblical figure), 60, 64, 111, 114,
    115, 119, 143

F

Faber & Faber, 15
Fascism, 16, 93
Faulkner, William, 16
Faure, Elie, 32–33, 51, 106, 132, 133, 141
Faust, as symbol, 35, 84
Faust (Goethe), 84
Fear of Flying (Jong), 19
Federal Bureau of Investigations, 16
Fénelon, François, 113
Ferguson, Robert, 21, 31, 132, 136
Finnegan's Wake (Joyce), 44, 57, 79, 105
"First Love" (Miller), 140
Fishbein, Leslie, 28
Fitzgerald, F. Scott, 14
Foucault, Michel, 8
Fraenkel, Michael, 7, 63, 131
Frank, Waldo, 4
Funk, J. K., 4

G

Gandhi, Mahatma, 45
Geddes, Alexander, 8
Gide, André, 16, 90, 134
Gilbert, Sandra M., 21, 131
Ginsberg, Allen, 20
Gnostic Mass, 73, 116, 137; *see also* Crow-
    ley; Ordo
Gnosticism, 30, 121, 144
Goethe, Johann Wolfgang von, 57
Golden Dawn, *see* Hermetic Order of
Goldman, Emma, 17, 29, 138
Golgotha, 58, 66, 82, 84, 87, 92, 97; *see also*
    Crucifixion; "Happy Rocks";
    Rocks
Gottesman, Ronald, 21, 131
"Grand Inquisitor" (Dostoyevsky), 107
Granta, 20
Great Mother, 53, 135; *see also* Whore of
    Babylon
Greenblatt, Stephen, 8, 130
Grimm, Brothers, 136
Grove Press, 18

Guattari, Felix, *see* Deleuze
Gubar, Susan, *see* Gilbert
Guiler, Hugo, 21
Gurdjieff, 4, 20, 27, 28–29, 129

H

Hagiographies, 5, 41; *see also* Autobiogra-
    phies; Confessions; Testaments
Hamilton, Roy (character), 100, 132; *see also*
    Challacombe
Hamsun, Knut, 16
Happiest Man Alive (Dearborn), 21, 22
"Happy Rock" (symbol), 10, 79–82, 85, 87,
    90, 95; *see also* Golgotha; Rocks
Happy Rock (Porter), 15
Harris, James B., 17–18
Heap, Jane, 4, 29
Heindel, Max, 3, 30
Hemingway, Ernest, 14, 16, 21
Henry and June (film), 21, 24
Henry and June (Nin), 21
Henry Miller: Asleep and Awake (film), 19
"Henry Miller, Emerson, and the Divided
    Self" (Jackson), 130
Henry Miller Literary Society, 18
Henry Miller Odyssey (film), 19
"Henry Miller's Divine Comedy" (Mathieu),
    139
Heraclitus, 36, 58, 97, 113
Hermaphroditic union, 10, 72, 81, 90, 123,
    136; *see also* Androgyny
Hermes Trimestigus, 31, 113
Hermetic Order of the Golden Dawn, 129
Hinduism, 45, 111, 112, 135
His World of Urania (Omarr), 18
Historia Calamitatum (Abelard), 71, 113
History of Art (Faure), 32–33, 133
Holy Rollers of Oregon, 76
Homer, 89
Homophobia, 21
Horne, Charles F., *see* Ellis, Edward
Humphrey, Robert, 27
Hymns of Orpheus, 134

I

Inferno (Dante), 45, 67–69, 135, 139, 140
Inferno (Strindberg), 56, 137

Index

"Inside the Whale" (Orwell), 15, 20
Institute for the Harmonious Development of Man, 4
"Into the Future" (Miller), 133
"Into the Night Life" (Miller), 143
Issac (Biblical figure), 111

J

Jackson, Paul R., 130
Jacobs, Lou, 138
Jensen, Finn, 130
Jesus (Biblical figure), *see* Christ
Jewel, 131
John the Baptist (Biblical figure), 43, 60
Jong, Erica, 1, 5, 19, 22–23, 136
Jours tranquilles à Clichy (film), 131
Joyce, James, 2, 14, 30, 44, 57, 79, 89, 105, 135
Judaism, 22, 23, 45, 51, 52, 64, 65, 75, 103, 111, 112
Jung, C. G., 3, 32, 33, 36–37, 38, 48, 50, 135, 142
Just Wild About Harry (Miller), 6

K

Kahane, Jack, 34
Kahn, Albert E., 16–17
Kandinsky, Wassily, 3
Kaufman, Philip, 21
Kellner, Carl, 129
Kerouac, Jack, 2, 20
Koenig, P. R., 30
Krishnamurti, Jiddu, 65
Kronski, Jean, 23, 65, 142; *see also* Anastasia
Kubrick, Stanley, 17–18
Kundara, Milan, 21

L

Lady Chatterley's Lover (Lawrence), 1, 15, 18
Lächeln am Fusse der Leiter (opera), 14
"Land of Fuck" (symbol), 70, 72, 73, 75–81, 86–87
Lao Tzu, 30
Lawrence, D. H., 10, 14, 18, 34–35, 37, 51, 127, 132, 135, 140
Leeds Art Club, 129
Letters to Anaïs Nin (Miller), 132, 134

Lewis, H. Spencer, 4
Lewis, Juliette, 24
Lewis, Wyndham, 14
Lewisohn, Ludwig, 37–38, 130, 134
Lilith, 90
Lindbergh, Charles, 94
Literature Without Qualities, 20
Little Review, 4, 28–29; *see also* Anderson, Heap
Logos, 30, 51, 58, 73–77, 81, 140
Lolita (film), 18
Longinus, 113
Lorris, Guillaume de, 124
"Love Song of J. Alfred Prufrock" (Eliot), 99
Lowell, Robert, 20
Lowenfels, Walter, 63, 139

M

M: The Studio for Henry Miller, 18, 131
Mademoiselle, 18
"Mademoiselle Claude" (Miller), 52
Magdalene, Mary (Biblical figure), 109
Mailer, Norman, 18, 20, 21, 131
Malatesta, Errico, 113
Man Cut in Slices, 58
Manifesto of Surrealism (Breton), 130
Mansfield, June, *see* Smerth
Mansfield, Katherine, 4, 28, 129
Mara (character), *see* Mona
"Marilyn" (Bern), 131
Marriage of Heaven and Hell (Blake), 8, 42, 136
Martin, Jay, 15, 17, 28, 29, 42, 65, 131, 133
Mary (Biblical figure), 109
Mathieu, Bertrand, 36, 139
Matisse, Henri, 57, 137
McGann, Jerome, 8, 130
Medeiros, Maria de, 21
Meister Eckhart, *see* Eckhart
Mensch ohne Namen, 65
Mesmerism, 3
Meun, Jean de, *see* Lorris
Mezzotints (Miller), 28
Miller, Beatrice Sylvas Wickens (first wife), 138, 139–140
Millett, Kate, 18, 19, 22
Mills, Benjamin Fay, 29, 112, 138, 143

Index

Milton, John, 43, 57, 68
Minor literature, 11
Minos, King, 53
Miriam (Biblical figure), 144
Modern Library, 24
Modernism, 4, 13, 14, 30, 60, 99, 127, 129
Moloch (Miller), 6, 21, 110, 132
Mona–Mara (character), 6, 41, 42, 46, 50,
    51, 54–55, 57, 67, 70, 72, 73,
    84, 85, 87–91, 94, 97, 99–100,
    102, 104, 106–110, 111, 114,
    115–124, 129, 134, 135, 139,
    141; *see also* Smerth
Montezuma, 113
Montrose, Louis, 8
Moricand, Conrad, 31, 63, 130, 131, 132,
    138, 142, 144
"Morning Song" (Jewel), 131
Moses (Biblical figure), 52, 80, 108, 111,
    114, 137
Mosher, Clint, 17
Motion Picture Association of America, 21
Müller, Gottlieb Leberecht (character),
    64–65, 72
Muller, Herbert, 95, 125
Munson, Gorham, 4, 129
"Murder the Murderer" (Miller), 15
My Life and Times (Miller), 19, 133

N

National Institute of Arts, 17
Nazi Party, 16
Nehemiah (Biblical figure), 111
New Age, 4; *see also* Orage
"New Cult of Sex and Anarchy" (Brady), 17
New Directions Press, 16
New Historicism, 8
New Jerusalem Church, 8
New Leader, 16
New Republic, 4
New Thought, 3, 29, 112, 143
New York Institute for Psychical Research, 4
New York Public Library, 24
New York Times, 24
Newsweek, 25
Nexus (Miller), 5, 6, 94, 96, 97, 106–112,
    113–114, 115, 118, 120, 121,
    122, 123, 125, 126, 129, 137,
    142, 143, 144, 145
Nexus 2 (Miller), 14, 18, 143
Nicolaus of Cusa, 113, 142
Nietzsche, Friedrich, 9, 34–36, 51, 106,
    133, 138
Niles, John Jacob, 113, 144
Nin, Anaïs, 7, 8, 19, 20, 21, 22, 23–24, 31,
    42, 57, 63, 128, 132, 133, 134
Niro, Robert de, 24
Noah's Ark, 75, 78–79, 83–84, 140, 141,
    142
Nolte, Nick, 24
Nostradamus, 102, 113
"Novena," 113

O

Oak Ridge National Laboratory, 15
Obelisk Press, 34, 135
Odyssey (Homer), 89
Olcott, Henry Steel, 3
Omarr, Sidney, 18
Omophagia, 36, 56
"On Turning Eighty" (Miller), 136
Opus Pistorum (Miller), 20
Orage, A. R., 4, 28, 129
Ordo Templi Orientis, 4, 31, 73, 116, 129,
    136, 137; *see also* Crowley
Orgone Energy, 142
Origen, 113
Orpheus, 36, 59, 134
Orwell, George, 14, 15, 20, 93
Osborn, Richard, 134
Ouija, 102
"Outside the Whale" (Rushdie), 20
"Ovarian Trolley, On the" (symbol), 68–69,
    74, 84–85, 139

P

Paracelsus, 31, 102, 113
Paradise Lost (Milton), 43, 68
"Paradise Lost" (Miller), 131, 138
Paradiso (Dante), 70, 113, 121, 139, 140
Paul (Biblical figure), 64, 80
Paulhan, Jean, 32
Pepper Pot, 28
Percy, Walker, 20

Index

161

Perles, Alfred, 7
Peters, Fritz, 29
Phrenology, 3, 138
Plath, Sylvia, 20
Plato, 31
Playboy, 19, 20
Plexus (Miller), 5, 6, 94, 95, 96, 97, 102–
      106, 113, 114, 115, 116, 118,
      119, 120, 123–124, 129, 133,
      137, 143, 144
Poe, Edgar Allen, 38
Porter, Bern, 15–16
Post-Impressionism, 60
Pound, Ezra, 14, 16, 30, 129
Powys, John Cowper, 29
Presbyterian Church, 22
Priapus, 76
Princeton University, 15
Prisoner of Sex (Mailer), 18
"Proem: To Brooklyn Bridge" (Crane), 69
Prometheus, 36, 89–90, 134
Prometheus Unbound (Shelley), 142
Protestantism, 9, 23
Prothero, Stephen, 129
Proust, Marcel, 2, 42, 56, 57, 66, 107, 130
Purgatorio (Dante), 139
Puritans, 5
Pynchon, Thomas, 20
Pythagoras, 113

Q

Queneau, Raymond, 13, 130
Quiet Days at Clichy (Miller), 6, 19, 131

R

Rabelais, François, 57
Ramakrishna, 3, 30; *see also* Vedanta
Rand School, 112, 143
Rank, Otto, 3, 32, 132
Read, Herbert, 14
Reds (film), 20
Reflections (Miller), 2, 134
"Reflections on the Maurizius Case"
      (Miller), 135
Reich, Wilhelm, 94, 142
Reinach, Salomon, 134
Remember to Remember (Miller), 7, 142

Remembrance of Things Past (Proust), 42,
      130
Resurrections, as symbol, 36, 38, 44, 66–67,
      82, 104, 125
Reuss, Theodor, 129
Rich, Adrienne, 20
Rivers, as symbol, 32–36, 41, 46–49, 56,
      58, 59, 64, 69–70, 74–75, 77–
      80, 82, 88, 95–97, 108–109,
      117, 135, 137, 139, 140; *see also*
      Elan vital; Water
Rocks, as symbol, 35, 48, 59, 76–85, 87, 91,
      95, 98, 108, 111, 137, 141; *see*
      also Golgotha; "Happy Rock"
Roman de la rose (Lorris), 124
Roosevelt, Theodore, 85
Roseland Ballroom, 28, 70, 86
Roses, as symbol, 70, 123–124
Rosicrucian Cosmo-Conception (Heindel), 30
Rosicrucian Fellowship, 3
Rosicrucians, 3–4, 27, 30–31, 63, 72, 80,
      81, 99, 116, 121, 124, 137
Rosy Crucifixion (Miller), 2, 5, 6, 7, 10, 11,
      16, 30, 67, 70, 72, 92, 93–126,
      129, 130, 139, 142–145; *see also*
      Nexus; Plexus; Sexus
Rudhyar, Dane, 3
Rushdie, Salman, 20
Ruth (Biblical figure), 111, 114, 144

S

Sacrifices, as symbol, 5, 9, 23, 34–35, 36–
      37, 58–60, 66, 67, 88, 111, 138
Sade, Marquis de, 102
Saladin, 113
Saint Augustine, 5, 113, 144
Saint Bernard of Clairvaux, 113
Saint Bridget, 142
Saint Francis de Sales, 113
Saint Francis of Assisi, 99, 113
Saint Hildegarde, 142
Saint Ignatius Loyola, 102
Saint Jerome, 113, 144
Saint John of the Cross, 142
Saint Vincent de Paul, 113
Saint-Martin, Claude, 102
Salome (Biblical figure), 109

Index

Samson (Biblical figure), 76–77, 140
Sampson, William T., 85
San Francisco Examiner, 17
Sartre, Jean-Paul, 13
Scarlet Whore, 90, 116, 137; *see also* Crowley; Ordo; Whore
Schiller, Tom, 20
Schley, Winfield Scott, 85
Schnellock, Emil, 31, 132
Schrank, Berthe, 142
Scorsese, Martin, 24
"Second Coming" (Yeats), 133
Secret Doctrine (Blavatsky), 30, 48, 93, 94
Secret of the Golden Flower, 94, 123, 124, 142
Secrets of Seduction (Venus), 131
Secrets of Seduction for Women (Venus), 131
Seinfeld (TV), 24
Semele, 117
Seraphita (Balzac), 125
Seventh Day Adventists, 76
Seward, Cora, 138, 140
Sextet (Miller), 7, 135, 136
Sexual Politics (Millett), 18
Sexus (Miller), 5, 6, 24, 29, 34, 94, 95, 96, 97–102, 112, 115, 117–118, 119–120, 121–122, 123, 124, 143, 144, 145
"Shadowy Monomania" (Miller), 133
Shakespeare, William, 8, 47, 113, 141
Shapiro, Karl, 18
Shaw, George Bernard, 14, 129
Shelley, Percy Bysshe, 142
Singer, Issac Bashevis, 20
Sinnett, A. P., 30, 132, 141
60 Minutes (TV), 19
Smerth, June, 21, 23, 28, 33–34, 38, 41, 51, 54, 57, 94, 95, 128, 139, 142, 143; *see also* Mona
Smile at the Foot of the Ladder (Miller), 6, 13
Snyder, Robert, 19, 131
Socialism, 16, 112
Solomon, King (Biblical figure), 111, 114, 144
Sophia, 121
Spencer, Herbert, 51
Spengler, Oswald, 28, 33, 35, 51, 105, 119, 132, 133

Spermatikos Logos, 73
Spinoza, Baruch, 9–10
Spiritualism, 3
Stand Still Like the Hummingbird (Miller), 7
Stern, Howard, 25
Stevens, Wallace, 3, 20
Stille dage i Clichy (film), 19
Stones, as symbol, *see* Rocks
Story of the World's Greatest Nations and the World's Famous Events (Ellis), 53
Streams, as symbol, *see* Rivers
Strindberg, August, 56, 90, 137, 141
Subterraneans (Kerouac), 2
Surrealism, 13, 29, 130
Swedenborg, Emanuel, 8, 31, 102, 113, 144

T

Tao te Ching (Lao Tzu), 112
Taoism, 94, 112, 123
Testaments, 5, 11, 34, 41, 43, 58, 67, 136; *see also* Autobiographies; Confessions; Hagiographies
Theosophical Review, 129
Theosophy, 3, 4, 27, 29–30, 63, 81, 88, 89, 93, 94, 112, 129, 132
There are Crimes and Crimes (Strindberg), 90, 141
Thiebaud, Twinka, 134
This is Henry Miller, Henry Miller from Brooklyn (Miller), 131
Thompson, E. P., 8, 130
Thousand Plateaus (Deleuze), 9–10
Time, 1
Time of the Assassins (Miller) 7
Toomer, Jean, 4
Torn, Rip, 19
Thurman, Uma, 21
Transcendentalism, 3, 5, 43
Tropic of Cancer (film), 19
Tropic of Cancer (Miller), 1, 2, 5, 6, 7, 10, 11, 13, 14–15, 17, 18, 20, 23–24, 32, 33, 34, 35, 36, 37, 38, 41–61, 63, 64, 66, 71, 72, 74, 77–78, 87, 89, 92, 95, 100, 101, 103, 105, 123, 129, 130, 131, 133, 134–138, 139, 141, 143

Index

163

Tropic of Capricorn (Miller), 2, 5, 6, 7, 10,
11, 15, 17, 48, 61, 63–92, 93,
94, 95, 97, 98, 100, 102, 113,
118, 132, 138–142
Two Essays on Analytical Psychology (Jung),
31, 135
Two Sources of Morality and Religion (Bergson)
32, 126, 137
Tzu, Lao, *see* Lao Tzu
Tzu, Chuang, *see* Chuang Tzu

U

Ulysses (Joyce), 79, 89
Unbearable Lightness of Being (film), 21
Unitarian Church, 29
"Universe of Death" (Miller), 133
University of California at Los Angeles, 15
University of California Radiation Labora-
tory, 15

V

Valentinus, 121, 124
Van Gogh, Vincent, 57, 96
Van Ruysbroeck, Jan, 113
Vedanta, 3, 112; *see also* Vivekananda
Venus, Brenda, 20
Virgil, 69, 107, 113
Viscomi, Joseph, 8, 130
Vita Nuova (Dante), 102, 110
Vivekananda, Swami, 3, 29, 112
Voice of the Silence (Blavatsky), 30, 88

W

Walker, Jean, 129
"Walking Up and Down in China" (Miller),
140

Ward, Fred, 21
"Waste Land" (Eliot), 58–59
Water, as symbol, 10, 45, 47–49, 54, 55,
58, 59, 66, 69, 70, 74–76, 78,
80, 81–84, 87, 88, 89, 108,
109, 110, 111, 115–116, 119,
135, 137, 140, 141, 145; *see
also* Rivers
Wells, H. G., 14
West, Herbert Faulkner, 16
Western Union Telegraph Company, 28;
see also Cosmodemonic
Whitman, Walt, 34, 37, 46, 101, 139
Whore of Babylon (Biblical figure), 54, 90,
115–117, 136
Wilcox, Ella Wheeler, 4
Wilhelm, Richard, 94, 142
William Blake's Circle of Destiny, 135
"William Wilson" (Poe), 38
Winslow, Kathryn, 131
Wisdom of the Heart (Miller), 7
Woolf, Virginia, 10
Worcester, Elwood, 3
Word, *see* Logos
World of Lawrence (Miller), 7, 34, 63, 133,
134
World of Sex (Miller), 1, 2, 7, 93, 134
World Parliament of Religions, 3

X

Xenophon, 113
Xerxes Society, 118, 136

Y

Yeats, W. B., 116, 127, 129, 133
Yoga (Eliade), 31